AN ELEMENTARY
MIDDLE ENGLISH GRAMMAR

Oxford University Press, Ely House, London W.1

GLASGOW   NEW YORK   TORONTO   MELBOURNE   WELLINGTON
CAPE TOWN   SALISBURY   IBADAN   NAIROBI   LUSAKA   ADDIS ABABA
BOMBAY   CALCUTTA   MADRAS   KARACHI   LAHORE   DACCA
KUALA LUMPUR   HONG KONG   TOKYO

AN ELEMENTARY
MIDDLE ENGLISH
GRAMMAR

BY

JOSEPH WRIGHT

Ph.D., D.C.L., LL.D., Litt.D., D.Litt.

FELLOW OF THE BRITISH ACADEMY; EMERITUS PROFESSOR OF
COMPARATIVE PHILOLOGY IN THE UNIVERSITY OF OXFORD

AND

ELIZABETH MARY WRIGHT

SECOND EDITION

OXFORD UNIVERSITY PRESS

FIRST EDITION 1923
SECOND EDITION 1928

REPRINTED LITHOGRAPHICALLY IN GREAT BRITAIN
AT THE UNIVERSITY PRESS, OXFORD
FROM SHEETS OF THE SECOND EDITION
1934, 1946, 1952, 1957, 1962, 1967

To the Revered Memory

OF

DR. HENRY BRADLEY

AND

DR. SIR JAMES MURRAY

WHO DEVOTED THEIR LONG AND STRENUOUS
LIVES TO PROMOTING THE STUDY OF ENGLISH
WORD-LORE THIS MIDDLE ENGLISH GRAMMAR
IS RESPECTFULLY DEDICATED

PREFACE TO THE FIRST EDITION

THE need of an elementary Middle English Grammar written on scientific and historical principles must long have been felt by pupils and teachers alike, and it is with a view of supplying this need that the present Grammar has been written. In writing it we have followed as far as possible the plan adopted in the *Elementary Old English Grammar*, our object being to furnish students with a concise account of the phonology and inflexions of the Middle English period. And in order that the book may form a kind of basis for the modern English period, we have in almost all cases chosen the examples illustrating the Middle English sound-changes from words which have survived in Modern-English. It will thus link up with a similar book dealing with the phonology and inflexions of New English, which is already in an advanced stage of preparation, and which will be published next year.

In dealing with the Middle English dialects, we have, as far as is possible in an elementary Grammar, endeavoured to exhibit the phonological and inflexional features of each group of dialects without attaching too great importance to any one of them. In this part of the work we have made considerable use of the modern dialects, as they help to throw much light upon many points of Middle English phonology.

As the book is not intended for specialists in English philology, some more or less important details have been intentionally omitted. All or most of them will doubtless be found in Morsbach's *Mittelenglische Grammatik*, Halle, 1896, and Luick's *Historische Grammatik der englischen Sprache*, Leipzig, 1914–21, if these two comprehensive grammars are ever completed, as well as some of them in *Chaucers Sprache und Verskunst* by B. ten Brink, third edition, edited by E. Eckhardt, Leipzig, 1920. We gratefully acknowledge our indebtedness to the above-mentioned works, and to Björkman's *Scandinavian Loan-words in Middle English*, Halle, 1900–2.

We are convinced that the student who conscientiously works through this book will find that he has gained a thorough general knowledge of Middle English sound-laws and inflexions, and has thereby, not only laid a solid foundation for further study of historical English grammar, but also for a fuller and more appreciative study of mediaeval English Literature.

In conclusion, we wish to express our sincere thanks to the Controller of the University Press for his great kindness in complying with our wishes in regard to special type, and to the Press reader for his valuable help with the reading of the proofs.

JOSEPH WRIGHT.
ELIZABETH MARY WRIGHT.

Oxford,
  October, 1923.

PREFACE TO THE SECOND EDITION

THE rapidity with which a large first edition of this Grammar has been exhausted would seem to indicate that there was a real need for such a book among beginners of the subject at our universities.

In preparing this new Edition for press we have adhered strictly to our original plan, viz. that of furnishing students with a concise account of the phonology and inflexions of the Middle English period. From our long experience as teachers of the subject, we are convinced that this is the only satisfactory method. To have overburdened the book with a large number of details would only confuse the student and render him unable 'to see the wood for the trees'. Although we have preserved the original number of paragraphs, many of these have been enlarged, and others have been entirely re-written, especially in the phonology of the vowels of accented syllables and in the chapter on verbs.

In conclusion, we beg to express our heartiest thanks to the reviewers of the first edition for their useful suggestions, especially to Professor E. Ekwall in *Beiblatt zur Anglia*, vol. xxxv, pp. 226-8, Professor F. Holthausen in *Literaturblatt für germanische und romanische Philologie*, Jahrgang xlv, Nr. 10-12 (cols. 302-5), Professor E. Kruisinga in *English Studies*, vol. vi, pp. 162-3, and Professor F. Wild in *Englische Studien*, vol. lix, pp. 96-9. And lastly, we gratefully acknowledge our indebtedness to the *Handbuch der mittelenglischen Grammatik,* Erster Teil: Lautlehre (Heidelberg, 1925), by our old friend the late Professor Richard Jordan, through whose untimely death the study of English Philology has suffered a great loss.

JOSEPH WRIGHT.

ELIZABETH MARY WRIGHT.

OXFORD,
  November, 1927

CONTENTS

ABBREVIATIONS, ETC.

AN.	= Anglo-Norman	MHG.	= Middle High German
Angl.	= Anglian		
C.Fr.	= Central French	Mod.	= Modern
dial.	= dialect	N. or n.	= Northern
ED.Gr.	= English Dialect Grammar	NE.	= New English
EM.	= East Midland	N. E. D.	= New English Dictionary.
ENE.Gr.	= Elementary Historical New English Grammar	NHG.	= New High German
		Nth.	= Northumbrian
		NW.	= north-west(ern
EOE.Gr.	= Elementary Old English Grammar	OE.	= Old English
		O.Fr.	= Old French
Fr.	= French	O.Icel.	= Old Icelandic
Goth.	= Gothic	ON.	= Old Norse
Ken.	= Kentish	S. or s.	= Southern
Lat.	= Latin	Sc.	= Scottish
M. or m.	= Midland	W. or w.	= West
ME.	= Middle English	WM.	= West Midland
		WS.	= West Saxon

ƀ	= v in **vine, five**	ž	= s in **measure**
ð	= th in **then**	dž	= j in **just**
ʒ	= g often heard in German **sagen**	š	= sh in **ship**
		tš	= ch in **chin**
ŋ	= n in **finger, think**	χ	= ch in German **nacht, nicht**

The sign ⁻ placed over vowels is used to mark long vowels. The sign ˛ placed under vowels is used to denote open vowels, as ę̄, ǭ, ęi, ǫi. The sign . placed under vowels is used to denote close vowels, as ẹ̄, ọ̄, ẹi, ẹu, ọu. Simple e in unaccented syllables denotes that the vowel was not pronounced, as **come, hevenes, livẹde.** The asterisk * prefixed to a word denotes a theoretical form, as **cladd** from older ***clādd,** *clothed.*

INTRODUCTION

§ 1. Middle English embraces that period of the English language which extends from about 1100 to 1500. The division of a language into fixed periods must of necessity be more or less arbitrary. What are given as the characteristics of one period have generally had their beginnings in the previous period, and it is impossible to say with perfect accuracy when one period begins and another ends. In fact many of the vowel-changes which are generally described as having taken place in early ME. did in reality take place in late OE., although early ME. writers often continued to use the traditional OE. spelling long after the sound-changes had taken place; this applies especially to ǣ, ȳ, ěa, ěo. And just as it is impossible to fix the precise date at which one period of a language ends and another begins, so also it is not possible to do more than to fix approximately the date at which any particular sound-change took place, because in most languages, and more especially in English, the change in orthography has not kept pace with the change in sound.

§ 2. For practical purposes Middle English may be conveniently divided into three sub-periods :—(*a*) Early ME. extending from about 1100 to 1250. (*b*) Ordinary ME. extending from about 1250 to 1400. And (*c*) late ME. extending from about 1400 to 1500.

(*a*) Early ME. 1100-1250. The chief characteristics of this sub-period are :—The preservation in a great measure of the traditional OE. system of orthography, and the beginnings of the influence of Anglo-Norman orthography. The change of æ to a (§ 43), ā to ǭ in the dialects south of the Humber (§ 51), the lengthening of a, e, o in open syllables of dissyllabic words (§ 77), the formation of a large number of new diphthongs of the -i and -u type (§§ 104, 105), the weakening of unaccented a, o, u to e (§ 134), the preservation for the most part of unaccented final -e (§ 139). The breaking up of the OE. inflexional system, especially that of the declensions of nouns, adjectives, and pronouns. The preservation of greater remnants of the OE. declensions of nouns, adjectives, and pronouns in the South than in the North and the Midlands. Grammatical gender was almost entirely lost in nouns (§ 314). Few Anglo-Norman loan-words found their way into the dialects of the South, still fewer into those of the Midlands, and hardly any at all into those of the north Midlands, and of the North.

(*b*) Ordinary ME. 1250–1400. The chief characteristics of this sub-period are :—The gradual formation of extensive literary dialect centres ; and in the fourteenth century, especially in the second half, the beginnings of a standard ME. which, excluding Scotland, became fully developed in the fifteenth century. The great influence of Anglo-Norman orthography upon the written language (§§ 7–21). Un-accented final -e had practically ceased to be pronounced in all the dialects. The limitation of the inflexion of nouns and adjectives chiefly to one main type in the North and the Midlands, and in the South to two main types— the strong with the inflexions of the old a-declension, and the weak. The introduction of a large number of Anglo-Norman words into all the dialects, even into those of the North.

(*c*) Late ME. 1400–1500. In this sub-period we can observe the gradual disappearance of the local dialect element from the literature of the period through the spread and influence of the London literary language. The close approximation of the system of inflexions to that of New English. The gradual cleavage between the Scottish and the northern dialects of England.

§ 3. In the present state of our knowledge it is not possible to give more than a rough-and-ready classification of the ME. dialects, because we are unable to fix the exact boundaries where one dialect ends and another begins. Nor shall we ever be able to remedy this defect until we possess a comprehensive atlas of the modern dialects such as has been produced by France and Germany of their dialects. An atlas of this kind would enable English scholars to fix the dialect boundaries far more accurately than is possible at present, and to show conclusively that there was no such thing as a uniform northern, north Midland, east Midland, west Midland, or south Midland dialect in the ME. period, but that within each principal division there were many sub-dialects each possessing clearly defined phonological peculiarities.

§ 4. ME. is usually divided into three large groups of dialects :—

1. The Northern Group, including the dialects of the Lowlands of Scotland, Northumberland, Durham, Cumberland, Westmorland, the whole of Yorkshire except the south, and north Lancashire. Roughly speaking, the Humber and the Ouse formed the southern boundary, while the Pennine Chain determined its limits to the West.

2. The Midland Group, including the dialects of south Yorkshire, the whole of Lancashire except the north, the counties to the west of the Pennine Chain, the East Anglian counties, and the whole of the Midland area. It corresponded roughly to the Old Mercian and East Anglian areas. The Thames formed the southern boundary of this extensive group of dialects. This group is generally further subdivided into the north Midland, east Midland, west Midland, and south Midland dialects.

3. The Southern Group, including the dialects of the counties south of the Thames, Gloucestershire, and parts of Herefordshire and Worcestershire. This group is often further subdivided into the south Eastern dialects, also

sometimes called Kentish or the Kentish group of dialects, and the south Western dialects.

§ 5. So far as is possible in an elementary grammar we have endeavoured to exhibit the phonological and morphological features of each of the various groups of dialects without attaching too great importance to any one of them. And with this end in view considerable use has been made of the modern dialects, as they undoubtedly help to throw light upon many debatable points of ME. phonology which can never be satisfactorily settled in any other manner.

PHONOLOGY

CHAPTER I

ORTHOGRAPHY AND PRONUNCIATION

1. ORTHOGRAPHY

§ 6. The following brief sketch of ME. orthography is merely intended to draw the student's attention to the subject in a connected manner. To enter into it here with any degree of completeness would necessitate the repetition of much that properly belongs to other chapters. Long vowels were, of course, not marked as such in ME. manuscripts, but in order to avoid confusion they are here generally marked long.

§ 7. The ordinary ME. orthography is based partly on the traditional OE. orthography and partly on the Anglo-Norman (AN.). OE. ǽ, ěa, and ěo continued to be written in early ME. long after they had changed in sound. æ had become a over a large area of the country in the early part of the twelfth century (cp. § 43), but it often continued to be written æ and by AN. scribes e until well on into the second half of the thirteenth century. ea became æ in Late OE., but the ea often continued to be written until a much later date. And then the æ had the same further fate as the ordinary OE. æ above. The old traditional spelling with ǣ was preserved in the *Ormulum* (c. 1200), *Laȝamon* (c. 1205), and the Proclamation of London (1258), but in other monuments it, as also ǣ from older ēa, was generally written ę̄ from about the end of the twelfth century. ēa had also become ǣ, except in Kentish, by about the beginning of the eleventh century, although the ēa often continued to be written until a much later period. This change of ǣ to ę̄ was merely a letter change due to the influence of AN. orthography ; the æ-sound itself remained in ME. until near the end of the fifteenth century when it became ẹ̄, see § 52, 2. Through ǣ and ēa falling together in sound in late OE. the ēa was sometimes written for old ǣ in the twelfth and thirteenth centuries, and also occasionally much later. At a still later period this writing of ēa for ǣ became the general way of expressing long open ẹ̄ of whatever origin, cp. NE. **leap, deal, eat**, ME. **lẹ̄pen, dẹ̄len, ẹ̄ten**, OE. **hlēapan, dǣlan, etan.** The old traditional spelling with **eo, ēo** was often preserved in the twelfth and thirteenth centuries, although the **eo, ēo** had become **e, ẹ̄** in sound in the northern and east Midland dialects, and **ö, ȫ** in the west Midland and southern dialects (except Kentish) in the twelfth century. And then through the influence of AN. orthography the **ö, ȫ** sounds came to be written **o, ue, oe** and sometimes **u**, see §§ 65, 198 ; and conversely **eo** occasionally came to be written for old **e** (§ 44) in those dialects where **eo** became **e** in early ME. The writing of **e** for ǣ (= OE. ǣ, ēa) and of **e** for ẹ̄ (= OE. ē, ēo) led to confusion in ME. orthography owing to long open ẹ̄ and long close ẹ̄ being written alike, cp. **leden, ded** = OE. **lǣdan** *to lead*, **dēad** *dead* beside **fet, crepen** = OE. **fēt** *feet*, **crēopan** *to creep*.

§ 8. Long and short y̆ (= ŭ) became unrounded to ĭ over a large part of the country during the OE. period. The result was that monuments written in these extensive areas during the ME. period have both **i** and **y** to represent old long and short ĭ. In the late ME. period an attempt was made by some writers to restrict the use of **y** to express old long ī.

§ 9. Many of the changes which the OE. vowel-system underwent in ME. were not due to sound-changes, but were merely orthographical changes introduced by Anglo-Norman scribes. Examples of such changes are:—In those areas where the OE. short **y** (= ü) remained in the ME. period it came to be written **u** (like the **u** in Fr. **lune**), and the long ȳ (= ū) came to be written u, ui (uy) from about 1170 onwards (§§ 49, 57). After the writing of u for y, and the u, ui (uy) for ȳ had become general in those districts where the long and short ŭ-sound had remained, the y began to be written for ĭ, especially before and after nasals, u (= v), w, and finally. This writing of y for ĭ gradually became very common, and by the time of Chaucer it was also used in other positions as well. From about the middle of the thirteenth century o came to be written for u before and after nasals, u (= v), and w. This writing of o for u in these positions became pretty general towards the end of the thirteenth century. The object of using y, o for i, u in the above positions was primarily to avoid graphical confusion. In late ME. o was also generally written for u when followed by a single consonant + vowel. v was often written for u initially, and u for v medially between vowels. The writing of ou (ow) for ū became fairly common in the second half of the thirteenth century, and in the fourteenth century it became general. By the time of Chaucer it was generally written ow when final and frequently also in open syllables, especially before l, n, and v, but in other positions it was mostly written ou. e came to be written for æ (later a), ǣ (see above) in early ME., and through the influence of Central O.Fr. orthography ie was sometimes written for ẹ̄ in later ME., especially after the sound ẹ̄ had become ī or was on the way to become ī, see §§ 50, 107, 2, and *ENE. Gr.* § 31.

§ 10. In later ME. ea was occasionally used for ẹ̄, oa (ao) for ǭ, and ou for ǭ in the fourteenth century before the ǭ had become ū (cp. § 50); the diphthongs ai, ei, oi, au, eu, ou were often written ay, ey, oy, aw, ew, ow finally and before n ; and ai (ay), ei (ey), ōi (oy) were written for ā, ē, ō in the northern dialects, see § 121.

§ 11. During the ME. period some attempt was made to distinguish between long and short vowels in writing, but

only Orm made a systematic attempt to indicate long vowels
by writing double consonants after short vowels. His system,
however, broke down when a short vowel was in an open
syllable. In this position he sometimes put a mark over
the vowel, thus dăle *valley*, to indicate that the vowel was
short. Orm's system was cumbersome, but it was not
more so than some of the other attempts which were made
to indicate long vowels. From the fourteenth century
onwards long ē and ō were often indicated by writing them
double in closed syllables and when final, but single in open
syllables, as dẹẹd *dead*, dẹẹd *deed*; but dẹlen *to deal*, mẹten
to meet; bọọt *boat*, fọọt *foot*; but grọpen *to grope*, brọþer
brother. ā was rarely written aa in closed syllables. The
reason why ā, ē, ō were not written double in open syllables
was doubtless due to the lengthening of early ME. a, e, o
in open syllables in the first half of the thirteenth century
(§ 78). These new long vowels were always followed by an
e in the next syllable, and this e came to be regarded as the
sign of a long vowel in the preceding syllable. And then
later the e came to be used in words to which it did not
etymologically belong for the purpose of indicating a preceding long vowel. Long and short ŭ came to be dis-
tinguished by writing the former ou (ow) and the latter
u (o). By some later ME. writers an attempt was made to
distinguish between long and short ĭ by writing the former
y and the latter i. This mode of indicating ī was very
common in Chaucer.

§ 12. In late ME. it became fairly common to double consonants after short stem-vowels in order to indicate that the preceding vowel was short, just as is the case in Modern German.

§ 13. The OE. consonant-system was very defective inso-
much as each of the letters c, f, g, h, n, s and þ was used
to represent two or more sounds, see *EOE. Gr.* § 7. The
ambiguity in the use of these consonants was chiefly due to
sound-changes which took place during the OE. period

without the corresponding changes in the orthography. Germanic **f, þ** and **s** became voiced in OE. between voiced sounds, and Germanic **ƀ, ʒ** became unvoiced when they came to stand finally, but no regular change took place in the orthography to indicate the change in pronunciation, see *EOE. Gr.* §§ 139, 172. Again Germanic **k, g** (which only occurred in the combination ng), **χ, ʒ** and **ng** became differentiated in OE. into gutturals and palatals, but the same letters were kept to indicate both kinds of sounds, see *EOE. Gr.* §§ 166, 168-70. Mainly through the influence of Anglo-Norman orthography many of the above ambiguities were got rid of in ME.

§ 14. **c** came to be used for the **k**-sound before guttural vowels and liquids, and **k** before palatal vowels and **n**, and from the beginning of the thirteenth century **ck** beside **kk** came to be used to express the double **k**-sound. The letter **c** was sometimes used for voiceless **s** initially before palatal vowels, and in AN. words both initially and medially, as **citee, recciven**. **c** was also sometimes used to express **ts**, as **blecen**, OE. **bletsian** *to bless*, **milce**, OE. **milts** *mercy*. The OE. combination **cw** was written **qu**. From about 1150 onwards it became common to write **ch** for the assibilated OE. palatal **c** (= **tš**), and **cch** (chch) when it was doubled.

§ 15. **v** was written initially in those ME. dialects where **f** had become voiced in this position. **u** later **v** came to be written medially for OE. voiced **f**, and **v** was often written for **u** initially.

§ 16. In OE. the explosive **g** and the spirant **ʒ** were written alike, but in ME. **g** came to be used exclusively for the explosive, and **ʒ** for the spirant, as **gōd, glad,** beside **ʒard, ʒernen,** early ME. **boʒe** = OE. **boga** *bow*. For initial **ʒ-** the letters **y·** and **i·** were also used, as **yaf, iaf** = **ʒaf**, OE. **geaf** *he gave*. At the end of words **ʒ** was sometimes used for **z** (= **ts**), and in late ME. for voiced **s**, through confusion with z, and conversely z for ȝ. Some scribes also used g for ȝ initially. The assibilated OE. palatal cg (= dž) came to be written gg, but this was not an improvement, because OE. did generally distinguish in writing between the guttural and palatal explosive gg by writing the former gg and the latter cg, as in dogga *dog*, beside licgan *to lie down*. In Fr. words dž was written j (also sometimes i) initially and g (gg) medially, as juge, chargen, plegge.

§ 17. In order to distinguish between the pronunciation of the aspirate h and the spirant h = χ, the h gradually became used for the aspirate only, and the spirant was represented by ȝ (also sometimes by c, g), later gh (also ch, especially in the Scottish dialects). This rule had become fully established by the time of Chaucer, who usually has gh. And as French scribes did not have the combination ȝt (ht) in their own language they sometimes substituted st for it, as pret. miste for miȝte *might*. OE. hw came to be written qu, qv, quh, qw, qwh in the northern dialects, especially the Scottish, and generally wh in the other dialects.

§ 18. s was generally written for both the voiced and the voiceless s, but z was occasionally used for the former, especially in late ME. sc was sometimes written for ss, as blisced *blessed*, and z for ts, as milze, OE. milts *mercy*.

§ 19. The š-sound from OE. sc was generally written sch in early ME., and later also ssh, sh, and in Ken. ss, as ssrīve, vless. Double šš was written schs, ssh, and also shs (§ 289).

§ 20. OE. þ, ð continued to be written side by side until well on into the thirteenth century, and then the latter went out of use. In the fourteenth century th gradually came to be used beside þ, but the þ often continued to be written beside th, especially initially, throughout the ME. period. In the best manuscripts of the *Canterbury Tales* th is generally used. In the early fourteenth century þ and

y had become so closely alike in form that in some manuscripts (e.g. the Cotton MS. of the *Cursor Mundi*, *c.* 1340)
they were indistinguishable, and in others a dot was sometimes placed over the y in order to distinguish it from the þ.
After 1400 þ fell more and more out of use, and in some
manuscripts was represented only by the y-form in demonstrative and pronominal words, as yᵉ, yᵗ, yᵐ, yᵘ = *the, that,
them, thou.* Two of these, yᵉ and yᵗ, were retained in printers'
types during the fifteenth and sixteenth centuries, and yᵉ is
still often used pseudo-archaically in shop-signs like Yᵉ Olde
Booke Shoppe. See *N.E.D.* sub y.

§ 21. The OE. rune Ƿ (= w) continued to be used occasionally until the end of the thirteenth century, but the
ordinary way of writing u-consonant was uu (also vv in
early ME.) and w.

2. PRONUNCIATION

A. The Vowels.

§ 22. ME. had the following simple vowels and diphthongs:—

Short Vowels a, e, i, o, u, ö, ü
Long   ,,   ā, ę̄, ē, ī, ǭ, ō, ū, ȫ, ṻ
Diphthongs ai, ęi, ei, ǫi, ui, au, ęu, eu, iu, ǫu, ou

NOTE.—With the exception of ę̄ and ǭ the short and long
vowels had the same sound-values as in OE. where ǽ, ȳ̆ = ME. ö̆,
ü̆. ę̄ is used in ME. to represent two slightly different sounds,
viz. a low-front-narrow vowel like OE. ǽ, and a mid-front-wide
vowel which arose in ME. by the lengthening of OE. e in open
syllables, see §§ 52, 78. The sound represented by ǭ did not exist
in OE. For the Kentish rising diphthongs which arose from OE.
ēo, ēa, see §§ 64, 67.

§ 23. The approximate pronunciation of the above vowels
and diphthongs was as follows:—

a like the a in OE. assa and NHG. gast, as **asse,
bladder, chapman, passen.**

e like the e in NE. met, as bed, fellen, gest, helpen, slepte.

i like the i in NE. bit, as bidden, children, niȝt *night*, sitten.

o like the o in NHG. Gott and nearly like the o in NE. dog, as dogge, gosling, hors, norþ.

u like the u in NE. full, as dust, ful, sunne (sonne) *sun*, wulf (wolf), see § 48.

ö (gen. written o, ue, and sometimes u) like the ö in NHG. götter, as chorl (churl), horte (huerte, hurte) *heart*, storre *star*, orþe (urþe) *earth*, see § 60.

ü (gen. written u) like the ü in NHG. füllen, as brugge *bridge*, duppen *to dip*, kussen *to kiss*, sunne *sin*, see § 49.

ā like the a in NE. father, as·āle, bāken, nāme, rāven.

ę̄ like the ai in NE. air, as lę̄den (OE. lǽdan) *to lead*, lę̄pen (OE. hlēapan) *to leap*; ę̄ten (OE. etan) *to eat*, mę̄te (OE. mete) *meat*, see §§ 52, 78.

ē̦ like the e in NHG. reh, as dēd *deed*, dēp, hēre, fēt, snēsen.

ī like the i in NE. machine, as bīten, fīnden, līf, tīde.

ǭ like the a in NE. all, as bǭte (OE. bāt) *boat*, cǭld (OE. ceald) *cold*; cǭle (OE. col) *coal*, þrǭte (OE. þrote) *throat*, see § 51, note.

ō̦ like the o in NHG. bote and the eau in Fr. beau, as brō̦þer, fō̦t, lō̦ken, sō̦ṅe.

ū (gen. written ou, ow), like the ou in Fr. sou, and nearly like the oo in NE. food, as doun, hous, hou (how), pound.

ȫ (gen. written o, ue, eo, and sometimes u) like the ö in NHG. schön, as cheose(n) chuse(n) *to choose*, duep (dup) *deep*, lof (luef, luf) *dear*, see § 65.

ǖ (gen. written u, ui, uy) like the ü in NHG. grün, as fur (fuir) *fire*, huden (huiden) *to hide*, mus (muis) *mice*, see § 57.

ai nearly like the ai in NE. aisle, as dai (day), hail, maiden, saide *he said*.

Early ME. ẹi nearly like the ay in NE. day, as clẹi, grẹi, lẹide *he laid*, plẹien *to play*, wẹi, see § 107.

Early ME. ẹi with ẹ like the é in Fr. été, as dẹien *to die*, ẹie *eye*, flẹien *to fly*, see § 107, 6.

ọi like the oy in NE. boy, as bọi (bọy), chọis, jọie, vọis.

au nearly like the ˙ou in NE. out, as drawen, fauȝt *he fought*, sauȝ *he saw*, tauȝte *he taught*.

ẹu like the n. dial. pronunciation of the ew in few, as dẹu (dẹw), fẹwe, hẹweṇ, schẹwen.

Early ME. ẹu with ẹ like the é in Fr. été, as hẹwe *hue*, knẹu (knẹw), nẹwe, pret. þrẹu (þrẹw), see § 112.

Early ME. iu (later written ew) nearly like the ew in NE. few, as sniwen *to snow*, spiwen, triwe *true*.

ọu with ọ like the o in NE. not, as bọwe (OE. boga) *bow*, pp. fọuȝten, knọwen, sọule, þọuȝte.

Early ME. ọu nearly like the o in NE. no, as bọwes *branches*, pl. inọwe *enough*, plọwes *ploughs*, see § 114, 2.

ui (= the u in NE. put + i) generally written oi, as enointen *to anoint*, point *point*, see § 207.

B. The Consonants.

§ 24. The ME. consonant-system was represented by the following letters:—b, c, d, f, g, ȝ, h, j, k, l, m, n, p, q, r, s, t, þ, v (u), w, x, y, z.

Of the above letters b, d, f, j, k, l, m, n, p, q, r, s, t, v (u), w, x, y had the same sound-values as in Modern English. The remaining letters require special attention, see §§ 13–20.

c had a threefold pronunciation : 1. Before guttural (back) vowels and liquids it had the k-sound, as cat, cọ̄ld, cuppe ; clẹ̄ne, craft. 2. Initially and medially before palatal vowels it had the sound of voiceless s in Fr. words, as citee, deceiven. 3. It was occ. used to represent the combination ts (= O.Fr. ts from Latin ce, ci, which later became s in sound), as blecen = OE. bletsian *to bless*, milce = OE. milts *mercy*. The simple affricata was written ch, and when doubled cch (chch), as chīld, kichene ; crucche, wrecche.

g had a twofold pronunciation : 1. Initially it was a voiced explosive (stop), as gāte, glad, gnat, gōd, grēne. 2. Medially before vowels it had the sound dž (= the affricata j and dg in NE. judge) in Fr. words, as chargen, jugen.   The combination ng had the sound ŋg beside ndž according as it represented OE. guttural or palatal ng, as long, singen, þing, beside crengen (cringen), sengen (singen) ; and similarly with double gg (= OE. guttural gg and palatal cg), as dogge, frogge, stagge, beside brigge, cuggele, seggen *to say*, and also in Fr. words, as plegge *pledge*.

ȝ had a threefold pronunciation : 1. Initially like NE. y in ye, as ȝard, ȝernen, ȝong.   2. In early ME. a voiced guttural or palatal spirant like the g often heard in NE. sagen beside siegen, as boȝe later bowe *bow*, draȝen later drawen, beside flēȝen later fleien *to fly*.   3. Finally and before t it was a voiceless guttural or palatal spirant like the ch in NHG. noch beside ich, as burȝ (burgh), douȝ (dough), douȝter (doughter), beside hēȝ (hēh) *high*, fiȝten (fighten).

Initial h (except in the combination hw· = χw·) was an aspirate like the h in NE. hand, as hand, hous.   In other positions it was a voiceless spirant like the ȝ in 3 above, which came to be written for it in early ME.

sch from OE. sc (gen. written sch in early ME., and later also ssh, sh, and in Ken. ss) was like the sh in NE. ship, as schaft, waschen, fisch ; ssrīve *to shrive*, vless *flesh*.

þ (th) was used to express both the voiceless and voiced sounds like the th in NE. thin, cloth ; father, then, as baþ, þing ; brōþer, Ken. þet *that*.

z had the ts sound in early ME., as milze = OE. milts *mercy* ; in later ME. it was also used for voiced s, especially in the *Ayenbite*, as zelver *silver*, þouzond.

§ 25. The accentuation in native ME. words was essentially the same as in OE., that is, in all uncompounded words the chief accent fell upon the stem-syllable and always remained there even when suffixes and inflexional endings followed it. In compound words the chief accent fell upon the stem-syllable of the first component part if the second part was a noun or an adjective ; and on the stem-syllable of the second part if this was a verb or derived from a verb.

CHAPTER II

THE OE. VOWEL-SYSTEM

§ 26. OE. had the following vowel-system :—

Short vowels **a, æ, e, i, o, u, y**
Long   ,,   **ā, ǣ, ē, ī, ō, ū, ȳ**
Short diphthongs **ea, eo, ie, io**
Long   ,,   **ēa, ēo, īe, īo**

In the next chapter we shall trace the ME. development of the above simple vowels and diphthongs of accented syllables. And in doing so we shall first deal with the independent and then with the dependent changes which they underwent in ME. By independent changes we mean those which took place independently of neighbouring sounds, and by dependent changes those which depended upon or were due to the influence of neighbouring sounds. But before entering upon the subject it will be useful to state here certain dependent changes which took place during the OE. period, as some of them are of special importance for ME.

§ 27. The diphthongs **ĕa, ĕo, ĭo** became monophthongs during the OE. period before **c, g, h, hs, ht**; before a liquid

+c, g, h ; and after the initial palatals c·, g·, and sc·. And then the resultant long or short vowels had the same further development in ME. as the corresponding older long or short vowels. See *EOE. Gr.* § 67 and notes.

§ 28. Before h and h + consonant ea became æ (= ME. a, §§ 43, 59) in Anglian, but e in late WS. and also in the eleventh century in Kentish, as sæh *he saw*, fæx *hair*, flæx *flax*, wæxan *to grow*, æhta *eight*, fæht *he fought*, hlæhtor *laughter*, mæht *might*, næht *night*, beside seh, fex, flex, wexan, ehta, feht, hlehtor, meht, neht. A few of these latter forms occur in Chaucer, as flex, wex, wexe(n) beside waxe(n). See §§ 107, 110.

§ 29. After initial palatal c·, g·, sc· ea generally became æ in Anglian (= ME. a), but e in late WS., whence a beside e in ME., as chaf (OE. ceaf) *chaff*, ȝaf *he gave*, ȝat *gate*, schal *shall*, beside chef, ȝef, ȝet, schel.

§ 30. Before ht eo became i in later WS. (rarely y), Ken. and the south Midlands when not followed by a guttural vowel in the next syllable, but became e in the north Midlands and the North (cp. *EOE. Gr.* § 67 and notes 1, 4), whence we have in early ME. riht beside reht (mod. n. dialects reit) *right*, but fehten (OE. feohtan) in all the early ME. dialects. The common form fiȝten was a ME. new formation.

§ 31. io became i in Anglian before c, h + s or t, and before a liquid + c, as birce *birch-tree*, milc *milk*, mixen *dunghill*, gebirhta(n) *to make light*, rihta(n) *to set straight*, see § 62 and *EOE. Gr.* § 67, note 1.

§ 32. The OE. eo, io which occurred after initial palatal sc·, g· were probably never either rising or falling diphthongs. The e, i merely indicated the palatal nature of the preceding sc·, g· as is shown by the ME. forms, and in OE. itself sco· occurs beside sceo·, as schort (OE. scort beside sceort), and similarly ME. bischop, schot *missile*, &c.; ȝon (OE. geon) *yonder*, Orm ȝocc (OE. geoc) *yoke*. And in like

manner OE. has **scu·, iu·** (i = ȝ) beside **sceo· (scio·), geo·
(gio·),** as **schulen** (OE. **sculon** beside **sceolon, sciolon**) *they
shall,* ȝung, ȝong (OE. **iung** beside **geong, giong**) *young.*

§ 33. The OE. initial combinations **scă·, scŏ·** were also
often written **sceă·, sceŏ·** with **e** merely to denote the
palatal pronunciation of the **sc·,** as **sceacan** beside **scacan**
(ME. **schāken**) *to shake,* **sceolde** beside **scolde** (ME. **schǫlde**
beside the unstressed form **schŏlde**) *should,* **sceōp** beside
scōp (ME. **schǫp**) *he created.*

§ 34. The **ēa** from older **ǣ** (= Anglian and Ken. **ē**) became
ē after the initial palatals **c·, g·, sc·** in some of the late WS.
dialects, which like Anglian and Ken. **ē** remained in ME.
(§ 52), as **cēp** *cheap,* **cēs** *he chose,* **gēfon** *they gave,* **gēr** *year,*
gēt *he poured out,* **scēp** *sheep,* **scēt** *he shot* = ME. **chēp** beside
chẹp, ȝēr, schẹp, &c.

§ 35. Before **c, g, h ēa** became **ē** through the intermediate
stage **ǣ** in late Anglian and WS., which remained in early
ME., as **bēcen** (earlier **bēacen**) *beacon,* **ēc** *also,* **lēc** *leek,* **bēg**
ring, **ēge** *eye,* **lēg** *he told lies,* **tēg** *rope,* **hēh** (older **hēah**) *high,*
tēh *he drew.* For the further development of the **ē** before
g, h, see § 107.

§ 36. In Anglian **ēo** became **ē** before **c, g, h,** and **h + s** or
t, and then the **ē** remained in early ME. like the **ē** from **ēo**
in other positions, see §§ 65, 107, as **rēca(n)** *to smoke,* **sēc**
(older **sēoc**) *sick,* **flēga(n)** *to fly,* **flēge** *fly,* **þēh** *thigh,* **wēx** *he
grew,* **lēht** which later became **līht, liht** *a light.*

§ 37. **īo** became **ī** in Anglian before palatal **c** and **ht,** as
cīcen, older ***kioken** from ***kiukīn** *chicken,* **līhta(n)** = WS.
līehtan *to give light.*

§ 38. **weo·** : The OE. initial combination **weo·,** of whatever origin, became **wu·** (rarely **wo·**) in late WS., and **wo·**
in late Northumbrian, but remained in Mercian and Kentish
(= ME. **we·**), and then the **·u·, ·o·, ·eo·** had the same further
-development in ME. as old **u** (§ 48), but generally written **o**
in the combination **wur·, o** (§ 47), and **eo** (§ 60). These

three different developments were preserved in these areas in ME., as **wurld**, generally written **world**, and similarly **work**, **worpen** *to throw*, **worþ**, **worþen** *to become*; **world**, **work**, **worpen**, **worþ**, **worþen**; **werld**, **werk**, **werpen**, **werþ**, **werþen**. And we also have **suster** older **swuster** (OE. **sweostor**), **swurd**, generally written **sword**, beside **soster** older **swoster**, **sword**, **swerd**.

§ 39. **wio·** : OE. **io** in the combination **wio·** generally became **wu·** in late WS. and Anglian, but remained in Kentish (= ME. **e**, **i**). And before gutturals it became **i** in Anglian (*EOE. Gr.* § 63 and note 2). The **wu·**forms generally remained in ME. In ME. we accordingly have **wu·**, **wi·** and **we·**forms representing the different areas, as **bitwux**, **bitwix**, **bitwex** *between*, **cude** (code, **o = u**), **cwide**, **cwede** *cud*, **cwuc**, **cwic**, **cwec** *alive*, **wuke**, **wike** (§ 85), **weke** *week*, **wodewe** (**o = u**), **widewe** (**widwe**) *widow*, **wude** (**wode**) *wood*, see § 85.

CHAPTER III

THE ME. DEVELOPMENT OF THE OE. VOWEL-SYSTEM OF ACCENTED SYLLABLES

1. INDEPENDENT CHANGES

A. THE SHORT VOWELS.

§ 40. OE. **æ** became **a**, and **y** was unrounded to **i** during the ME. period in those areas where it had remained in OE. (§ 49), but the vowels **a**, **e**, **i**, **o**, **u** underwent no independent changes.

a

§ 41. OE. **a** in closed syllables = ME. **a**, as **asse** (OE. **assa**), **cat** (OE. **catte**), **sak** (OE. **sacc**), and similarly **asche**, **castel**, **crabbe**, **fals** *false*, **mattok**, **palme**, **stagge**, **waschen**.

basken (ON. baðask) *to bathe*, casten (ON. kasta), flat
(ON. flatr), happe (ON. happ) *good luck*.

§ 42. Before nasals Germanic a became rounded in early
OE. to a sound intermediate between the o in NE. on and
the a in NHG. mann. In the oldest OE. it was nearly
always written a, in the ninth century it was mostly written
o, but in late OE. it became pure a again except in some
parts of Mercia (west Midlands) where it became full o, and
has remained as such in many of the dialects in this area
down to the present day. Examples in closed syllables
before a single or double nasal, and a nasal + a voiceless consonant are : man, mon; þank, þonk ; and similarly anker,
bank, bigan, camp, can, pret. drank, hamme *ham*, plante,
ram, ran, swam, swan, pret. wan, wanten. ransaken
(ON. rannsaka). For OE. a(o) before a nasal + a voiced
stop see §§ 72–4.

Note.— þenne, þen *then*, whenne, when *when*, beside þanne,
þan, whanne, whan were the unstressed forms. The preterites
cam *he came*, nam *he took* beside cǭm (OE. c(w)ōm), nǫm (OE.
nōm) were ME. new formations.

æ

§ 43. æ had become a sound lying between e and æ
(generally written e) during the OE. period in Kent and the
districts bordering on it, and also in the sw. Midlands, as
feder *father*, gled, smel, þet, wes, weschen *to wash*. From
about 1300 the e was supplanted by a in the sw. Midlands,
and also in Kent and the districts bordering on it from about
1400. This change of e to a was to some extent not a sound-
change, but merely a letter-change imported from those
parts of the country which regularly had a from older æ, as
is evidenced by the preservation of the e-sound in some of
the dialects, especially the Kentish, down to the present day.
In all the other parts of the country OE. æ, of whatever
origin, became a in the early part of the twelfth century,

although the æ often continued to be written until a much
later date, e. g. in the Proclamation of London (1258).
Examples in closed syllables are : **appel** (OE. **æppel**, **æpl**),
baþ (OE. **bæþ**), **craft** (OE. **cræft**), **þat** (OE. **þæt**), and
similarly **after, at, ax** *axe,* **bak, blak, fasten, fat** *vat,* **glad,
glas, gnat, gras,** pret. **hadde (hafde)** pp. **had, harvest,
hat, paþ, sad, smal, staf, what,** pret. **bad** (OE. **bæd**), and
similarly **bar, brak, brast, sat, spak, was.** For OE. **æ** in
open syllables see § 79, 3.

NOTE.—1. ME. **whether** (OE. **hwæþer**) is the unstressed form
which became generalized. **hedde** (OE. **hæfde**) *had,* **wes** (OE.
wæs) *was* beside **hadde, was** were the unstressed forms. South
Midland pret. sing. forms like **breek, seet, speek** were new
formations with the long vowel of the plural levelled out into the
singular. The northern form **quās (quhās)**, and the Midland and
southern **whǭs whǫs** (OE. **hwæs**) were new formations from the
nom. **quā (quhā)**, **whǭ whǫ** (OE. **hwā**) *who.* Northern forms
like **efter, gres, seck (sekk)** beside **after, gras, sak** *sack* were
ON. loan-words, and they are still in common use in the modern
dialects of this area, see Index to *ED. Gr.*

2. Forms like west Midland **elder, fellen** beside **alder, fallen**
had **e** beside **æ** also in OE., see *EOE. Gr.* § 57 note 1.

e

§ 44. OE. **e** in closed syllables = ME. **e,** as **bed** (OE.
bedd), **better** (OE. **bet(e)ra, bettra**), **helpen** (OE. **helpan**),
and similarly **benche, bersten** *to burst,* **beste, delven,
fresch, helle** *hell,* **helm, henne, melten, men, nest, net,
quenchen, sellen, senden, steppen, swelten** *to die,*
tellen, þreschen, wegge *wedge,* **west, egg** (ON. **egg**), **legge**
(ON. **leggr**) *leg.* For OE. **e** before **ld, nd, ng,** see §§ 71,
73, 74.

NOTE.—In some parts of the se. Midlands early OE. **æ** (= the
i-umlaut of **a(o)** before nasals, *EOE. Gr.* § 57) remained until the
early part of the twelfth century, and then became **a** at the same
time as ordinary OE. **æ** (§ 43), as **ande** *end,* **man** *men,* **panewes**

panes pans *pennies, pence,* **sanden** *to send,* &c., but these and
similar a-forms were ousted by the e-forms of the neighbouring
dialects during the latter half of the fourteenth century.

i

§ 45. OE. **i** = ME. **i** in closed and generally also in open
syllables (see § 85), and was often written **y** before and after
nasals, **u** (= **v**), **w**, and finally, as **bidden** (OE. **biddan**) *to
pray, bid*, **cribbe** (OE. **cribb**), **grim** (OE. **grimm**), **milken**
(OE. **milcian**), **sinken** (OE. **sincan**), **þing** (OE. **þing**), and
similarly **biginnen**, **bil** *axe*, **bitter**, **brid** *bird*, **bringen**, **chin**,
crisp, **disch**, **drinken**, **finger**, **fisch**, **flicche** *flitch*, **his, is**,
lid, lippe, middel, ribbe, ring, schilling, schip, schrinken,
sitten, spinnen, springen, stingen, stinken, swimmen,
twig, þis, þridde *third*, **winter**; hider *hither*, **liver**, sive *sieve*,
þider *thither*, **witen** *to know*; pret. pl. and pp. of strong
verbs belonging to class I (§ 396), as **biten** (OE. **biton**,
biten), and similarly **biden, driven, gliden, riden, risen**,
schinen, writen. **hitten** (ON. **hitta**) *to hit*, **ill** (ON. **illr**),
skil (ON. **skil**), **skin** (ON. **skinn**). For OE. **i** before **ld, mb**,
nd, see §§ 71–3.

§ 46. Late OE. **i**, of whatever origin, + **ht** remained
throughout the ME. period in the northern and north
Midland dialects, but in the south Midland and southern
dialects it became lengthened to **ī** with gradual loss of the
spirantal element from about the end of the fourteenth
century, as **niht, niȝt, night, nīght** (early OE. **neaht** later
niht), and similarly **miȝt** sb., **miȝti** adj., pret. **miȝte**; **kniȝt**
(early OE. **cneoht** later **cniht**) *boy*, and similarly **riȝt**; **siȝt**
(early WS. **gesiehþ** later **gesihþ**, **-siht**) *sight*; **diȝten** (OE.
dihtan from Lat. **dictāre**) *to set in order*, and similarly
pliȝt, wiȝt *thing, creature*, &c.

o

§ 47. OE. **o** in closed syllables = ME. **o**, as **borwen** (OE.
borgian) *to borrow*, pp. **holpen** (OE. **holpen**), **þorn** (OE.

þorn), and similarly pp. borsten (brosten) *burst*, box, broþ,
colt, corn, flok, folk, folwen *to follow*, forke, fox, frogge,
frost, god, hoppen, horn, hors, knotte *knot*, lok, morwe
(morwen, morȝen) *morning, morrow*, norþ, ofte, orchard,
oxe, port *harbour*, sorwe (sorȝe) *sorrow*, stork, storm, top.

u

§ 48. OE. u = ME. u in closed and generally also in open
syllables (see § 85). From about the middle of the thirteenth
century o came to be written for u before and after nasals,
u (= v), and w. The writing of o for u in these positions
became pretty general towards the end of the century. In
late ME. o was also generally written for u when followed
by a single consonant + vowel (§ 9). This use of o for u is
later than that of u for y = ü (§ 49), but earlier than the
writing of ou for ū (§ 56). Examples are : bukke (OE.
bucca), ful (OE. full), hunger honger (OE. hungor), and
similarly butter, clubbe (ON. klubba), cursen, ȝung ȝong
young, huntere hontere, plukken, pullen, sum som *some*,
sunne sonne *sun*, tunge tonge *tongue*, wulf wolf, wulle
wolle *wool*, pret. pl. and pp. of strong verbs belonging to
Class III (§§ 403-4), as runnen ronnen (OE. runnon,
runnen), and similarly bigunnen bigonnen, drunken
dronken, sungen songen, wunnen wonnen ; cumen
comen (OE. cuman) *to come*, dure dore (OE. duru) *door*,
and similarly huni honi *honey*, luve love, nute note,
sumer somer, sune sone *son*.

y

§ 49. OE. y appears in ME. partly as i, partly as e, and
partly as ü (written u from about 1100 onwards).

1. It became unrounded to i in late OE. or early ME. in
all the northern counties, in a great part of the east Midland
counties, including Lincolnshire, Norfolk, and the districts
bordering on these counties, as well as in parts of the south-

western counties, especially Devonshire, Dorsetshire, and Wiltshire.

2. It became **e** in Kent and parts of Middlesex, Sussex, Essex, and Suffolk during the OE. period, and remained as such in ME. and also in many of the modern dialects of this area, see *ED. Gr.* § 109. In Chaucer the forms with **e** are nearly as numerous as those with **i**. A few of the **e**-forms have crept into standard NE., as **fledged** (mod. n. dialects **fliġd**), **kernel, knell, left** adj.

3. In all other parts of the country, including the west Midlands, it remained and was written **u** until about the end of the fourteenth century and then became unrounded to **i**; see, however, § **125**. The London dialect also belonged to the **ü**-area in early ME. as is evidenced by the **ü**-forms in the Proclamation of London (1258). The writing of **u** for **y** is earlier than that of **o** for **u** (§ **9**), both of which are due to the influence of Anglo-French orthography.

Examples are: **brigge bregge brugge** (OE. **bryċg**) *bridge*, **dippen deppen duppen** (OE. **dyppan**) *to dip*, **kin (kyn) ken kun** (OE. **cynn**) *race, generation*, **kissen kessen kussen** (OE. **cyssan**) *to kiss*, **sinne (synne) senne (zenne) sunne** (OE. **synn**) *sin*, and similarly **birþe, chirche, cripel, dine** *din*, **dint, disi** *foolish*, **fillen, fixene** *vixen*, **first, hil, hippe, hirdel, kichene, king, kirnel, listen** *to please*, **listen** *to listen*, **lift** *left*, **mille, pit, rigge** *ridge*, **schitten** *to shut*, **sister** (ON. **syster**), **stiren, þinken** *to seem*, **þinne (þynne)**, **winne (wynne)** *joy*. For the writing of **y** for **i** see § **45**. For OE. **y** before **nd** see § **73**.

B.   The Long Vowels.

§ 50. During the ME. period OE. **ā** became **ǭ** in the dialects south of the Humber, **ō** became **ü** in the dialects north of the Humber, and **ȳ** was unrounded to **ī** in those areas where it had remained in OE. (§ 57), but the vowels ǣ, ē, ī, and ū underwent no independent changes. In the course of the fifteenth century, however, the vowels ī, ū (south of the Humber) began to undergo diphthongization, and ē, ō (south of the Humber) had become ī, ū in sound before the end of the century, see *ENE. Gr.* §§ 71, 73, 75, 77.

ā

§ 51. OE. ā had become long open ǭ in all the dialects south of the Humber by about the year 1225. The change of ā to ǭ did not take place throughout this large area at one and the same time. In some dialects, especially the southern, it undoubtedly took place in the latter half of the twelfth century and in others later, e. g. it had not taken place in the east Midland dialect of Orm at the time he wrote the *Ormulum* (about 1200). But it must have taken place before the influx of early French loan-words like dāme, fāble, rāge (§ 195), and before the lengthening of early ME. ă in open syllables, as nāme, māken, &c. (§ 79), otherwise these two types of words would also have been included in the change of ā to ǭ. The ǭ was sometimes written oa (ao) and from the fourteenth century onwards it was very often written oo in closed syllables and when final. In the dialects north of the Humber the ā remained until about the end of the thirteenth century, when it became long open ę̄, although the ā was mostly retained in writing, and from the time of Barbour (1375) it was often written ai, ay (cp. § 121). Throughout this large area OE. ā, the long ā in early French loan-words, and early ME. ă in open syllables all fell together in ę̄. This great characteristic difference between the ME. development of OE. ā in the dialects north and south of the Humber has been preserved in the modern dialects right down to the present day. On the other hand the modern dialects north of the Humber still preserve the distinction in development between OE. ā and early ME. ŏ in open syllables (§ 81), whereas in the other dialects they have generally fallen together just as in the standard language. Examples are : bǭn bǫǫn bān (OE. bān) *bone*, bǭt bǫǫt bāt (OE. bāt) *boat*, grǭpen grāpe (OE. grāpian) *to grope*, mǭre māre (OE. māra) *more*, tǭ tǫǫ tā (OE. tā) *toe*, and similarly bǭr, bǭþe *both*, brǭd, clǭþ, fǭm *foam*, gǭn *to go*, gǭst *ghost*, gǭt, hǭl *whole*, hǭm, hǭt, lǭf, nǭn *none*, ǭn *one*, ǭte *oats*, ǭþ, rǭd, rǭp *rope*, sǭr, strǭken, tǭde *toad*, þǭs *those*, wǭ *woe*, wǭt *I know* ; the pret. sing. of strong verbs belonging to class I (§ 396), as arǭs, bǭd, bǭt, drǭf, schǭn, slǭd, smǭt, strǭd, wrǭt.

Note.—The ǭ from OE. ā was probably a low-back-narrow-round vowel like the a in NE. all, whereas the ME. ǭ which arose from OE. ŏ in open syllables was probably a mid-back-wide-round vowel (§ 81). Although the two sounds have fallen together in the NE. standard language they are still kept apart in some of the north Midland dialects, the former having become uə (oə) and the latter ǫi, as uəm ǫəm (OE. hām) *home*, but þrǫit (OE. þrote) *throat*.

æ

§ 52. In dealing with the history of OE. ǣ in ME. it is necessary to distinguish between ǣ = Germanic ǣ and the ǣ = the i-umlaut of ā.

1. Germanic ǣ had become long close ē in the non-WS. dialects in early OE., but by the end of the OE. period the ǣ had spread again to Middlesex, Essex, parts of the south Midland counties, and parts of East Anglia. From these latter areas words containing this ǣ-sound gradually crept into most of the other areas during the ME. period as is evidenced by the modern dialects.

2. ǣ = the i-umlaut of ā became long close ē in Kentish during the OE. period, and remained as such throughout the ME. period. In all the other dialects the ǣ-sound (= ę̄) generally remained in ME. until near the end of the fifteenth century when it became ę̄, see § 63 note.

In consequence of the spreading of ǣ in 1, Chaucer sometimes has ę̄ beside ę̄, as dę̄ęd beside dēęd *deed*, generally
rę̄den, wę̄re(n) beside drę̄de *dread*, slę̄pen; and probably
through the influence of Kentish ę̄ in 2 he occasionally has
ę̄ beside ę̄, as clę̄ne, lę̄den, lę̄ren *to teach*, beside clę̄ne,
lę̄den, lę̄ren.

In those areas where the ǣ-sound in 1 and 2 had remained
throughout the OE. period the ǣ was preserved in writing
until about the end of the twelfth century, and occasionally
even later, as in the Proclamation of London (1258). In the
Ormulum (about 1200) it was also used to express Germanic
ǣ as well, although this ǣ had become ę̄ in Orm's dialect
hundreds of years before his time. This was due to Orm
having adopted the classical WS. system of orthography.
Through the influence of Anglo-Norman orthography the ǣ
was generally supplanted by ę̄ from about the end of the
twelfth century, and from the fourteenth century onwards
it was very often written ee in closed syllables and when
final. After OE. ēa had been monophthongized to ǣ (§ 63)
the ēa came to be written sometimes for old ǣ in the twelfth
and early thirteenth centuries, and occasionally also in the
fourteenth century. This change of ǣ to ē (ee), generally
written ę̄ (ęę) in grammars, was not a sound-change, but
merely an orthographical change. The sound itself, viz.
a low-front-narrow vowel like the ai in NE. air, remained
in ME.

In those areas where the long close ę̄ had remained at the
end of the OE. period, it also remained in ME. and was
written e. From the fourteenth century onwards it was
very often written ee in closed syllables and when final. In
grammars it is generally written ę̄ (ęę).

Examples of 1 are: dēd (Angl. and Ken. dēd) dę̄d (WS. dǣd)
deed, slēpen (Angl. and Ken. slēpan) slę̄pen (WS. slǣpan)
to sleep, and similarly bę̄re *bier*, ę̄l, ę̄ven *evening*, hę̄r *hair*,
hę̄ring, lę̄ten, mę̄de *meadow*, mę̄l *meal, repast*, nę̄dle, rę̄den, .

sēd, spēche, strēte, þēre *there*, þrēd, wēpen, whēre,
wēte *wet* ; pret. pl. of strong verbs belonging to classes IV
(§ 407) and V (§ 408), as bēren, ēten, sēten, wēren, &c.
mēden (WS. mæden) *maiden*, pret. sēde (WS. sæde) *he
said*.

Examples of 2 are : dēlen (Angl. and WS. dælan) dēlen
(Ken. dēlan) *to divide*, clēne (Angl. and WS. clæne) clēne
(Ken. clēne), and similarly blēchen, brēde *breadth*, ēni *any*,
ēvre *ever*, hēlen, hēte, hēþ, lēden, lēne *lean*, lēnen *to lend*,
lēren *to teach*, lēven, rēchen, rēren *to rear*, sē *sea*, sprēden,
swēten, tēchen, whēte.

NOTE.—1. The ę̄ = OE. ǣ was a low-front-narrow vowel like the
ai in NE. air, whereas the ME. ę̄ which arose from OE. ě in open
syllables was probably a mid-front-wide vowel (§ 80). Although
the two sounds have fallen together in standard NE. they are still
kept apart in many of the north Midland dialects, the former
having become iə and the latter ei, as liəd (OE. lǣdan) *to lead*,
but eit (OE. etan) *to eat*.

2. In parts of the se. Midlands (Middlesex, Essex, Herts., &c.)
it became usual to write ā for ę̄ (= Germanic ǣ and the i-umlaut
of OE. ā, as dād, lāten ; lāden, tāchen) from about 1100 until
well on into the thirteenth century, and then the ā was gradually
ousted by ę̄. The writing of ā for old ǣ in these parts was only a
letter-change. The ǣ could not have become ā in sound, otherwise it would have fallen altogether with old ā ; and furthermore
the modern dialects in these parts have no trace of ME. ā for ǣ,
but see, however, LUICK, *Hist. Gr.*, pp. 345-6.

ē

§ 53. OE. long close ē, of whatever origin, = ME. long
close ę̄ (cp. § 50). From the fourteenth century onwards it
was very often written ee in closed syllables and when final,
and in later ME. it was often written ie through the influence
of French orthography. Examples are : 1. Germanic ē, as hēr
hēre (OE. hēr) *here*, mēde (OE. mēd) *meed, reward*. 2. The
pret. of strong verbs belonging to class VII (§ 414), as lēt

(OE. lēt) *he let*, and similarly hēt *he was called*, slēp *he slept*. 3. The i-umlaut of OE. ō, as dēmen (OE. dēman) *to judge*, fēt (OE. fēt) *feet*, and similarly bēche, blēden, fēden, fēlen, gēs, grēne, grēten, hēden, kēne *keen*, kēpen, mēten, quēne, sēken (sēchen), sēmen, spēde *success*, swēte, tēþ, wēpen *to weep*. 4. In Latin loan-words, as bēte (OE. bēte, Lat. bēta) *beetroot*, crēde (OE. crēda *creed*, Lat. crēdō *I believe*). 5. OE. lengthened ē in monosyllables, as hē *he*, mē *me*, þē *thee*, wē *we*. For forms like bēken *beacon*, ēk *also*, lēk *leek*, see § 35.

ī

§ 54. OE. ī = ME. ī (cp. § 50) which was very often written y before and after nasals, u (= v) and w (§ 9), and in Chaucer y is also very common in other combinations, as fīf fīve (OE. fīf) *five*, sīde (OE. sīde) *side*, tīme tȳme (OE. tīma) *time*, þīn þȳn (OE. þīn) *thine*, wīs wȳs (OE. wīs) *wise*, and similarly blīþe, īren, īs *ice*, īvi, knīf (ON. knīfr), līf, līken *to please*, līm, mīle, pīpe, swīn, tīde, whīle, whīt, wīf, wīn; in the present of strong verbs belonging to class I (§ 396), as bīten (OE. bītan) *to bite*, and similarly bīden, chīden, drīven, glīden, rīden, schīnen, smīten, strīden, þrīven, wrīten.

ō

§ 55. In the dialects south of the Humber OE. long close ō = ME. long close ǭ (cp. § 50), also very often written oo in closed syllables and when final from the fourteenth century onwards. In the dialects north of the Humber the ǭ became ü through the intermediate stage ȫ about 1300, and was generally written u through the influence of Anglo-Norman orthography, and sometimes o, later also ui, oi (cp. § 121), but it was not written o before nasals, u (= v), after w, and when final. Many of the northern dialects, especially the Scottish, have preserved the ü- or ö-sound down to the present day. Examples are: bǭk bŭk later buik (OE. bōc) *book*, gǭs gŭs later guis (OE. gōs) *goose*, lǭken lüke(n) later luike(n) (OE. lōcian) *to look*, and similarly blǭd, brǭd, brǭk, brǭm, brǭþer, cǭk, cǭl, dǭm, dǭn (dǭ), flǭd, fǭde, fǭt, gǭd, hǭd, hǭk, mǭder, mǭne *moon*, mǭneþ, nǭn, ǭþer, pǭl rǭf, rǭk, rǭte, schǭ, sǭne, sǭt, spǭn, stǭl, tǭl, tǭþ; the pret. of strong verbs belonging to class VI (§ 411), as awǭk, forsǭk, schǭk, schǭp *he created*, stǭd, swǭr, tǭk. Pret. sing. cǭm (OE. c(w)ōm), nōm (OE. nōm) *he took*, beside the ME. new formations cam com, nam nom.

ū

§ 56. OE. ū = ME. ū. Through the influence of Anglo-Norman orthography it was often written ou (ow) from the second half of the thirteenth century and became general in the fourteenth. By the time of Chaucer it was generally written ow when final and frequently also in open syllables, especially before l, n, and v, but in other positions it was mostly written ou (§ 9). Examples are : brū brow (OE. brū) *brow*, dūn doun down (OE. dūn) *down*, hūs hous (OE. hūs) *house*, mūþ mouþ (OE. mūþ) *mouth*, and similarly abouten *about*, broun, cloud, clout, cou (cow), croume *crumb*, douke *duck*, douve *dove*, foul, goune, hou (how), loud, louken *to close*, lous, mous, nou (now), oule (owle), our, out, ploume *plum*, proud, rouȝ *rough*, roum, schour, schroud, scoulen (ON. skūla), souken *to suck*, souþ, toun, þou (þow), þoume (þoumbe) *thumb*, þousend.

ȳ

§ 57. The development of OE. ȳ in ME. went parallel with that of short y (§ 49), viz. it appears in ME. partly as ī, partly as ē̦, and partly as ū (written u, ui, rarely uy from about 1100 onwards, see § 9).

1. It became unrounded to ī in late OE. or early ME. in all the northern counties, in a great part of the east Midland counties, including Lincolnshire, Norfolk, and the districts bordering on these counties, as well as in parts of the south-

western counties, especially Devonshire, Dorsetshire, and Wiltshire.

2. It became ę̄ in Kent and parts of Middlesex, Sussex, Essex, and Suffolk during the OE. period, and remained as such in ME. In the modern dialects of this area the ę̄ has become ī, as mīs = ME. męs *mice*.

3. In all other parts of the country including the west Midlands, it remained and was written u, ui (rarely uy), until about the end of the fourteenth century and then became unrounded to ī.

Examples are: brīde brę̄de brūde (OE. brȳd) *bride*, fīr fę̄r (vę̄r) fūr (OE. fȳr) *fire*, hīden hę̄den hūden (OE. hȳdan) *to hide*, and similarly hīde, hīre, hīve, līs, mīs, prīde, whī *why*; līþen (ON. hlȳðа) *to listen*, mīre (ON. mȳrr) *mire*, skīe (ON. skȳ *cloud*) *sky*.

C. THE DIPHTHONGS.

§ 58. All the diphthongs ĕa, ĕo, ĭo became monophthongs in late OE. except in Kentish, although they mostly continued to be written long after this sound-change had taken place. ĭe, which only occurred in the WS. area, had become monophthongized to y̆, ĭ by the time of Alfred, although the ĭe mostly continued to be written until a very much later date.

1. *The Short Diphthongs.*

ea

§ 59. OE. ea, of whatever origin, became æ in the early part of the eleventh century, although the old spelling with ea was often preserved in writing until a much later date. This æ fell together with old æ and along with it became a in the early part of the twelfth century (§ 43). Examples are: all (OE. eall) *all*, fallen (OE. feallan) *to fall*, barn (OE. bearn) *child*, and similarly calf (see § 284), callen, chalk, half, halle *hall*, pret. halp *he helped*, malt, salt,

scharp, swal(e)we *swallow*, wall; arm, dar(r) *I dare*, ȝard,
hard, harm, sparke, sparwe *sparrow*, sward, swarm,
warm; chaf, ȝaf *he gave*, ȝat *gate*, schadwe *shadow*, schaft,
schal.

eo

§ 60. eo, of whatever origin, became ö in late OE. in all
the dialects, although the eo was often preserved in writing
until well on into the ME. period. The ö then became unrounded to e during the twelfth century in the northern,
east Midland, and south Midland dialects, but remained in
the west Midland and southern dialects (except Kentish)
until about the end of the fourteenth century, when it also
became unrounded to e. In these latter dialects the ö-sound
was written eo and later through the influence of Anglo-
Norman orthography o, ue and sometimes u. Examples
are: herte, heorte horte huerte hurte (OE. heorte) *heart*;
erþe, eorþe urþe (OE. eorþe) *earth*, and similarly berken
to bark, cherl *churl*, derk, erl *Earl*, ernest, ferre *far*,
kerven *to carve*, self (for silf, sülf see *EOE. Gr.* § 311),
smerten, sterre *star*, sterven *to die*, ȝel(o)we *yellow*, hert
hart, heven(e), seven(e), werk *work*.

ie

§ 61. WS. ie, of whatever origin, was monophthongized
to y, i by the time of Alfred, although it generally continued
to be written until a very much later date, cp. § 49 and
EOE. Gr. § 67. The chief sources of the ie were: 1. The
i-umlaut of ea after initial palatal c-, g-, sc-; 2. the i-umlaut
of ea which arose from breaking; 3. the i-umlaut of io; and
4. Germanic e after initial palatal c-, g-, sc-. For 1, 2, and
4 the other dialects regularly had e in OE. and ME., but for
2 the west Midland had a (before l + cons.) in early ME.
which was later supplanted by the e of the other dialects, and
for 3 they had io (eo) in OE. and i (e) in ME., see § 62. In
ME. the y had the same further development as old y (§ 49).

Examples are: chüle chile, chele *cold, coldness*; güst gist, gest *guest*; schüppen schippen, scheppen *to create*; chürren chirren, cherren *to turn*; dürne, derne *dark, hidden*; üldre, eldre, aldre *elder*; füllen, fellen, fallen *to fell*; süllen sillen (WS. siellan, syllan, sellan), sellen *to sell*; ȝürnen ȝirnen, ȝernen *to desire*; hürde hirde, herde *shepherd*; ürre irre, erre *anger*; bigüten bigiten, bigeten *to beget*; ȝüllen, ȝellen *to yell*.

io

§ 62. **io,** of whatever origin, had become **eo** during the OE. period except in Northumbrian and a part of n. Mercian where the **io** remained. In ME. the **eo** had the same development as old **eo** (§ 60), and the **io** became i, as melk, milk (OE. miol(u)c, meol(u)c) *milk*, and similarly selk, silk, selver, silver; hirde (Nth. hiorde) *shepherd*, and similarly irre *anger*.

2. *The Long Diphthongs.*

ēa

§ 63. **ēa,** of whatever origin, became ǣ in Anglian and WS. in the early part of the eleventh century, and thus fell together with old ǣ = the i-umlaut of ā (see § 52 and note 1), although the ēa was often preserved in writing until well on into the ME. period. Through the influence of Anglo-Norman orthography the ǣ was generally supplanted by ę̄ from about the end of the twelfth century, and from the fourteenth century onwards it was very often written ee in closed syllables and when final. This change of ǣ to ę̄ (ęę), generally written ę̄ (ęę) in grammars, was not a sound-change, but merely an orthographical change. The sound itself, viz. a low-front-narrow vowel like the ai in NE. air, remained in ME. until near the end of the fifteenth century when it became ē̦, see note. In Kentish ēa became a rising diphthong in the second half of the twelfth century, which was generally written ea, ia, ya, yea, and in the fourteenth century e, rarely ye, which seems to indicate that by this time it had become long ē. Examples are : dẹd, dead dyad dyead (OE. dēad) *dead* ; lẹpen, leapen lyapen lyeapen (OE. hlēapan) *to leap,* and similarly bẹm, bẹne *bean,* bẹten, brẹd, chẹpe *cheap,* dẹf, dẹþ, drẹm, ẹre *car,* ẹst, flẹ *flea,* grẹt, hẹp, hẹved (hẹd) *head,* lẹf, rẹd *red,* slẹn *to slay,* stẹm, stẹp, strẹm ; pret. chẹs *he chose.*

NOTE.—In both native words (cp. §§ 52. 2, 80) and Fr. loan-words (cp. §§ 196, 205. 3, 217, 223) the ẹ, of whatever origin, became ē towards the end of the fifteenth century, that is, soon after old ę̄ had become ī (§ 50), see *ENE. Gr.* § 72.

§ 64. The non-WS. dialects had ẹ for early WS. ēa (= Germanic ǣ, § 52) after initial palatal c-, g-, sc-, which remained in ME., as chẹke *check,* ʒẹr *year,* ʒẹven *they gave,* schẹp *sheep,* cp. § 34.

ēo

§ 65. ēo, of whatever origin, became ȫ in Anglian and WS. in late OE., although the ēo was often preserved in writing until well on into the ME. period. The ȫ then became unrounded to close ẹ during the twelfth century in the northern, east Midland, and south Midland dialects, but remained in the west Midland and southern dialects (except Kentish, see § 67) until about the end of the fourteenth century, when it also became unrounded to ẹ. In these latter dialects the ȫ-sound was written eo and later through the influence of Anglo-Norman orthography o, ue and sometimes u, w, we, cp. § 112. The ẹ was very often written ee in closed syllables and when final, and in later ME. also often ie (§ 9). Examples are : dẹp diep, deop duep dup (OE. dēop) *deep* ; þẹf þief, þeof þuef þuf (OE. þēof) *thief,* and similarly bẹ *a bee,* bẹden *to bid,* bẹn *to be,* clẹven *to cleave,* crẹpen, dẹr *deer,* fẹnd *fiend,* flẹn *to flee,* flẹs *fleece,* frẹnd *friend,* frẹsen, knẹ, lẹf *dear,* lẹsen *to lose,* rẹd *reed,* rẹken *to smoke,* schẹten *to shoot,* sẹke beside sike *sick* (§ 99), sẹn *to see,*

sēþen, snēsen, wēde *weed*; the pret. of strong verbs
belonging to class VII (§ 414), as bēt *he beat*, hēld *he held*,
lēp beside lepte *he leapt*, wēp beside wepte *he wept*.

NOTE.—In some words the éo became a rising diphthong eó
which in ME. became ǭ by absorption of the first element. This
often gave rise to double forms, as chǭsen, schǭten beside
chēsen, schēten; ʒǭde beside ʒēde (OE. ge-eóde beside ge-éode)
he went.

īe

§ 66. WS. īe, of whatever origin, was monophthongized to
ȳ, ī (cp. § 9 and *EOE. Gr.* § 67) by the time of Alfred,
although it generally continued to be written until a very
much later date. The chief sources of the īe were : 1. The
i-umlaut of īo = īo (ēo) in the other dialects (cp. § 67) ; and
2. the i-umlaut of ēa = ē in the other OE. and ME. dialects.
In ME. the ȳ had the same further development as old ȳ
(§ 57). Examples are : dēre, düre dīre (OE. dīore, dēore,
dīere) *dear*, hēren, hüren huiren (§ 9) hīren (OE. hēran,
hīeran) *to hear*, and similarly alēsen *to deliver*, bēʒen later
beien (cp. § 107, 6) *to bend*, bilēven *to believe*, chēse, ēken
to increase, nēde, slēve, stēle *steel*, stēpel.

īo

§ 67. Old īo had become ēo in all the dialects except the
Kentish before the end of the OE. period, and then had the
same further development in these dialects as old ēo (§ 65).
On the other hand old ēo had become īo (also written īa) in
Kentish by the end of the OE. period, and then had the same
further development as old īo. The īo became īe in early
ME. Then it became a rising diphthong medially, written ie,
ye and sometimes i, e, which became ē in the fourteenth
century, but remained finally and then later became ī also
written ȳ. Examples are: diep dyep (OE. dēop) *deep*,
diere dyere (OE. dīore, dēore, WS. dīere) *dear*, and
similarly liese lyese *to lose*, lyeve lēve *dear*, viend vyend

fiend, but **bī bȳ** (OE. **bīon, bēon**) *to be*, **vlȳ** (OE. **flēon**) *to flee*, **vrī vrȳ** (OE. **frīo, frēo**) *free*, **zī zȳ** *to see*. See LUICK, *Hist. Gr.*, p. 338.

2. DEPENDENT CHANGES

(1) THE LENGTHENING OF SHORT VOWELS BEFORE CONSONANT COMBINATIONS.

§ **68.** From our knowledge of ME. phonology it is clear that short vowels and short diphthongs must have been lengthened some time during the OE. period before certain consonant combinations, especially before a liquid or a nasal + a homorganic voiced consonant, that is, before **ld, rd, nd, mb, ng, rl, rn,** and probably also before **rþ, rs** + vowel. This lengthening of short vowels and short diphthongs took place some time before the end of the ninth century. But the lengthening did not take place when the consonant combination was immediately followed by another consonant, as pl. **lambru : lāmb** *lamb*, comp. **lengra : lāng** *long*, **heardra : hēard** *hard*, pret. **sende** from *senddе : inf. **sēndan** *to send*, pl. **cildru : cīld** *child*, **hundred : hūnd** *hundred*, pl. **sculdru : scūldor** *shoulder*, **wundru : wūndor** *wonder*, &c. ; nor in unstressed forms, as **sceolde** *should*, **under, wolde** *would*.

§ **69.** In the transition period from OE. to ME., in early ME., and during the ME. period the long vowels were shortened again before some of the combinations, especially before **rd, rl, rn, rþ,** and **rs,** so that the combinations with which we are specially concerned are only **ld, mb, nd,** and **ng.** And even before these latter combinations shortening began to take place before **mb, nd,** and **ng** in the course of the late twelfth, thirteenth, and fourteenth centuries.

§ **70.** From what is said below it will be seen that whether the long vowels were preserved or became shortened again depended partly upon the nature of the following consonant

combination, partly upon the nature of the vowel, and partly
upon difference of dialect. The lengthening before ld was
generally preserved in all the dialects. Shortening had
taken place before nd, ng, and rd (see below) in Orm's
dialect before he wrote the *Ormulum*, as senndenn *to send*,
brinngenn *to bring*, harrd *hard*. For OE. a(o) before
nasals (§ 42) Chaucer has o before nd, ng, but ǫ before mb,
as hond, lond, stondon, but cǫmb, pret. clǫmb *he climbed*,
lǫmb, wǫmb. In his dialect long ę̄ (= OE. īo (ēo), ē)
remained before nd and ng, as fę̄nd *fiend*, hę̄ng *he hung*,
and also ī before mb, nd, as clīmben, fīnden, but i before
ng, as bringen ; ū remained before nd, as ground, but was
shortened before mb, ng, as pp. clomben (o = u, § 9)
climbed, songen *sung* ; a was short before rd, as hard,
warde, but OE. lengthened ō remained long, as bǫrd *board*,
hǫrd *hoard*, and similarly in Orm's dialect. For ę̄ (= early
OE. ea, later ēa) before rd he has ę̄, as bę̄rd *beard*, yę̄rd
yard, and similarly before rn, as bę̄rn *child*, fę̄rn *fern*, but
for OE. ē he has e, as pret. herde (OE. hērde) *he heard*, pp.
herd (OE. hēred), pret. ferde (OE. fērde) *he behaved*. ī, ū
were shortened to i, u in all the north Midland and northern
dialects and are still short in all the modern dialects of this
area, but remained long in the other dialects, as bīnden,
pp. bounden. Long vowels and diphthongs before the
consonant groups which originally caused lengthening were
shortened in monosyllabic forms during the late OE. period
in Kentish, but were preserved in the inflected forms, as
lamb : lāmbe, hand : hānda, hund *hound* : hūndas, eald :
ēalde which in ME. became ealde, yalde (cp. § 63). This
gave rise in ME. to many new formations through levelling
out in different directions.

§ 71. ld : The lengthening before ld was generally preserved in all the dialects.

Anglian ā from older a (= early WS. and Ken. ea, later
ēa) remained in early ME. in the northern dialects, but in

the Midland and some of the southern dialects it became
ǭ at the same time as old ā became ǫ (§ 51). In the other
southern dialects the later WS. ēa became ę̄ at the same
time as old ēa became ę̄, but the ēa remained a diphthong in
Kentish (§ 63). A few of these southern forms with ę̄ are
found in Chaucer, as hę̄lde *to hold*, wę̄lde *to rule*, although
the ę̄ had generally been ousted by the ǭ of the other
dialects in the early part of the thirteenth century. Examples are: cǭld, northern cāld, southern chę̄ld, Ken.
chealde *cold*, and similarly bǭld, fǭlden, hǭlden, ǭld, pret.
sǭlde, tǭlde, pp. sǭld, tǭld.

ę̄, also written ee, as fę̄ld (early OE. feld, later fēld) *field*,
chę̄lde *cold* sb., ę̄lde *old age*, ȝę̄lden *to recompense*, sę̄ld
seldom, schę̄ld *shield*, wę̄lden *to wield*.

ī, as chīld (early OE. cild, later cīld), and similarly mīlde,
wīlde.

ǭ, as gǭld (early OE. gold, later gōld) = early NE. gūld,
Gould, beside gŏld = NE. gold, and similarly mǭlde *mould*;
pret. schǭlde, wǭlde beside the unstressed forms schŏlde
(Orm shollde), wolde (Orm wollde).

§ 72. mb: cǭmb (cp. § 51), northern cāmb (early OE.
camb, later cāmb), and similarly lǭmb, later lamb, formed
from the pl. lambren, wǭmb (see § 128), pret. clǭmb *he
climbed*.

ī, as clīmben clȳmben (early OE. climban, later
clīmban).

ū, as dūmb doumb *dumb*, beside pp. clomben (o = u)
climbed.

§ 73. nd: Before nd all vowels were short or became
shortened in the late twelfth and the early thirteenth centuries in the northern and north Midland dialects. In the
other Midland and the southern dialects they all, except ī
(= early OE. i, y) and ū, became shortened during the ME.
period, but the approximate date of this shortening is
difficult to fix.

The ǫ from older OE. **a** (o) before nasals remained until well on into the ME. period in the south Midland and the southern dialects, and then became shortened to **o**, hence Chaucer has **o**, but we have **a** in the north Midland and the northern dialects. And then the forms with **o** were gradually ousted by those with **a** towards the end of the fourteenth century. Examples are : Early ME. **hǫnd, hānd,** later **hond, hand** ; **stǫnden, stānden,** later **stonden, stan-den,** and similarly **band** sb., pret. **band** *he bound,* **land, sand, strand,** &c.

ę̄, as early ME. **ę̄nde** (early OE. **ende,** later **ēnde**) *end,* **bę̄nden** *to bend* ; later **ende, benden,** and similarly **blenden, renden, spenden** ; **sę̄nden,** later **senden,** but pret. always **sende** from older *sendde, and similarly with the preterite of the other verbs. The ME. **ę̄** from OE. **īo** (**ēo**), see § 65, seems not to have been regularly shortened before **nd,** as **frę̄nd** (OE. **frīond, frēond**) beside **frend** formed from the compound **frendschipe** (§ 92, 2), but always **fę̄nd** (OE. **fīond, fēond**), because there was no compound beside it.

ī, as **blīnd, blind** (early OE. **blind,** later **blīnd**), and similarly **līnde** *lime-tree,* **rīnde, wīnd** ; inf. **bīnden, binden** (early OE. **bindan,** later **bīndan**), and similarly **fīnden, grīnden, wīnden,** &c. ; **kīnde, mīnde.**

ū, as **grūnd** (generally written **ground**), **grund** (early OE. **grund,** later **grūnd**), and similarly **hound, pound, sound** *healthy,* **wounde** *wound,* past participles like **bounden, founden, wounden** *wound.*

§ 74. ng : The OE. lengthened **ī, ū** became short again in early ME. in all the dialects, as **finger, ring, þing** ; **ȝung** (**ȝong**) *young,* **hunger** (**honger**), **tunge** (**tonge**) *tongue* ; inf. **singen,** pp. **sungen,** and similarly **springen, stingen, wringen.**

The OE. lengthened **ā** (**ō**), **ē** became short again in the latter part of the thirteenth and early part of the fourteenth centuries, as **lāng, lǫng,** later **lang, long,** and similarly

hongen *to hang*, strong, þong, wrong.　lenger *longer*,
lenþe (§ 263), mengen (mingen) *to mix*, streng (string)
string, see § 132.

§ 75.　Neither in OE. nor in ME. were short vowels
lengthened when the consonant combination which usually
caused lengthening was followed by a third consonant, see
§ 68.　Examples are: Orm allderrmann : āld *old*; comp.
eldre eldere *elder*, seldere : sēld *seldom*; pl. children
childre : chīld, wildernesse : wīld; sing. and pl. schul-
dre (Orm sing. schulldre) *shoulder*.　dumbnesse : doumb
dumb, whence the back-formation dumb; pl. lambre, lambren : lāmb, whence the back-formation lamb; timbre
timber; slumbren.　candle, gandre (OE. gandra), wan-
dren; hindren, spindle; blundren, hundred, wundren,
pl. wundres, from which a new singular wunder was
formed.　þunder always had short u, because it was from
OE. þunor.　Pl. engles, whence new sing. engel *angel*.
Many exceptions to the above arose in ME. through new
formations from the simple forms which regularly had long
vowels, as chīldhēde, -hōde : chīld; frēndli beside frendli :
frēnd; sēlden (Ellesmere MS. seelden) beside selden :
sēld, &c.

§ 76.　Long vowels also arose in early ME. through the
loss of þ in the medial combinations -þn-, -þr- of words
which had accented and unaccented forms side by side, as
hĕn (ON. heþan) *hence*, sĕn, sĭn (OE. siþþan, sioþþan)
since, þĕn (ON. þeþan) *thence*, wĕn, earlier wheþen (ON.
hvaþan) *whence*, whĕr (OE. hweþer) *whether*, ŏr, early ME.
oþ(e)r.　Then after the analogy of forms like ME. hider,
þider, whider with i were formed hiþen, þiþen, whiþen,
which also became hĭn, þĭn, whĭn.　Cp. § 249.

(2) The Lengthening of Short Vowels in Open Syllables.

§ 77. ME. short vowels, of whatever origin, were lengthened in open syllables of dissyllabic forms during the thirteenth century. The lengthening of a, e, o to ā, ẹ̄, ǭ took place in all the dialects, whereas that of i, u to ẹ̄, ǭ only took place in some of them. And as the lengthening of a, e, o took place earlier than that of i, u and with an entirely different result, we shall deal with them in two separate groups.

1. a, e, o

§ 78. The lengthening of a, e, o to ā, ẹ̄, ǭ took place somewhat earlier in the dialects north of the Humber than in those south of it, but in both areas the vowels had been lengthened before the end of the first half of the thirteenth century. In the dialects north of the Humber the new ā fell together with old ā (§ 51), but in the dialects south of it they were kept apart, because old ā had become ǭ (§ 51) before the lengthening of a to ā took place. The new ẹ̄, ǭ differed in quality from the ME. ę̄ which arose from OE. ǣ, ēa (§§ 52, 63), and the ǭ which arose from OE. ā (§ 51 and note). The new ẹ̄, ǭ were probably mid-front-wide like the long of the short e in standard NE. **men,** and mid-back-wide-round like the first element of the diphthong in standard NE. **so,** and the older ę̄, ǭ were low-front-narrow like the **ai** in standard NE. **air** and low-back-narrow-round like the **a** in standard NE. **all.** Although the two pairs have fallen together in standard NE. and may also have fallen together in the south Midland and southern dialects during the ME. period, they certainly did not fall together in the north Midland and northern dialects, because they are still kept apart in the modern dialects of this area, e.g. in Yks., Lanc., Derb., Stf. the new ẹ̄ has become **ei,** but the old ę̄ has become **iə** or some such diphthong. The new ǭ has become ǫi and the older ǭ has become uə, ǫə or some such diphthong.

ā

§ 79. 1. From OE. a, as bāken (OE. bacan), hāre (OE. hara), and similarly āpe, awāken, bāþen, cāre, drāke, hāten *to hate*, lāke, māken, nāked, rāke, sāke, spāde, wāden, wāven. bāre (OE. masc. pl. bare) *bare*, dāle (OE. pl. dalu), gāte (OE. pl. gatu), and similarly blāde, glāde *glad*, grāve, lāte, smāle *small*, tāle. tāken (ON. taka), and similarly cāke, gāsen *to gaze*, gāpen *to gape*.

2. From OE. a (o) before nasals, as nǎme, but nǫme in the west Midlands (OE. nama), see § 42, and similarly gāme, lāme, lāne, schāme, &c.

3. From OE. æ, south-eastern dialects e (§ 43), as fāder, fēder, vēder (OE. fæder, feder) *father*, rāven, rēven (OE. hræfen, hrefen) *raven*, see § 102 ; and similarly āker *acre, field*, brāsen *brazen*, hāsel, pl. pāþes, wāter, &c.

4. From OE. ea, of whatever origin (§ 59), as āle (OE. ealu) *ale*, bāle (OE. bealu) *bale, evil*, and similarly cok-chāfer, māre *mare*, schāde, schāken, &c.

Note.—1. In both native and Fr. loan-words (§§ 195, 216) the ā became fronted to ǣ (= ę̄) in the fifteenth century, although the a was mostly retained in writing, see *ENE. Gr.* § 69.

2. For māken, tāken the northern and north Midland dialects had mak, tak through early loss of the final -en, and these forms are still preserved in the modern dialects of this area. The pret. and pp. māde, mād (maad) for older mākede, māked arose from the loss of intervocalic k. From the new pret. and pp. was then formed a new present mā(n), after the analogy of which was formed a new present tā(n) for tāken. These presents are also still preserved in the modern north Midland dialects.

3. hǎven, hǎvest, hǎveþ (haþ) beside bihāven are the unstressed forms.

ę̄

§ 80. 1. From OE. e, as bēren (OE. beran) *to bear*, mēte (OE. mete) *meat*, stēlen (OE. stelan) *to steal*, and similarly

bḗre *bear*, brḗken, ḗten, ēven *even*, knēden, mḗte *meat*,
pḗre *pear*, spḗken, spḗre *spear*, swēren, tēren, trēden,
wēren *to wear*, wēven. gēten (ON. geta), lēken (ON.
leka) *to leak*. See §§ 11, 63 note.

2. From OE. eo, of whatever origin (§ 60), as bēver (OE.
beofor) *beaver*, mēde (OE. meodu) *mead (drink)*, and similarly mēle, smēre *ointment*, tēre *tar*, &c. See § 63 note.

NOTE.—For brēken, gēten, lēken the northern and north
Midland dialects had brek, get, lek through early loss of the
final -en, and these forms are still preserved in the modern
dialects of this area. For early west Midland and Southern forms
like bōre *bear*, ōten *to eat*, stōlen *to steal*, mōle *meal*, cp. § 60.

Ǭ

§ 81. The ǭ from OE. o was very often written oo from
the fourteenth century onwards, as flǭten flǫǫten (OE.
flotian) *to float*, þǭlen (OE. þolian) *to bear, suffer*, þrǭte
(OE. þrote) *throat*, and similarly fǭle *foal*, hǭpen, nǭse, ǭpen,
ǫver, rǭse, smǭke. Pp. bǭren (OE. boren), and similarly
brǭken, forlǭren, stǭlen, swǭren *sworn*. cǭle (OE. col,
gen. coles) with the vowel of the inflected form levelled
out into the uninflected, and similarly hǭle (OE. hol), see
§ 103.

§ 82. Lengthening also took place in dissyllables with two
consonants belonging to the second syllable, as nāvle, also
written nāvele (OE. nafola) *navel*, wāvren, also written
wāveren (ON. vafra) *to waver*; gen. ȝēstes beside nom.
ȝest, from which was formed a new nom. ȝēst *yeast*,
cp. § 97.

§ 83. Just as long vowels were shortened before single
consonants in trisyllabic forms, so also short vowels remained unlengthened before a single consonant in trisyllabic
forms, see § 87. Examples are: feþere beside early ME.
feþer (OE. feþer) *feather*, gaderen (OE. gaderian) *to gather*,
and similarly berie *berry*, scateren, stameren, þe latere

(NE. latter) beside lāter (NE. later), &c. bǫdi (OE. bodig) *body*, beside pl. bŏdies from which a new singular bŏdi was formed ; māni (OE. manig) beside early ME. pl. manie (OE. manige) from which a new singular mani was formed, and similarly with a large number of other words, as peni, popi; disi *foolish*, bisi *busy*, hevi, stedi, &c.

NOTE.—Beside the accented form mani there was also an unaccented form moni which was very common, especially in the northern dialects, and which has been preserved in a large number of dialects down to the present day, see *ED. Gr.* p. 521.

2. i, u

§ 84. The result of the lengthening of i, u to ẹ̄, ǭ through the intermediate stage ī, ū was entirely different from that of a, e, o to ā, ẹ̄, ǭ. In the latter case there was only a change in quantity, but in the former case there was a change both in quantity and quality of the vowels. This change of i, u to ẹ̄, ǭ took place in the dialects north of the Humber and in parts of the north Midland dialects in the latter half of the thirteenth century, and in the East Anglian dialects about a century later. In the Scottish dialects the ẹ̄, ǭ were later written ei, oi (ui), see § 10.

§ 85. In dealing with the lengthening of i, u to ẹ̄, ǭ it is necessary to distinguish two types of words :—

1. Old dissyllabic forms which lost their final -e before lengthening in open syllables took place, so that in this type lengthening only took place in the inflected forms, as wik (OE. wice) *week* : pl. wẹ̄kes, sun (OE. sunu) *son* : pl. sǭnes, from which new singulars were often made, as wẹ̄k, dǭr, sǭn, &c.

2. Old uninflected dissyllabic forms which became trisyllabic when inflected or had suffixes, as ẹ̄vel (OE. yfel, ifel) *evil* : gen. iveles, sẹ̄ker (OE. sicor) *secure* : sikerli, sǭmer (OE. sumor) *summer* : pl. sumeres, from which new

uninflected forms were often made, as bisi *busy*, mikel, widow ; sumer, þun(d)er, &c.

Other examples of type 1 are: northern gif : gēves *he gives*, lif : lẹves *he lives* ; schip, smiþ, wik : pl. schẹpes, smẹþes, wẹkes ; cum : cǭmes *he comes* ; dur *door*, wud *wood* : pl. dǭres, wǭdes ; and of type 2 : northern bẹsi *busy* : bisiness, mẹkel : mikelnèss, wẹdow : pl. widowes. East Anglian clẹpe(n) *to call*, lǭve(n) *to love* ; northern and East Anglian bẹtel *beetle*, crẹpel *cripple*, wẹvel *weevil*, &c. The past participles of strong verbs belonging to class I (§ 396) also regularly had ẹ, as drẹven *driven*, rẹsen *risen*, wrẹten *written*, but they generally came to have i through new formations. Already in late OE. the past participles with ·t· often had ·tt· beside ·t·, as bitten, written beside biten, writen, which gradually gained the upper hand, and then the ·i· in this type of verb was extended analogically to the other verbs, as driven, riden, risen, &c.

NOTE.— The ǭ which arose from u became ü in the northern dialects at the same time as old ǭ became ü about 1300, see § 55.

(3) THE SHORTENING OF LONG VOWELS.

§ 86. Long vowels and long diphthongs were shortened before certain consonant combinations during the OE. period and especially in late OE. :—(a) Before combinations of three consonants, as pl. bremblas beside sing. brēm(b)el *bramble*. (b) Before two consonants in trisyllabic and polysyllabic forms, as enlefan from older *ǣnlefan *eleven*, hlammæsse beside older hlāfmæsse *Lammas*, samcucu (from *sāmi·, older *sǣmi·) *half dead*, gen. twentiges : nom. twēntig *twenty*, blissian beside older blīþsian *to rejoice*, pl. deorlingas : dēorling *darling*. (c) Before double consonants + r, as gen. attres beside nom. ātor, whence new nom. attor beside ātor *poison* ; blæddre,

næddre beside older blǣdre *bladder*, nǣdre *adder*, comp.
hwittra : hwīt *white*, gen. foddres beside nom. fōdor,
whence new nom. foddor beside fōdor *fodder*, comp.
deoppra : dēop *deep*, see *EOE. Gr.* § 146. (*d*) Before
double consonants, as acc. ænne, enne beside older ǣnne
one, þrittig beside older þrītig *thirty* ; wimman beside older
wīfman *woman*. (*e*) In trisyllabic forms before single consonants, as haligdōm : hālig *holy*, pl. ænige, -u : sing.
ǣnig *any*, pl. cicenu : sing. cīcen *chicken*, whence new
singular cicen, suþerne : sūþ *south*, pl. heafodu : hēafod *head*. (*f*) And in late OE. and early ME. long vowels
began to be shortened before the consonant combinations
which caused lengthening in early OE., see § 68.

§ 87. In the following treatment of the shortening of
long vowels, we shall, as a rule, not distinguish between
shortenings which took place in OE. and those which only
took place in ME. So far, then, as ME. is concerned it may
be said that all long vowels, whether original long vowels or
long vowels which arose from old long diphthongs, were
shortened in late OE. and early ME. before double consonants and before all consonant combinations other than
those which caused the lengthening of short vowels (§ 68).
Long vowels were also shortened before single consonants
in trisyllabic forms of which many arose in ME. from the
development of svarabhakti vowels, as in brẹþeren from
older brẹþren (§ 152, 1), or were new formations made from
the uninflected forms, as in the pl. wẹpenes for older
wẹpnes formed from the sing. wẹpen *weapon*. This kind
of shortening took place in the thirteenth century, as Orm
still preserved the long vowels in this position. And just
as long vowels were shortened in words of this type, so also
short vowels remained unlengthened before single consonants in trisyllabic forms (§ 83).

§ 88. Before dealing with the shortening of the various
separate long vowels before consonant combinations we will

deal with the shortening in trisyllabic forms, as **clavere**
beside **clọver** (OE. **clāfre**) *clover*, see § 51; **laverke** later
larke (OE. **lāwerce**) *lark*; **erende** beside older **ẹrende** (OE.
ǣrende) *errand*, and similarly **evere** (§ 152, 1), pl. **heringes,
nevere, redili** beside **rẹdi, selinesse** beside **sẹli, sẹli** *happy*,
pl. **wepenes** from older **wẹpenes** *weapons*; pl. **stirọpes**
(OE. **stīrāpas**) *stirrups*; **breþeren** from older **brẹþeren**;
slumeren : OE. **slūma** *slumber*. From the trisyllabic were
often made new disyllabic forms with short vowel, as **hering,
redi, wepen,** &c., beside **hẹring, rẹdi, wẹpen,** &c.

§ **89.** In dealing with the shortening of long vowels before
consonant groups it is necessary to take into consideration
the question of chronology. When **ǣ** was shortened in OE.
it became **æ** and then **a** in ME. (§ 43), but when ME. **ẹ** from
OE. **ǣ** was shortened in ME. it became **e,** whence we have
forms side by side in ME. with **a** and **e.** And similarly
when **ēa** was shortened in OE. it became **ea** and then **a** in
ME. (§ 59), but when ME. **ẹ** from OE. **ēa** (§ 63) was shortened
in ME. it became **e,** whence we have forms side by side in
ME. with **a** and **e.** When **ēo** was shortened in OE. it
became **eo** and then **e** in ME. (§ 60), and when ME. **ẹ** from
OE. **ēo** (§ 65) was shortened in ME. it became **e,** so that in
this case the result was the same.

§ **90. ā** became **a,** as **axen, asken** (OE. **āxian, āscian**)
to ask, pp. **clad** from *clādd (OE. **clāþod**) *clothed*, **hatte**
(OE. **hātte**) *is* or *was called*, **halwen** (OE. **hālgian**) *to hallow*,
halwes (OE. **þā hālgan**) *Hallows*, **lammasse** (OE. **hlāfmæsse**) *Lammas*. In comparatives like **bradder** : **brād,
brọd,** beside the new formation **brọder**; **hatter** : **hāt, họt**
beside the new formation **họter** later **hotter,** see § 51.

§ **91. ǣ** became **a, e.** It should be remembered that late
OE. **ǣ** is of threefold origin, viz. Germanic **ǣ** (§ 52), the
i-umlaut of **ā** (§ 52), and late OE. **ǣ** from older **ēa** (§ 63).
Germanic **ǣ** became **ẹ** in Anglian and Kentish in early OE.,
so that the shortening in these dialects is always **e,** whether

it took place in OE. or ME. ǣ the i-umlaut of ā became ę̄ in early Kentish (§ 52), so that the shortening is always e in this dialect. In all the dialects we have a or e from late OE. ǣ (= early OE. ēa) according as the shortening took place in OE. or ME. Examples are:—

1. **bladder, bledder** (late OE. **blæddre** older **blǣdre**) *bladder*, pret. **dradde, dredde**, pp. **drad, dred** *dreaded*, and similarly **ampti, em(p)ti** *empty*, **medwe** (OE. inflected form **mǣdwe**) beside **mę̄de** (OE. **mǣd**) *meadow*, **nadder, nedder** *adder*, pret. **radde, redde** *he read*, pret. **slepte, wrastlen, wrestlen** *to wrestle*.

2. **clansen, clensen** (OE. **clǣnsian**) *to cleanse*, **fat, fet** (OE. **fætt**) *fat*, and similarly **clanli, clenli** *cleanly*, **helþe** *health*, **laddre, leddre** *ladder*, **lafdi, lefdi** *lady*, pret. **lafte, lefte** *he left*, **lasse, lesse** *less*, **lasten, lesten** *to follow*, **wraþþe, wreþþe** *wrath*; pret. **ladde, ledde** (OE. **lædde** older **lǣdde**), pp. **lad, led** *led*, and similarly **cladde, cledde, clad, cled**; pret. **lente**, pp. **lent** (OE. **lǣned**) *lent*; **spradde spredde, sprad, spred**; **swatte, swette** *sweated*; **ę̄ni** (OE. **ǣnig**) *any* beside ME. pl. **anie, enie** from which was formed a new singular **ani, eni** (cp. § 83).

3. **biraft, bireft : birę̄ven** (OE. **berēafian**) *to deprive, rob*, **chapman, chepman** (OE. **cēapman**), and similarly **grattre, grettre** *greater*, **laþer** (OE. **lēaþor**, gen. **lēaþres**) *lather*, **schepherde, þratte, þrette** *he threatened*.

§ 92. Late OE. ę̄, of whatever origin, became e:—

1. ę̄ = i-umlaut of ō, as pret. **bledde** (OE. **bledde**, older **blēdde**) *he bled*, and similarly **fedde, grette** *he greeted*, **kepte, mette**; **demde**, forms like **dę̄mde, wę̄nde** *he hoped* were ME. new formations from the present; **blessen, breþeren. twenti, ten** (Orm **tenn**) is a back-formation from forms like **tenþe, tenfǫld**.

2. ę̄ = OE. ēo (§ 65), as **devel** (OE. **dēofol**, gen. **dēofles**) *devil*, **lemman** (OE. **lēofmann**) *sweetheart*, and similarly **deppre** *deeper*, **ferþing, frendschipe**, whence the back-

formation frend beside frẹnd (§ 73), seknesse, stepfader; pret. fell (OE. fēoll) *he fell*, and similarly crepte, lepte.

3. Non-WS. ēo (īo) = early WS. īe, as derling (OE. dēorling, dīerling) *darling*, and similarly depþe *depth*, derre *dearer*, þefte.

4. ON. ē, as felaӡe, felawe (O.Icel. fēlage) *fellow*.

5. OE. i-umlaut of ēa, as grettre (OE. grīetra) *greater*.

§ 93. ī became i, as children, childre : chīld, fifte (OE. fīfta) *fifth*, and similarly Cristmesse, cristnen, fifti, liӡt light *a light*, liӡt light *light*, litel, lütel (OE. lītel, lȳtel, gen. lītles, lȳtles), whence the ME. new formation litel, lütel *little*, stiffer, whence the new formation stif (OE. stīf) *stiff*, wimman, wisdọm.

§ 94. ọ became o, as fodder (OE. fōdor, gen. fōdres), gosling : gọs, pret. schodde, pp. schod : schọn *to shoe*, and similarly blostme, blosme *blossom*, bosme *bosom*, softe. For the late OE. combination oht from older ōht see § 113, 5.

§ 95. ū became u, as dust (OE. dūst) *dust*, husbonde : hūs (hous), rust (OE. rūst) (see § 97), þursdai (OE. þūres-dæg) O.Icel. þōrs-dagr *Thursday*, þuӡte (OE. þuhte, older þūhte) *it seemed*, udder (OE. ūder, gen. ūdres).

§ 96. Late OE. ī, ē, ü from early OE. ȳ (§ 57) were regularly shortened to i, e, ü (written u), as fist, vest, füst (early OE. fȳst), and similarly filþe, þimel (early OE. þȳmel, gen. þȳmles) *thimble*, wischen; pret. hidde, hedde, hüdde (early OE. hȳdde), pp. hid, hed, hüd (early OE. hȳded) *hid*, and similarly kidde, pp. kid *made known*.

§ 97. Long vowels were regularly shortened in closed syllables before such combinations as ·sch, ·st, but remained long in open syllables through the consonant combinations belonging to the second syllable. This gave rise to double forms in ME. according as the vowel of the uninflected forms was levelled out into the inflected forms or as the vowel of the inflected forms was levelled out into the uninflected forms. Regular forms were: flesch (OE. flǣsc), gen. flēsches; brest (OE. brēost), gen. brēstes, whence flesch, brest beside flēsch, brēst. At a later period one or other of the forms became generalized. Examples of the former are: blast (OE. blǣst) *blast*, brest (OE. brēost), dust (OE. dūst), rust (OE. rūst), fist, vest, füst (early OE. fȳst), flesch (OE. flǣsc), mesch (OE. mǣsce), wisch, wesch, wüsch (early OE. wȳsc). Examples of the latter are: gāst, gǭst (OE. gāst) *ghost*, Crīst, ēst (OE. ēast) *east*, prēst (OE. prēost) *priest*. For forms like brust *breast*, prust *priest* in the west Midland and Southern dialects, see §§ 60, 65.

§ 98. From numerous examples given in the previous paragraphs it will be seen that long vowels were regularly shortened in derivatives and compounds when the stem-syllable was followed by one or more syllables with a strong secondary accent, as in alderman : ǭld, older āld, chapman : OE. cēap, Cristmesse : Crīst, frendli, frendschipe : frēnd, halidai : OE. hālig *holy*, lavedi, lafdi (Orm laffdig) : OE. hlǣfdige *lady*, wildernesse : wīlde, wisdǭm : wīs, &c. This rule was, however, very often broken through new formations made from the simplex, as frēndli, kīndnesse, wīsli, &c. Cp. § 75.

§ 99. Through causes which have never been satisfactorily explained a few ME. words have i beside e for the shortening of ē, ę̄, as briþeren beside breþeren, pret. fil beside fel (OE. fēoll) *he fell*, gritte beside grette *he greeted* (§ 425), hild beside older hēld *he held* (§ 414), kipte beside kepte (§ 424), þifte beside þefte (§ 92, 3), hipbrembles beside hepbrembles (OE. hēopbremblas) *dog-roses*, from which were formed the simplex hipe beside hepe (mod. dialects ep), hēpe *hip*, and similarly siknesse beside seknesse (OE. sēocnes), whence sik beside sek, sę̄k, silinesse beside selinesse (OE. gesǣlignes), whence sili beside seli, sę̄li, sę̄li.

F

§ 100. Through causes which have never been clearly defined there was a tendency from about the beginning of the thirteenth century onwards in some dialects to shorten long vowels before a single consonant in monosyllables. And this kind of shortening became quite common in the fifteenth century. It is possible that the shortening started out from such monosyllables being used in the sentence before other words beginning with a consonant, and that then the shortened forms came to be used in other positions. Examples from the *Ormulum* are: **dæþþ** (OE. **dēaþ**) beside **dǣþ** *death*, pret. **drohh** (OE. **drōh**) beside **drōh** *he drew*, **comm** (OE. **c(w)ōm**) *he came*, **toþþ** (OE. **tōþ**) *tooth*, **watt** (OE. **wāt**) beside **wāt** *he knows*, &c. ; and from other ME. texts : **bred** *bread*, **ded** *dead*, **fott** *foot*, **godd** *good*, **hedd** *head*, **þeff** *thief*, &c. Forms like **grat, gret** (OE. **grēat**) *great*, **hat** *hot*, **stif** (OE. **stīf**), **swet** *sweet* were new formations from the comparative **gratter, gretter**, &c.

§ 101. Long vowels were also shortened in unaccented forms, as **an** (OE. **ān**) *one, an*, but beside **būt** (OE. **būtan**) *except*, **nat, not** (OE. **nāwiht, nōwiht, nāht, nōht**) *nothing, not*, **scholde** (Orm **shollde, sollde**) beside **schǫlde** *should*, **us** (Orm **uss**) beside **ūs**, Orm **þehh** (OE. **þēah**) beside **þohh** (ON. **þōh*) *though*, **wham, whom** beside **whǫm** (OE. **hwām**) *whom*, **wolde** (Orm **wollde**) beside **wǫlde** *would*; and similarly with personal pronouns like **mě, wě, þǔ, ȝě, hě**.

(4) Variable Vowel Length in Stem-syllables.

§ 102. In ME. dissyllabic nouns and adjectives ending in **-el, -em, -en, -er** the vowel in the second syllable belonged originally to the uninflected forms only, see *EOE. Gr.* § 96. But already in OE. the vowel in the uninflected forms was generally levelled out into the inflected forms when the stem-syllable was short, as nom. sing. **æcer, cradol, efen**, gen. **æceres, cradoles, efenes** beside **æcres, cradles, efnes**.

And so also in ME. we have side by side forms with and
without the medial vowel, as **akeres, cradeles, evenes**
beside **akres, cradles, evnes.** ME. short vowels in open
stem-syllables regularly remained short in trisyllabic forms
(§ 83), so that lengthening of the stem-vowel took place
regularly in the uninflected forms only, but regularly
remained short in the inflected forms. Then. one of two
things happened: Either the long vowel of the uninflected
forms was levelled out into the inflected forms or the short
vowel of the inflected forms was levelled out into the uninflected forms. This often gave rise to double forms in
ME. itself, as **crādel, wāter, ēven, ōpen** beside **cradel,
water, even, open,** and similarly **fāder** beside **fader** from
the inflected forms **faderes, fadres.** During the ME. period
one or other of the doublets usually became generalized.
And this difference in the stem-vowel of words of this type
is reflected in standard NE. down to the present day, cp.
**acre, brazen, cockchafer, cradle, hazel, ladle, maple,
raven, staple, taper**; **beaver** (ME. **bēver** beside **bever**),
besom, evil, even, weasel; open; beside **fathom, hammer,
madder, saddle, shackle, swaddle, wattle; eleven,
heaven, kettle, leather, nettle, seven, weather; bottom,
copper, hovel, otter.** The modern dialects have often
preserved the forms which have not survived in the standard
language, as **brăzen, stăple, ĕven, ŏpen.**

The past participles of strong verbs, just like dissyllabic
nouns and adjectives ending in -en, had double forms in
ME., as **tāken, trēden, gēten, brōken, stōlen** beside **tăken,
trĕden, gĕten, brŏken, stŏlen (stŏln).** At a later period
one or other of the forms became generalized, e. g. stems
ending in -r, -d, -t generally had the short vowel, as **bŏren
(bŏrn), gĕten, sŏden,** and the others generally had the long
vowel, as **tāken, brōken, stōlen,** &c., which more or less
agrees with the development in the NE. standard language.
On the other hand the modern dialects, especially the

northern and north Midland, have usually generalized the
forms with short vowels, as tăken, ĕten, brŏken, chŏzen,
spŏken, trŏden, &c.

§ 103. OE. monosyllabic nouns and adjectives containing
an æ (a), e, or o in the stem-syllable gave rise to double
forms in ME. according as the vowel of the inflected forms
was levelled out into the uninflected forms, or as the vowel
of the uninflected forms was levelled out into the inflected
forms. Examples of such double forms are:— bāre beside
bar (OE. bær, gen. bares) *bare*, lāte beside lat (OE. læt,
gen. lates) *late*, and similarly cǫle beside col (OE. col, gen.
coles) *coal*, smāle beside smal, whāle beside whal, &c.
During the ME. period one or other of these forms became
generalized. Examples of the former kind of levelling are :
bāre, dāle, gāte, grāve, lāte, smāle, tāme, whāle; cǫle,
hǫle *hole*, ʒǫke beside Orm's ʒocc. And examples of the
latter kind of levelling are: bak, baþ, blak, bras, glad,
glas, gras, paþ, staf; broþ, God, lok, &c.

(5) The Formation of New Diphthongs in ME.

§ 104. One of the great characteristic differences between
OE. and ME. is the monophthongization of the typical OE.
diphthongs in ME. (§ 58), and the development of a large
number of diphthongs of an entirely different type, the
second element of which contained an i (y) or u (w).
Although late OE. had a small number of such diphthongs,
e. g. dæi (Ken. dei) *day*, Ken. meiden beside older megden
maiden, mǣw, mēu *seagull*, gen. sāwle, sāule beside sāwol
soul, cp. *EOE. Gr.* § 79, the number became greatly increased
through sound-changes which took place in early ME.,
especially the vocalization of intervocalic palatal and guttural
ʒ, and the development of glides between a vowel and
a following palatal and guttural h (= χ), written h, ʒ or gh
in ME.

In OE. the ·i (y) and ·u (w) type of diphthong only occurred finally and before consonants, and this must also have been the case in the earliest ME. period, but already in early ME. diphthongs seem to have arisen before a following vowel through a change of syllabic division in the combination vowel + ʒ (= i·consonant) or w + vowel whereby the ʒ or w was transferred from the second to the first syllable. When the first element was originally long it became shortened at the time the diphthong was formed. When such diphthongs are marked as long in ME. grammars the sign of length merely indicates that the first element was long before the formation of the diphthongs. It was very common, especially finally and before n, to write y for the second element of i·diphthongs and w for the second element of u·diphthongs. The new diphthongs which arose in ME. were all falling diphthongs. On the other hand the Kentish diphthongs of the ME. period which arose from the OE. falling diphthongs ēa, īo (ēo) were rising diphthongs, see §§ 63, 67.

§ 105. The formation of new diphthongs in ME. was mainly due to the following causes :—

1. Intervocalic and final postvocalic w combined with the preceding vowel to form a diphthong of the u·type in the first half of the twelfth century.

2. The vocalization of palatal and guttural ʒ to i· and u· consonant respectively. In the former case the i·consonant combined with the preceding vowel to form a diphthong of the i·type, and in the latter case a diphthong of the u·type was formed. The vocalization of palatal ʒ to i·consonant took place already in late OE. after palatal vowels finally and before consonants, and in early ME. also medially between vowels. The medial guttural ʒ began to become w after back vowels before the end of the twelfth century and then later it combined with the preceding vowel to form a diphthong of the u·type.

3. A great many of the ME. diphthongs arose from the development of a glide between a vowel and a following palatal and guttural h (= χ) in the thirteenth century. In the former case the glide eventually became i-consonant, and in the latter u-consonant which combined with the preceding vowel to form diphthongs of the i- and u-type.

The new diphthongs which arose in the native element of the language in the early ME. period were:—ai, ei, au, ęu, eu, ǫu, ǫu, iu. Through sound-changes which took place during the ME. period the number of diphthongs became somewhat reduced. The ei, of whatever origin, generally became ai about 1300 and thus fell together with old ai, although the ei was often retained in writing until a much later date. ęu and iu fell together in iu about the end of the thirteenth century. In some dialects, e. g. Chaucer's, ǫu and ǫu fell together in ǫu in the early fourteenth century, but they did not fall together in all the dialects as is proved by their being still kept apart in many of the modern dialects, see *ED. Gr.* §§ 127–8, 166–8. To the above list of diphthongs may be added the ǫi, ui in French loan-words (§§ **206, 207**).

ai

§ **106**. OE. æ + palatal g (= ȝ) became æi partly in late OE. and partly in early ME, and then the æi became ai (§ 43), also written ay, as mai may (OE. mæg) *he may*, fai(e)r (OE. fæger) *fair*, hail (OE. hægl) *hail*, main (OE. mægen) *power*, saide (OE. sægde) *he said*, and similarly brain, dai (gen. sing. and the new nom. pl. daies dayes formed direct from the singular), fain, pret. lai, maiden, nail, snail, tail; pp. said, slain.

Note.—In some parts of the North, Midlands, and the South a became ai before sch in the thirteenth century, as aische (OE. æsce, asce) *ashes*, waischen (OE. wascan) *to wash*, and the ai is still preserved in some of the north Midland and south-western dialects down to the present day (*ED. Gr.* § 27).

ei

§ 107. Early ME. **ei,** also written **ey,** was of various origins, and in most cases it became **ai,** also written **ay,** about 1300.

1. From OE. e+palatal **g** (= ӡ), as **wei** (OE. **weg**) *way,* pp. leӡen leiӡen lei(e)n ley(e)n (OE. **legen**) *lain,* pleӡen pleiӡen pleien (OE. **plegian**) *to play,* and similarly **eie** *awe,* **rein** beside Southern **rēn** (WS. **rēn**), **seil** *sail,* pp. **sei(e)n sey(e)n** (Anglian **gesegen**) *seen,* **weien** *to weigh* ; **leiest, leiþ,** pret. **leide** beside Southern **lēde** (WS. **lēde**), pp. **leid** *laid.* The ME. northern and Midland infinitives **leyen** (**lei, lai**) and **seyen** (**seyn, sei, sai**) beside the southern regular forms **leggen, seggen** were new formations made from the second and third persons singular **leyest, leiþ** and **seyest, seiþ,** and similarly the first pers. singular, the regular forms of which would be **legge** (OE. **lecge**), **segge** (OE. **secge**).

2. From Ken. e+palatal ӡ = WS. æ+palatal ӡ (§ 43), as **dei** *day,* **lei** *he lay,* **meiden, seide** *he said.*

3. From Ken. e+palatal ӡ = WS. y+palatal ӡ (§ 49), as **reie** (Ken. **rege,** WS. **ryge**) *rye,* and similarly **beien beyen** *to buy* (see **leyen** above).

4. From late OE. e (= early WS. **ea**)+h or ht (§ 28), as **eiӡte eighte** (early WS. **eahta**) *eight,* and similarly **feight** *he fought,* **leighter** *laughter,* pret. **seiӡ seigh** (Chaucer also **say**) *he saw,* **streight** *straight.*

5. From OE. **ǣ** or **ēa**+palatal **g** (= ӡ), as **clei cley** (OE. **clǣg**) *clay,* **neien** (OE. **hnǣgan**) *to neigh* ; **dreiӡ** *he endured,* and similarly **ei ey** *egg,* **eiþer** *either,* **grei, kei key** *key,* pret. pl. **leien** *they lay,* **seien** (OE. **sǣgon**) *they saw,* **weie** *weighing-machine,* **whei whey,** cp. § 35.

6. Late OE. **ē̆,** of whatever origin, + **g** (= ӡ) or **h** (written **h, ӡ, gh** in ME.) had various developments in ME. which

were due partly to the position of the ȝ and h in the word,
partly to difference of dialect, and partly to new formations
through levelling out in different directions :—

When the ēȝ stood before a following vowel at the time
of the formation of diphthongs it generally became ei in the
North and Midlands, but ī, mostly written y, through the
intermediate stage īȝ in some parts of the Midlands, especially
the south Midlands including the dialect of Chaucer, and the
South, but the modern dialects show that the ī did not occur
in the north Midlands, otherwise it would have become ai
whereas they have ī from older ē in words of this type.
Examples are :—M. deien, S. dīen dȳen (late OE. dēgian)
to dye; eie, ȳe (late OE. ēge, § 35) *eye*; fleien, flȳen (late
OE. flēgan) *to fly*, and similarly deien, dȳen *to die*; dreie,
drȳe *tedious, dree*; fleie, flȳe *fly*; leien, lȳen *to tell lies*;
pret. pl. seien, sȳen *they saw*, from which was formed a new
sing. sȳ beside the regular form seih, seiȝ (late OE.
seh) ; teien, tȳen *to tie* ; wreien (cp. NE. be-wray), wrȳen
to accuse. Cp. § 118.

NOTE.—In some parts of the North, Midlands, and the South e,
of whatever origin, became ei before sch in the thirteenth century,
as fleisch *flesh* (cp. § 97), freisch *fresh*, neisch *tender*, þreischen
to thresh, which has been preserved in some dialects down to the
present day, see Index to *ED. Gr*.

§ 108. In the northern and north Midland dialects the ēȝ
in the above and similar forms had come to stand finally
through early loss of the following syllable. These dialects
accordingly had ēȝ (= ēχ, generally written ēgh), and later
ē with loss of the gh in pronunciation in the first half of the
fourteenth century, as dēgh *to dye*, ēgh *eye*, flēgh *to fly*, lēgh
he lied, later dē, ē, flē, lē which have regularly become dī, ī,
flī, līd in the modern dialects of this area. But when the
following vowel was preserved these dialects also had ei, like
the Midland, as eien eies *eyes*, fleies *he flies*, leies *he tells lies*,

&c. And then new formations often took place through levelling out in different directions, as **flei** formed from **fleies**, and **flēghes** formed from **flēgh**; &c.

§ 109. Medially before consonants and finally late OE. **ēh** (cp. §§ 35, 36) generally became **eih**, mostly written **eigh**, in the dialects south of the Humber, and then later **īgh** in some of the southern dialects. When the **ei** came to stand before vowels through the addition of inflexional endings it became **ī**. Regular forms were e.g. **heigh** (mod. n. Midl. dialects **ei**) *high* beside pl. **hīe,** and then through levelling out in both directions either the **ei-** or the **ī-form,** usually the latter, became generalized, as in Chaucer **hīgh hȳ** beside **heigh, nīgh nȳ** beside **neigh** (mod. n. Midl. dialects **nei**) *nigh, near,* and similarly **slīgh slȳe slȳ** beside **sleigh** (ON. slœgr), **þīgh** beside **þeigh, heighte** (mod. n. Midl. dialects **eit**) beside **hiȝte hīghte** due to the influence of **hīgh.**

In the northern and some of the north Midland dialects the **ēh** (generally written **ēgh**) remained in the above and similar forms, as **þēh þēgh** (mod. dialects **þī**) *thigh.*

au

§ 110. ME. **au,** also written **aw,** was of various origins:—

1. From OE. antevocalic **a + w** or **f** (= v), as **awel aul awl** (OE. **awul, awel**) *awl,* **clawe clau claw** (late OE. **clawu** beside the regular nom. **clēa**), **strau straw,** formed from the OE. inflected forms like gen. **strawes,** and similarly **rau raw;** **þawen** (OE. **þawian**) *to thaw;* **hawek** later **hauk** (OE. **hafoc**), **nauger** (OE. **nafogār**) *auger.*

2. From OE. **ā + w** in the dialects north of the Humber, as **blawe blau** (OE. **blāwan**) *to blow,* **snau** (OE. **snāw**) *snow,* **auþer** (OE. **āwþer**) *either,* and similarly **crawe crau** *to crow,* **knawe knau** *to know,* **saule** *soul,* **slau** *slow.* See § 113, 1.

3. From OE. **a + guttural g** (= ȝ), as **drawen** (OE. **dragan**) *to draw,* pl. **dawes** (OE. **dagas**) beside **daies,** formed from

the sing. dai *day*, hawe (OE. hagu) *haw*, and similarly
gnawen, lawe *law*, mawe *stomach*, sawe *a saw*, pp. slawen
from OE. slagen beside slain from slægen.

4. From OE. ā + guttural g (= ȝ) in the dialects north of
the Humber, as āȝen awe (OE. āgan) *to possess*, awen auen
aun (OE. āgen) *own*, sawen (OE. sāwon) *they saw* from
which was formed the singular saw, þrawe (OE. þrāg)
space of time.

5. From Anglian æ (§ 43) = WS. ea before h and ht, as
saugh (Angl. sæh, WS. seah) *he saw*, faught (Angl. fæht,
WS. feaht) *he fought*, and similarly aughte *eight*, laughter,
maught *might*, naught *night*, straught *straight*, straughte
he stretched. But the northern dialects did not develop
a glide before h and ht, as saȝ sagh, aȝte aghte, faȝt faght,
laȝter laghter, maȝt maght, naȝt naght, slaȝter slaghter.

6. From late OE. æ (§ 43), a, older ǣ, ā before ht, as
aught (OE. āht) *aught, anything*, rauȝte raughte (OE.
rǣhte, rāhte) *he reached*, and similarly tauȝte taughte *he
taught*, nauȝt naught *naught, nothing*.

NOTE.—A new au arose in late ME. through the development
of a glide between a and a following 1 + consonant. This glide
eventually became full u-consonant, and then combined with the
preceding a to form the diphthong au, as aull *all*, faull(e) *to fall*,
haulf *half*, taulk(e) *to talk*, see *ENE. Gr.* § 102.

ęu

§ 111. ME. ęu, also written ęw, was of various origins :—

1. From OE. ǣ and ēa (§ 63) + w, as slęuþe (OE. slǣwþ)
sloth, dęu dęw (OE. dēaw) *dew*, fęwe fęu (OE. fēawe) *few*,
hęwen hęu (OE. hēawan) *to hew*, and similarly pret. ręu
he rued, schęwen *to show*, þęu þęw *custom*. For the falling
diphthong in the above and similar words Ken. also had
a rising diphthong, written yau, eau (eaw), as dyau, sseawy
to show, see § 63.

2. From OE. ĕow, as ęwe (OE. eowe) *ewe*, sęwen sęu (OE. seowian) *to sew*, stręwen (OE. streow(i)an) *to strew*.

3. From OE. antevocalic e + f (= v), as ęwte older evete (OE. efete) *newt*.

NOTE.—In a few words the OE. éa became a rising diphthong eá which in ME. became ā (later ǭ § 51) by absorption of the first element. This gave rise to double forms like schǫwen beside schęwen *to show*; and similarly with eów beside éow in sǫwen, strǫwen beside sęwen, stręwen.

ęu

§ 112. The chief sources of ęu, also written ęw, are : OE. ēow (cp. § 65), and the Non-WS. ēow, īow = WS. īew (§ 66). The ęu became iu about 1300 and thus fell together with iu from OE. īw (§ 116), although the eu was mostly retained in writing, but was also sometimes written iw, as briwen, &c.

1. From OE. ēow, as bręwen bręu (OE. brēowan) *to brew*, and similarly chęwen chęu *to chew*, ręwen ręu *to reu*; pret. of the old reduplicated strong verbs (§ 414), as blęu blęw (OE. blēow) *he blew*, and similarly gręu, knęu, þręu.

2. From Non-WS. īo (ēo) + w = WS. īe + w, as nęwe niwe (Non-WS. nīowe, nēowe) *new*, and similarly clęwe *clew*, hęu hęw hęwe *hue*, ręuþe *ruth*, tręwe *true*, tręwen *to trow*.

For forms like bruwen, ruwen, bluwe blwe *blew*, knuwe knwe *knew*, huwe hwe *hue*, nuwe nwe *new*, truwe trwe trw *true* in the southern and west Midland dialects see § 65.

NOTE.—1. In a few words OE. initial ēow became a rising diphthong, as ʒọu (OE. acc. ēow) *you*, ʒọwer ʒọur (OE. ēower) *your*, and then later the ʒọu· became ʒū-, although the old spelling was generally preserved.

2. In some words OE. medial éow became a rising diphthong eów which in ME. became ou (ọw) by absorption of the first element. This often gave rise to double forms in ME., as chǫwen

beside che̦wen, and similarly fo̦wer foure *four*, rowen *to rue*,
tro̦wen, tro̦uþe *truth*. For the later change of ou to o̦u, cp.
§ 114, 1, and for the further change of o̦u to au in some dialects,
as fauer faur, trawþe trauþe, see § 113 note.

o̦u

§ 113. ME. o̦u, also written o̦w, was of various origins:—

1. ME. ǭ + w = OE. ā + w in the dialects south of the
Humber (§ 51), as blo̦wen (OE. blāwan) *to blow*, sno̦w (OE.
snāw) *snow*, so̦wle so̦ule (OE. sāwol, gen. sāwle) *soul*,
and similarly cro̦we *crow*, cro̦wen, kno̦wen, mo̦wen,
o̦uþer *either*, no̦uþer *neither*, slo̦w, ro̦we *row*, so̦wen,
þro̦wen.

2. From OE. o + guttural g (= ȝ), as bo̦ue, bo̦we (OE.
boga) *bow*, pp. flo̦wen flo̦u(e)n (OE. flogen) *flown*, pl.
tro̦wes (OE. trogas) *troughs*.

3. From early ME. ǭ + ȝ = OE. ā + guttural g (= ȝ) in
the dialects south of the Humber (§ 51), as o̦wen (OE. āgan)
to possess, o̦wen (OE. adj. āgen) *own*, þro̦we (OE. þrāg)
time, period; lo̦we (O.Icel. lāgr) *low*.

4. From OE. o + h or ht, as tro̦uȝ tro̦ugh (OE. troh,
trog) *trough*, do̦uȝter do̦ughter (OE. dohtor) *daughter*, pp.
fo̦uȝten fo̦ughten (OE. fohten) *fought*, and similarly pret.
wro̦ughte (but west Midland warhte wrahte), pp. wro̦ught.

5. From ōht which was shortened to oht during the OE.
period, as o̦uȝt o̦ught (OE. ōht, oht) *anything*, pret. bro̦uȝte,
bro̦ughte (OE. brōhte, brohte) *he brought*, pp. bro̦uȝt
bro̦ught (OE. brōht, broht), and similarly no̦ught *naught*,
so̦ughte, so̦ught; þo̦ughte, þo̦ught.

NOTE.—The ǭu in 1. became au in some dialects, especially in
the Kentish and parts of the n., nw. and w. Midland in the fourteenth century; and the o̦u in 2. also became au in the nw.
Midland. Examples are: blawe(n) *to blow*, knawe(n) *to know*,
saule (Ken. zaule) *soul*, snau *snow*, þrawe(n) *to throw*, &c.;
bawe *bow*, flawe(n) *flown*, &c. See § 114, 1.

ọu

§ 114. ọu, also written ọw, was of various origins :—

1. From OE. ō + w, as blọwen (OE. blōwan) *to bloom,
blossom,* flọwen (OE. flōwan) *to flow,* and similarly glọwen,
grọwen, lọwen *to low,* rọwen, stọwe *place.* In some
dialects, e. g. Chaucer's dialect, the ọu became ọu in the
early part of the fourteenth century, and thus fell together
with the ọu in § 113, but they did not fall together in all the
dialects as is evidenced by many of the modern dialects
which still keep them apart.   In the north and north-west
Midlands, for example, the ọu has become ọu (flọu, grọu,
&c.), but the ọu has become ọə, ọ̄ (krọə *crow,* nọə *to know,*
&c.) from older au, see § 113 and note.

2. From OE. ō + final guttural ·h (= ·χ) and medial
guttural ·g· (= ·ʒ·), cp. *EOE. Gr.* § 172.   It is necessary to
distinguish between the final and the medial position,
because the development in ME. was not the same in both
cases :—

(*a*) Final ·ōh regularly became ·ọuh (also written ·ọuʒ,
·ough) which later became ·ọugh as in 1. above, as bọugh
(OE. bōh) *bough,* inọugh (OE. genōh) *enough,* þọugh (ON.
*þōh) *though,* and similarly drọugh *he drew,* lọugh *he laughed,*
plọugh, slọugh *he slew,* tọugh, &c.

(*b*) Medial antevocalic ·ōʒ· became ọu, also written ·ow·,
which then became ·ū·, although the ·ou·, ·ow· were retained
in writing through the influence of the Anglo-Norman
system of orthography (§ 9), as pl. bowes (OE. bōgas)
boughs, drowen (OE. drōgon) *they drew,* and similarly
lowen *they laughed,* plowes *ploughs,* slowen *they slew,* &c.
Cp. § 120.

(*c*) Then new uninflected forms were often made by
levelling out the ou (ow) = ū of the inflected forms, as bow
beside bọugh, drou drow beside drough, inou inow beside
inọugh, plow beside plọugh, slow beside slọugh, &c.

§ 115. The combinations -ōh and -ōȝ- had an entirely different development in the dialects north of the Humber. Here as in the paragraph above it is also necessary to distinguish between the final and the medial position :—

(a) Final -ōh, generally written -ōȝ, -ōgh, remained until about the end of the thirteenth century, and then became -ūgh (= ūχ), although the old spelling was mostly preserved, see § 55, as bōgh, enōgh, plōgh, slōgh *he slew*, &c.

(b) Medial -ōȝ- became üu through the intermediate stage óu (cp. § 55) and was generally written ou (ow), and then in the fifteenth century the üu became iu by the unrounding of the first element, and was generally written ew (cp. § 116), as pl. bowes, enowe, plowes, slowen, &c., later bewes, enewe, plewes, slewen, &c.

(c) Then new uninflected forms were often made by levelling out the ew (= iu) of the inflected forms, as bew, enew, plew, slew, beside the older forms bōgh, &c.

iu

§ 116. The chief source of early ME. iu (written iw) is OE. ī + w, as sniwen (OE. snīwan) *to snow*, spiwen (OE. spīwan) *to spew, vomit*, stiward (OE. stīweard older stigweard) *steward*, Tiwesdai (OE. Tīwes dæg) *Tuesday*. But after eu had become iu about the end of the thirteenth century (§ 112) the iw came to be written ew in the above and similar words, as snewen, spewen, steward, Tewesdai.

§ 117. In the southern dialects of the south-western area ē̜, ǭ initially and after initial h- became the rising diphthongs ȝē̜, wǭ, written ȝe- ye-, wo-, who-, in the latter part of the fourteenth century, as ȝē̜r yē̜r beside ē̜re *ear* in the other dialects, and similarly ȝē̜rb yē̜rb *herb*, ȝē̜si yē̜si *easy*, ȝē̜ven yē̜ven *even* ; whǭl beside hǭl, hāl *sound, whole*, in the other dialects, wǭld beside ǭld, āld *old* in the other dialects, and similarly **whǫm** *home*, **whǫt** *hot*, **wǫn** *one*, **wǫtes** *oats*. And the rising diphthongs in the above and similar words have been preserved in the modern dialects of this area, see Index to *ED. Gr.*

(6) THE MONOPHTHONGIZATION OF ME. DIPHTHONGS.

§ 118. In parts of the Midlands, especially the south Midlands, and the South, early ME. antevocalic **ēʒ** became **ī** (mostly written **y**) through the intermediate stage **īʒ** in the second half of the thirteenth century, see § 107, 6, as **īe**, **ȳe** (late OE. **ēge** older **ēage**) *eye*, **flīen**, **flȳen** (OE. **flēogan**, Anglian **flēga(n)**) *to fly*, **dīen**, **dȳen** (late OE. **dēgian**) *to dye*, and similarly **dīen** *to die*, **sīen** *they saw*, **tīen** *to tie*, &c.

§ 119. Final and anteconsonantal **eigh** from OE. **ēh** became **īgh** in some of the southern dialects, see § 109, as **hīgh** beside **heigh** *high*, and similarly **hīghte** *height*, **nīgh** *nigh, near*, **slīgh** *sly*.

§ 120. In the dialects south of the Humber ME. antevocalic **ǫu** from OE. -**ōʒ**- became **ū**, written **ou, ow** (§ 9) in the second half of the thirteenth century, see § 114, 2 (*b*), as pl. **bowes** (OE. **bōgas**) *boughs*, and similarly pl. **inowe** *enough*, **drowen** *they drew*, **plowes** *ploughs*, **slowen** *they slew*, &c.

§ 121. In many Scottish dialects, e. g. Barbour's dialect, the diphthongs **ai, oi, ui** (= Anglo-Norman **ui** for older **ǫi**), of whatever origin, became **ā, ǫ, ū** in the latter part of the fourteenth century, although the **ai, oi, ui** were very often retained in writing. This led to the **i** being regarded as the sign of long vowels, and then old long vowels also came to have **i** written after them to indicate that they were long, as **mair** = **mār** *more*, **seik** = **sēk** *sick*, **boik buik** = **būk** *book* (§ 55). Examples are : **fār** beside **fair** (OE. **fæger**, § 106) *fair*, **hāl** beside **hail** (OE. **hagol**) *hail*, **mā** beside **mai** (OE. **mæg**) *he may*, **rāss** beside **raiss** (ON. **reisa**) *to raise*, **trātour** beside **traitour** (O.Fr. acc. traitor), **chǫss** beside **choiss** (O.Fr. **chois**) *choice*, **jǭ** beside **joi** (O.Fr. **joie**) *joy*, **vǫce** beside **voice**, **pūnt** beside **puint** *point*, **pūsoune** beside **puisoune** (mod. northern dialects **puizn**) *poison*.

(7) Fusion.

§ **122.** Fusion arose from the merging together of OE. ĭ, y̆ (= ŭ) + palatal ʒ and ŭ + guttural ʒ after the ʒ had been vocalized to i- and u-consonant (cp. § 105, 2). The fusion of ĭ + ʒ took place partly in late OE. and partly in early ME., but the fusion of y̆ + ʒ and ŭ + ʒ did not take place until the early ME. period. Examples are:—

1. OE. i + ʒ became ī, also written ȳ, as **nīne** (OE. **niʒon**) *nine*, **līest lȳest** (OE. **liʒest**) *thou liest down*, and similarly **stī** *pig-sty*, **stīle** *stile*, **tīle** *tile*.

2. OE. ī + ʒ became ī, as **stīen stȳen** (OE. **stīgan**) *to ascend*, **wī** (OE. **wīg**) *battle*, and similarly **Frīdai** *Friday*, **hīen hȳen** *to hie, hasten*; **twīes** (OE. **twīga** + adverbial gen. ending -es), Orm **twigess twiggess** *twice*, and similarly **þrīes** *thrice*.

3. OE. **y** (§ 49) + ʒ became **üi, ī**, as **lüie, līe, lȳe** (OE. **lyge**) *a lie*, and similarly **büiest, bīest, bȳest** *thou buyest*, **rüie, rīe, rȳe** *rye*.

4. OE. **ȳ** (§ 57) + ʒ became **üi, ī**, as **drüie, drīe, drȳe** (OE. **drȳge**) *dry*, **büien, bīen** (OE. **bīegan**, later **bȳgan**, **bīgan**) *to bend*.

5. OE. u + ʒ became **ū**, later written **ou, ow** (§ 9), as pl. **mouen, mowen** (OE. ***muʒon**) *they may*, **fūel, fou(e)l** (OE. **fugol**) *bird, fowl*, and similarly ·ʒūþ ʒouþ *youth*, **sow(e)** (OE. **sugu**) *sow*.

6. OE. **ū** + ʒ became **ū**, later written **ou, ow**, as **būen bouen bowen** (OE. **būgan**) *to bend, bow*, **trūen trouen trowen** (OE., Anglian **trŭgian**) *to trust*.

(8) OTHER DEPENDENT CHANGES.

§ 123. The initial **wur·** in the late OE. combination **wur** + consonant from older **wyr** + consonant (*EOE. Gr.* § 63) was generally written **wor·** in ME., as **worchen, wurchen** (early OE. **wyrcan**) *to work*, and similarly **worm, wurm ; worse, wurse ; wort, wurt** *root.*

§ 124. The initial combination **wim·** became **wum·** (also written **wom·**) in early ME., as **wum(m)an** (OE. **wimman**, older **wifman**) *woman*, although the old writing with **wim·** was often retained.

§ 125. In those parts of the country where OE. **y** remained in early ME. (§ 49) the **ü** about the beginning of the thirteenth century became **u** (often written **o**, § 9) before **š** (= sch), **tš** (= ch in chin), **ltš, ntš**, and **dž** (= the j in just), as **bluschen** (OE. **blyscan**) *to blush*, **crucche** (OE. **crycc**) *crutch*, **muchel** later **much(e)** (OE. **mycel**) *much*, **unche** beside **inche** (OE. **ynce**) *inch*, **cuggel** (OE. **cycgel**) *cudgel*, and similarly **rusche, þrusche, wusch** *wish* ; **clucchen, kuchen** *kitchen*, **swuche** later **suche, whuch** *which* ; **brugge** *bridge*, **rugge** *ridge*.

§ 126. The **ü** in the above area also became **u** in the neighbourhood of consonants which favoured rounding, viz. after labials and **sch**, before **r** and especially between such sounds as **burþen burden** (OE. **byrþen**) *burden*, **churche** (OE. **cyrice, cirice**) *church*, **gurdel** (OE. **gyrdel**) *girdle*, **schuttel** (OE. **scytel**) *shuttle*, and similarly **churn, hurdel, hurst** *copse*, **schutten**, &c., see LUICK, *Hist. Gr.* § 397.

§ 127. Before and after certain consonants **e** became **i** in the thirteenth and fourteenth centuries in the North and some parts of the Midlands, especially the east and south-east Midlands, as **briþren** (mod. dialects **briðə(r)z**) beside **breþren**, and similarly **brist** *breast*, **bristen** *to burst*, **ʒit** *yet*, **linþ(e)** *length* (cp. § 263), **prist** *priest* (cp. § 97), **rist** (mod.

dialects **rist, rust)** *rest,* **strinþ(e)** *strength* (cp. § 263), **togidre** *together* (cp. § 99).

§ 128. Postconsonantal **wǫ** from OE. **wā** (§ 51) became **wǭ** in a great part of the Midlands in the thirteenth century, as **twǭ** (OE. **twā**) *two,* **whǭ** (OE. **hwā**) *who,* and similarly **swǭpen** *to sweep,* **swǭt** *sweat,* **wǭmb** (cp. § 72).

§ 129. ME. **e,** of whatever origin, became **a** before **r** belonging to the same syllable in the fourteenth and fifteenth centuries, although the **e** was very often retained in writing, as **marre** (OE. **merran**) *to mar,* **starte** (ON. **sterta**) *to start,* and similarly **harvest, yard** *rod, staff*; **farre** older **ferre** (OE. **feorr**) *far,* and similarly **dark, harte** *heart,* **starre** *star,* **starve** *to die* ; **darling** (early OE. **dēorling,** later **deor-ling**), and similarly **farþing, starbord** ; **parsoun** (O.Fr. **persone**) *person, parson,* and similarly **sarve** *to serve,* **sarvise, warre** *war,* &c.

§ 130. **ri** in the combination consonant + **ri** + dental became **ir** (**ur**) in the early part of the fifteenth century, as **bird burd** beside older **brid** *bird,* **birne** *to burn,* **birste** *to burst,* beside **burne, burste, Cursmas** (mod. n. dialects **kāsməs**) beside older **Cristes messe** *Christmas,* **dirt durt,** older **drit, þirde þurde,** older **þridde** (OE. **þridda**) *third.*

§ 131. During the ME. period **i** was probably lowered in closed syllables, especially before and after labials, liquids, and nasals, to a mid-mixed-narrow vowel like the **e** in German **gabe.** It was often written **e,** especially in the Midland and northern dialects, and in some dialects it became a full mid-front-wide vowel like the **e** in standard NE. **set,** as is shown by its development in the modern dialects, e. g. in the south of Scotland, n.Nhb., n.Cum., Dor. and w.Som., see *ED. Gr.* § 68. Examples are : **bigenne(n)** *to begin,* **fenger, leppis** *lips,* **reng** *ring,* **sweftli, wekked** *wicked,* **welle** *will,* **wemmen** *women.* What is written **i** often rhymes with **e** from the thirteenth century onwards, as **childre : eldre, stille : telle,** &c.

§ 132. e became i during the ME. period before **nk, ng,** palatal **ng** (= **ndž**) and **ntš**, as þinken (OE. þencan) *to think*, flingen (ON. flengja) *to fling*, inglisch (OE. **englisc**) *English*, singen (OE. **sengan**) *to singe*, drinchen beside drenchen (OE. drencan) *to drown*, and similarly **link, winge** (ON. **væ̈ngr**) *wing*.

§ 133. The o which arose from older ǭ before **ng** (§ 74) became u (generally written o, § 9) during the ME. period in the west Midland dialects, and the u-sound or its further development has been regularly preserved in the modern dialects of this area, and has even spread to other areas, see *ED. Gr.* § 32. Examples are: **amonge, long, mongere** *merchant*, **song, strong, tonge** *a pair of tongs*, **þrong, wrong,** of which **amonge** and **mongere** have crept into standard NE.

CHAPTER IV

THE ME. DEVELOPMENT OF THE OE. VOWELS OF UNACCENTED SYLLABLES

1. The Weakening of Vowels in Unaccented Syllables.

§ 134. One of the characteristic differences between OE. and ME. is the weakening of the OE. vowels to **e** in un-accented syllables, and its eventual disappearance in most cases. The weakening of **a, o, u** to **e** had begun to take place in late OE., and final -i had already become -e in the seventh century. It is impossible to determine what was the precise quality of this **e**. In final syllables it must have been a kind of ə-sound and have varied in quality according to the nature of the surrounding sounds something like the **a** in standard NE. **china, cathedral.** This no doubt accounts for its being sometimes written **i, u.** These variations in writing were common from the end of the thirteenth century; the **u** was especially common in the

west Midland dialects and the i in the northern dialects.
Examples in final syllables are :—

(*a*) When final, as sǭne (OE. sōna) *soon*, eiȝte (OE.
eahta) *eight*, nom. sing. of masc. n-stems, as dogge (OE.
dogga) *dog*, the ending of the gen. pl. of nouns and
adjectives, as stǭne (OE. stāna), gǭdre (OE. gōdra), the
comparative of adjectives, as gretter(e) (OE. grīetra)
greater, dat. sing. of u-stems, as sune (OE. suna). Nom.
sing. of wa-, wō-stems, as bāle (OE. bealu, -o) *evil*, schāde
(OE. sceadu, -o) *shadow*, nom. sing. of short ō-stems, as
tāle (OE. talu) *tale*, *number*, nom. acc. sing. of short
u-stems, as sune sone (OE. sunu) *son*; OE. gearu, -o
ready, pl. gearwe regularly became ȝare, ȝarwe, and then
from the latter was formed a new singular ȝaru, and
similarly buru *burrow*, holu *hollow*, naru *narrow*, schadu
shadow, soru *sorrow*, &c., see § 241. Nom. sing. of masc. ja-
stems, as ende (OE. ende), nom. acc. sing. of short i-stems,
as dęne *valley*, spęre *spear* (OE. dene, spere), nom. sing.
of fem. n-stems, as tunge (OE. tunge) *tongue*, nom. acc. pl. of
strong adjectives, as blĭnde (OE. blinde), &c.

(*b*) In final syllables ending in a consonant, as nom. acc.
pl. of masc. a-stems, as stǭnes (OE. stānas), acc. gen. dat.
sing. and nom. acc. pl. of masc. and fem. n-stems, as
doggen (OE. doggan), tungen (OE. tungan), the inf. of
strong and weak verbs, as helpen, dęlen, māken (OE.
helpan, dǣlan, macian), ending of the second and third
pers. sing. of the present of the second class of weak verbs,
as mākest, mākeþ (OE. macast, macaþ), the ending of the
pres. plural of strong and weak verbs, as helpeþ, mākeþ
(OE. helpaþ, maciaþ). hęved later hęd (OE. hēafod) *head*,
sadel (OE. sadol), brǭþer, mǭder (OE. brōþor, mōdor),
superlative of adjectives gladest (OE. gladost), pp. of the
second class of weak verbs, as māked (OE. macod) *made*,
the pret. pl. of strong and weak verbs, as bounden, mākeden
(OE. bundun, -on, macodun, -on), the dat. pl. of nouns and

adjectives, stǭnen, tungen, blĭnden (early OE. stānum, tungum, blindum, late OE. ·un, ·on, ·an § 259), here the ending ·en mostly disappeared in early ME.

From the examples given in (*a*) and (*b*) it will be seen that the OE. stem-formative or inflexional endings ·a, ·an, ·as, ·ast, ·aþ; ·ol, ·on, ·or, ·ost; ·u, ·um (see § 259), ·un all became in ME. ·e, ·en, ·es, ·est, ·eþ; ·el, ·en, ·er, ·est; ·e, ·en.

(*c*) In medial syllables, as gen. sing. hevenes (OE. heofones), pret. sing. māked(e), pl. māked(en) (OE. macode, macodun, ·on), &c.

2. The Development of ME. Svarabhakti Vowels in Final Syllables.

§ 135. In late OE. or early ME. the vocalic nasals and l developed an e before them and then became consonantal, as bǭsem (OE. bōsm) *bosom*, hasel (OE. hæsl) *hazel shrub*, sweven (OE. swefn) *dream*, and similarly blossem, botem, hūsel *Eucharist*, setel *seat*, tǭken *token*, &c.

§ 136. Final ·els became ·eles, as birieles berieles bürieles (OE. byrgels) *tomb*, and similarly rēcheles rēkeles *incense*, rēdeles rēdeles *riddle*, &c.

§ 137. In late OE. and early ME. a vowel was developed between r and a following gutteral spirant, as ME. nom. sing. buruʒ (OE. burug, buruh beside burg, burh), inflected form burǫwe (with w from older ʒ, § 105), from which a new nom. sing. burǫugh was formed, and similarly furǫugh, holǫugh *hollow*, marǫugh *marrow*, sorǫw(e) *sorrow*, &c., cp. *EOE. Gr.* § 102.

3. The Weakening of Vowels in Syllables with a Secondary Accent.

§ 138. The vowel in suffixal and derivative syllables was generally weakened to e just as in the inflexional syllables, but in some suffixal and derivative syllables which had a secondary accent the vowel was not weakened to e. This was especially the case with derivatives in -dŏm, -ĕr(e) (denoting *nomina agentis*), -fast, -fǫld (-fāld), -ful, -hǫde (-hęde), -i (older -ī = OE. -ig), -ing, -isch, -lęs (OE. -lēas), -līche, -ling, -lok (OE. -lāc), -schipe, -sum, -ung, and -ward. The long vowels in the above were shortened during the ME. period. Examples are:—

kinedŏm, wisdŏm; bākĕre (OE. bæcĕre), drinkĕr(e) (OE. drincĕre); stędefast (OE. stedefæst); Orm ānfāld (OE. ānfeald); þankful (OE. þancfull); chīldhǫde, -hęde (OE. cildhād); bodi, hǫli hāli (OE. bodig, hālig), hęring (OE. hǣring) *herring*, englisch (OE. englisc), faderlęs, hǫmlęs (OE. fæderlēas, hāmlēas); hevenlīch(e) (OE. heofonlīc) *heavenly*; schilling (OE. scilling); wedlŏk (OE. wedlāc); frendschipe (OE. frēondscipe); langsum longsum (OE. langsum) *tedious*; chępung (OE. cēapung) *trading*; afterward (OE. æfterward).

The OE. ending -ende of the present participle became -and(e) in the North (probably of ON. origin, O.Icel. -ande), -end(e) in the Midlands, but ind(e) in the south-west Midlands, and -ind(e) in the South, as helpand(e), helpend(e), helpind(e) *helping*.

4. The Loss of Final -e.

§ 139. The loss of final -e took place at various periods and under various conditions, e.g. it ceased to be pronounced much earlier in the North than in the South, and much earlier in unaccented than in accented words, but it is only possible to fix approximate dates for its loss. This is in a great measure due to the laxity in the metrical construction of much of the ME. poetry and to the great conservatism exhibited by some of the best poets. The importance attached to metre and rhyme is sometimes exaggerated. What the student of the English language wants to know is not so much what poets like Orm, Chaucer, Barbour, &c.,

wrote in their metre, as how they actually pronounced their
words in speaking.   Good metre is always a valuable
auxiliary aid in helping to confirm results which have been
arrived at by other means, but when it is used as the chief
or sole means for arriving at results, we are merely making
use of what might be called letter-language instead of spoken
language.

§ 140. In treating the history of final ·e in ME. it is important to remember that a large number of ME. words have
a final ·e which did not belong to such words in OE., the e
of the inflected forms having been levelled out into the uninflected forms, as **bāre** (OE. **bær**, pl. **bare**), **brīde** (OE.
brȳd), **chępe** (OE. **cēap**), **cǫle** (OE. **col**, gen. **coles**), **lǫre**
(OE. **lār**), **nędle nędle** (OE. **nǣdl, nēdl**), **sęke** (OE. **sēoc**)
sick, **tīde** (OE. **tīd**), &c., see § 103.   This final ·e had the
same further development in ME. as in words with final ·e
from OE. ·a, ·e, ·o, ·u.

§ 141. The final ·e disappeared or rather ceased to be
pronounced earlier in dissyllabic forms with a short stem-
syllable than in those with a long stem-syllable, as in **bitę**
(OE. **bite**) *bite, bit*, **sunę sonę** (OE. **sunu**), beside **nędle
nędle, tīde**.   In both categories of words the ·e continued
to be written long after it had ceased to be pronounced.   In
late ME. the ·e in dissyllabic forms with a short stem-
syllable was generally omitted in writing, as in **bit, son,**
but in dissyllabic forms with a long stem-syllable it was
generally retained in writing to indicate that the preceding
vowel was long.   It ceased to be pronounced earliest in the
Scottish and northern dialects, later in the Midland dialects,
and latest of all in the southern dialects, especially the
Kentish dialect.   In all the dialects it disappeared in pronunciation earlier in nouns and verbs than in adjectives, and
earlier in the strong than in the weak declension of adjectives.

In the Scottish and northern dialects it had ceased to be

pronounced in all forms by about the middle of the thirteenth
century.

In the Midland dialects it had ceased to be pronounced in
all forms by about the middle of the fourteenth century, but
the loss of final -e in pronunciation began in some parts of
this large area at a much earlier date. Already in the
Ormulum (about 1200) it was often unpronounced when
the next word in the same sentence began with a vowel, in
the dat. sing. of strong nouns and adjectives, and in the
imperative singular of verbs. In the poetry of the fourteenth
century it had become optional to retain or omit the final -e
in most forms. But the full process of its loss in pronunciation was not completed until about one hundred years
later than in the Scottish and northern dialects.

As Chaucer (1340–1400) is by far the most important ME.
poet it will be useful to give here a brief summary of his
retention and omission of the final -e. It should, however,
be remembered that he was a very conservative poet, and
that consequently his metrical forms are no sure guarantee
of how he actually pronounced such forms in his spoken
language. In his poetry the final -e was generally pronounced in dissyllabic forms with a long stem-syllable at the
end of the line, but was often not pronounced in other
positions. It was not pronounced in the following categories
of forms :—In the pp. of strong verbs when the final -n had
disappeared, as **comę, drivę, stǭlę** ; in the second pers. sing.
of the preterite of strong verbs, as **bę̄rę, tǭkę,** &c. ; in nouns
with a short stem-syllable, as **sonę, wonę** *custom,* and also
in the dat. singular of such nouns. It was generally pronounced in the following categories :—In the plural of
attributive adjectives, and in the infinitive of verbs, as
bę̄re, māke. It was sometimes pronounced and sometimes
omitted in the following categories :—It was often omitted
in the present indicative and the imperative, more seldom in
the present subjunctive, and sometimes in the syncopated

forms of the singular and plural of the preterite of weak
verbs. It was omitted in nouns with a short stem-syllable,
but rarely in nouns with a long stem-syllable. In the dat.
singular of nouns ending in a consonant it was generally
omitted in pronunciation. It was often unpronounced in
the singular of the weak declension of adjectives.

In the southern dialects the final -e ceased to be pronounced
in all forms in the second half of the fourteenth century.

§ 142. The loss of final -e in trisyllabic forms can only be
partially treated here as we shall have to return to it when
dealing with -e- in medial syllables (§§ 153–4). It began to
disappear in early ME. when the first syllable was long and
the second syllable had a secondary accent, but the secondary
accent in the second syllable remained longer in some types
of words than in others, and in poetry the final -e often continued to be pronounced until the fifteenth century, whence
such double forms as **frendschipe, hei3liche** *highly*, **siknesse,** pl. **wurþie** *worthy*, beside **frendschip, hei3lich,
sikness, wurþi.** This explains why the final -e disappeared
so early in the inflected forms of dissyllabic adjectives, as
pl. **lēred** *learned*, **wurþi.** The -e regularly remained in early
ME. in verbs of the type **lovẹde** (OE. lufode), cp. § 153, but
in verbs of the type **mākede** (OE. macode) it only remained
for a time through the influence of dissyllabic preterites like
dẹmde (OE. dēmde) *he judged*, **hĕrde** (OE. hīerde, hērde)
he heard, cp. § 153.

5. THE LOSS OF e IN FINAL SYLLABLES ENDING
IN A CONSONANT.

§ 143. Endings like -es, -ed were in some dialects written
-is (-ys), -id (-yd), -us, -ud, see § 134, and Chaucer sometimes
used these i-endings for the sake of rhyme.

§ 144 e disappeared in early ME. between a diphthong
and a following liquid or nasal, as **drawn** beside older

drawen, dra3en (OE. dragen) *drawn*, fain (OE. fægen) *joyful*, fair (OE. fæger) *beautiful*, seil (OE. segel, segl) *sail*, and similarly hail, fǫur *four*, pp. lein lain, leir *lair*, main *power*, awn ǫwn *own*, rein *ruin*, pp. slein slain, tail, wain *wagon*.

§ 145. **e** also disappeared in early ME. in the combination vowel + e + consonant, as foul from older fuwel fu3el (OE. fugol) *bird, fowl* (§ 122), twīs *twice*, þrīs *thrice*, beside older twīes, þrīes.

§ 146. **-es.** This ending occurs in the gen. sing. of the strong declension of nouns and adjectives and in the plural of nouns except the weak declension, in adverbial genitives, in the second and third pers. singular and the plural of the present in the northern dialects. In the northern and north Midland dialects the **e** began to be syncopated in the early part of the fourteenth century and this process was completely carried out by the end of the century, as dai(e)s, wai(e)s, clāþ(e)s; adv. ell(e)s *else*, ǭns *once*; verbs, as cum(e)s com(e)s, bẹr(e)s, &c. When unsyncopated forms are found after the above date in monuments belonging to the Scottish and northern dialects, they are due to the imitation of Chaucerian forms. The syncope in nouns and adjectives took place much later in the Midland and southern dialects.

§ 147. **-en.** This ending occurs in the weak declension of nouns and adjectives, in the infinitive, in the past participle of strong verbs, in the present plural of the subjunctive, in the preterite plural of strong and weak verbs, and in the Midland dialects in the present plural of the indicative. The final -n in some of these categories disappeared during the OE. period in the northern dialects. The final -n also generally disappeared early in the southern dialects, but see § 247. After the loss of the final -n the **e** also gradually disappeared. When preceded by a diphthong the **e** was regularly syncopated in the infinitive, as lein leyn *to lay*, sein seyn *to say*. It was also syncopated between r–n, and l–n in the past participle of strong verbs, as bǫrn, tǫrn, stǫln, and also between a diphthong and the n, as pp. slain slayn (OE. slægen) *slain*, see § 144.

§ 148. -er. This ending chiefly occurs in the comparative of adjectives. The OE. ending was -ra. In passing from OE. to ME. the glide vowel e was developed between a preceding consonant and the r which gave in early ME. the ending -ere. And then the final -e disappeared, whence the ordinary ME. ending -er, as OE. grīetra = ME. gretter, OE. brādra = ME. brāder brǫder·; and similarly with the ending of the gen. plural of strong adjectives (OE. -ra), cp. Chaucer oure aller cok, alderbest, alderfirst.

§ 149. -est. This ending occurs chiefly in the superlative of adjectives, and corresponds to the OE. ending -est(a), -ost(a). In ME. the -e- was never syncopated.

§ 150. -est, -eþ. These endings occur in the second and third pers. sing. of the present indicative, for the plural ending -eþ, see below. Here a distinction must be made between the different dialects. In the OE. period syncope was general in the strong verbs in WS. and Kentish, but in the Anglian dialects the forms without syncope were almost entirely generalized. This distinction was also preserved in the ME. period, that is, syncope regularly took place in the southern dialects, but generally not in the Midland dialects, and not at all in the northern dialects. In the Midland dialects syncope was far more common after long than after short stems. Chaucer has double forms in the third pers. singular, as comþ, mākþ, lovẹþ, beside comeþ, mākeþ, loveþ. Syncope did not take place in any of the dialects in the second pers. sing. of the second class of weak verbs, as lovest, lǫkest, OE. lufast, lōcast. The e in the ending -eþ of the plural of the present indicative was never syncopated in the southern dialects.

§ 151. -ed. This ending of the pp. of weak verbs corresponds to the OE. endings -ed, -od. The -ed regularly

remained in ME., but there are many new formations which
were formed direct from the ME. preterite.   Regular forms
were : **māked** (OE. **macod**), **kīþed** (OE. **cȳþed**) *made known*,
wẹred (OE. **wered**) *defended*, &c.   New formations were :
hĕrd (OE. **hīered, hēred**) : **hĕrde, maad** : **māde**, beside the
regular form **māked, clept** : **clepte**, beside the regular form
clẹ̄ped.

6. The Development of ME. Svarabhakti Vowels in Medial Syllables.

§ 152.   Many words which were dissyllabic in OE. became
trisyllabic in ME. through the development of a glide
vowel between a consonant and a following liquid, nasal
or **w** :—

1. An **e** was developed about 1200 in the combination
open voiced consonant + a liquid or nasal in dissyllabic forms
with shortening of a preceding long vowel, as **breþeren**
beside older **brẹ̄þren**, pl. **develes** beside older **dẹ̄vles**,
evere (OE. **ǣfre**) *ever*, **slumeren** *to slumber*.

2. An **o** was developed between a liquid and a following
w from older **ʒ** (§ 298), as **borǫwen** beside older **borʒen**
(OE. **borgian**) *to borrow*, and similarly **folǫwen, halǫwen**
to hallow, **morǫwe** *morrow*.

7. The Loss or Retention of Medial and Final e in Trisyllabic Forms.

§ 153.   It is necessary to distinguish between trisyllabic
forms with a short stem-syllable and those with a long stem-
syllable.   When the stem-syllable was short the medial **e**
regularly disappeared, and when it was long the final ·**e**
disappeared.   This loss of the medial or final **e** began to take
place in early ME.   Examples with short stem-syllables are :
þanne þonne (OE. **þanone**) *thence*, pl. **fadres** (OE. **fæderas**),
gen. and dat. sing. **watres, watre** (OE. **wæteres, wætere**),

pl. develes, hevẹnes, pl. munkes monkes (OE. munecas)
from which was formed a new singular munk monk, and
similarly hemp, mint *coin*, &c.   The forms with syncope
are very common in the *Ormulum*, as pl. effne beside sing.
efenn, gaddrenn, niþþrenn *to humble*, oppnenn, wattrenn,
gen. werrldess beside nom. werelld *world*, but even in the
Ormulum we occasionally find new formations, especially in
the preterite of weak verbs, as lufede, oppnede, &c. ; in fact
forms of the type lufde were rare in ME., because the medial
e was mostly preserved through the influence of the e in the
past participle.   It should be noted that the medial e in
preterites like havẹde (OE. hæfde), livẹde (OE. lifde) was
never pronounced in the spoken language.   Examples with
long stem-syllable are : pl. helpers, maiden(e)s beside the
new formation maidnes, pret. māked (OE. macode), lōked
(OE. lōcode), but preterites of the type lōked, māked
preserved the final -e for a time through the influence of
dissyllabic preterites like dẹmde, hĕrde, cp. § 142.   During
the ME. period the above sound-laws became to some extent
obliterated through analogical formations in both directions.
In the northern dialects the loss of the final -e in forms
with a short stem-syllable became more general.   In the
southern dialects the loss of the medial e in forms with a
long stem-syllable became more general.   In Chaucer double
forms are sometimes found side by side, as wẹrẹde beside
wẹred, clepte beside clẹped.   The trisyllabic forms are very
rare in late ME. poetry.

§ 154. In trisyllabic forms containing a secondary accented
syllable it is necessary to distinguish whether the secondary
accent was on the second or on the third syllable.   When it
was on the second the final -e regularly disappeared, but
when it was on the third the medial e disappeared.   Examples
of the former are : *Ormulum* allmess (OE. ælmesse) *alms*,
laffdiȝ (OE. hlǣfdige) *lady*, frendschip, heiȝlich, sikness,
beside older frendschipe, &c., see § 142.   This explains

why adjectives like **englisch, hǫli, riʒtfull, wurþi,** &c., superlatives like **fairest, hardest,** derivatives in -**ung,** -**ing,** &c., remained uninflected in the oblique cases. Examples of the latter are: **Frīdai** (OE. **Frīgedæg**), **kindom** (OE. **cynedōm**), **neighbour** older **nehhebour** (OE. **nēahgebūr**), **quinstrẹ** beside older **quinestrẹ** *quince-tree*. This syncope of medial **e** is not common in early ME., and in the *Ormulum* it does not take place at all, but at a later date numerous analogical formations are found.

8. THE TREATMENT OF UNACCENTED e IN POLYSYLLABIC FORMS.

§ 155. In forms of the type ×́×̀×× the medial **e** disappeared in the first instance and then with the loss of the secondary accent in the third syllable the final -**e** also disappeared, as **mínchène** (OE. **mynecenu**), later **mínchen** *nun*, **hérbèrwe** (OE. **hereberge**) later **hérber** *harbour, inn*, **wébstère** (OE. **webbestre**) with -**è**- due to the influence of **webbere**, later **wébster** *female weaver*, and similarly **bakster, dáisì(e)** *daisy*, **minter, sempster,** &c. Preterites like **gaderede, scaterede** and those of the type **ánswèrède, wítnèssède** preserved the stronger secondary accent and had the endings -**ede,** -**ed,** -**de** apparently used indiscriminately.

9. THE TREATMENT OF VOWELS IN PREFIXES.

§ 156. In the treatment of prefixes it is necessary to distinguish between original nouns and adjectives on the one hand, and verbs on the other. In OE. as in the other Old Germanic languages original nouns and adjectives containing a prefix had the principal accent on the prefix. This rule was preserved in ME. and accordingly the prefixes generally underwent no change, cp. **after-ward** (OE. **æfter-weard**), **unfair** (OE. **unfæger**), &c. On the other hand in OE. as in the other old Germanic languages verbs containing an

inseparable prefix had the principal accent on the verbal
element. This rule was also preserved in ME. with the
result that prefixes containing a long vowel in OE. were
shortened in ME., as abīden, arīsen = OE. ābīdan, ārīsan,
to-brēken = OE. tō-brecan *to break to pieces*. With the
exception of OE. æt-, be-, ge-, of-, on-, ond-, the prefixes
containing a short vowel generally underwent no change in
ME., as forbēren (OE. forberan) *to forbear*, fulfillen (OE.
fulfyllan) *to fulfil*, mislīken (OE. mislīcian) *to displease*,
undōn (OE. undōn) *to undo*.   æt- became at-, as athālden,
-hǫlden *to withhold*.   be- became bi-, as bicumen (OE.
becuman), bihāten (OE. behātan) *to promise*.   ge- became
i- (also written y-) through the intermediate stages ʒi-, ī-, as
iholpen (OE. geholpen), inǫugh (OE. genōg, genōh)
enough, iwis (OE. gewiss) *certain*.   of-, on-, ond- became a-,
as adoun (OE. ofdūne) *down*, aþirst (OE. ofþyrst) *thirsty*,
abouten (OE. onbūtan) *about*, along (OE. ondlong, and-
lang) *along*.

10. The Treatment of Unaccented Words.

§ 157. This subject has been partly dealt with under the
shortening of long vowels, see § 101, and we shall have to
return to it when dealing with the pronouns and auxiliary
verbs.   By referring to Chapter XI of the *EOE. Gr.* it will
be seen that many of the pronouns had double forms in OE.,
and similarly in ME. we also have accented beside unaccented
forms, as wē, ŭs, năt, nŏt beside nauʒt, nǫuʒt, ăn, ă beside
ān, ǫn.   Final -e disappeared in early ME. in unaccented
forms, as ʒes *yes*, sǫn *soon*, þan (þen), whan (when), &c.,
beside the accented forms ʒese, sǫne, þanne (þenne),
whanne (whenne), &c. ; in the inflected forms of words
like ān, mīn, þīn, &c., and also between l or n, and s in
final syllables, as els *else*, hens *hence*, sins *since*, whens
whence, beside older elles, hennes, sinnes (siþnes),

whennes. The ·e in the def. article often disappeared when the next word began with a vowel, as þende *the end*, þōþre *the other*. This elision of the e has become generalized both before vowels and consonants in all the modern English dialects from Northumberland to Nottinghamshire, that is, it has become þ (never ð) or t, see *ED. Gr.* § 312.

CHAPTER V

THE SCANDINAVIAN AND FRENCH ELEMENTS IN ME.

1. THE SCANDINAVIAN ELEMENT IN ME.

§ 158. This is a wide and important subject and at the same time a difficult subject, because of the very large number of words which were entirely alike or nearly alike in the Old English and Old Scandinavian languages. And we should now be unable to tell from which language they came if we had no English records before the invasions of the Scandinavians took place. The consequence was that an Englishman in those days would have no greater difficulty in understanding a Viking than a Yorkshire dialect speaker would have in understanding a Somersetshire peasant of to-day. And we even possess historical evidence that the old Scandinavians looked upon the English language as one with their own. In Chapter VII of the *Saga of Gunnlaugr Ormstunga* it is stated that there was at that time (eleventh century) 'the same tongue in England as in Norway and Denmark'.

§ 159. The Scandinavian loan-words found their way into English in different strata and at different periods, which in some measure accounts for the same word appearing in various forms in ME., as **gauk, gǫwk, gōk** *cuckoo*,

laus, lǫus, lōs *loose*, naut, nǫut *cattle*, &c.   These periods
may be conveniently divided into :—

1. From 787 to about 860.   During this period the in-
vaders merely made raids for the sake of plunder, and no
loan-words worth mentioning came into the language.

2. From 860 to about 990.   During this period a very
large number of Scandinavians settled permanently in this
country, and the foreign idiom was spoken over large tracts
of the country.

3. From about 990 to 1016.   This was a period of political
conquest and of the importation of large numbers of loan-
words into the language.

4. From 1013 to 1042 England was entirely under
Danish rule.   During this period English was spoken at
Court, and by this time the foreign idiom had practically
ceased to be spoken.   An important factor which helped to
bring about the complete fusion of the Scandinavian settlers
and the English was the Norman Conquest in 1066, when
both the Scandinavians and the English combined together
to combat the invader.

5. From 1050 to 1150, when the English and Scandinavian
peoples were completely merged together.   This was the last
and most important period of influx, and a very large
number of loan-words found their way into the language
during these years.

§ 160. The area over which the loan-words extended in
OE. and ME. and still extends in the modern dialects was
the northern, the north and east Midland counties down to
East Anglia, and the north-western counties. The great
bulk of the loan-words must have come into the language in
the course of the tenth and especially the eleventh century,
but they do not appear in great numbers in the literature
until the ME. period. This was due to the fact that literature
in late OE. was mainly written in the WS. dialect. We
know that the Scandinavian influence was least of all in the

southern and south-western dialects, hence naturally very
few loan-words would be found in the WS. dialect of
the OE. period.　Thus in Laȝamon's *Brut* (about 1205), the
language of which keeps up much of the traditions of the
WS. literature, there are very few Scandinavian words, while
in the east Midland *Ormulum* (about 1200) the Scandinavian
element is considerable, viz. about 250 such words.

§ 161.　The number of Scandinavian loan-words in ME.
must have been very much greater than what appears in
ME. literature.　This is proved by the fact that the modern
dialects contain thousands of such words including all parts
of speech.　In this connexion we will only mention one
important piece of evidence showing how great the Scandinavian element is in the modern dialects.　In the modern
dialects OE. initial **sc·** (= **sk·**) has become **sh·** in native
words just as in the standard language, as shade, ship, &c.,
whereas in words of foreign origin it has remained in the
dialects just as in the standard language, as **scaffold, school,
score, skill, skin, skirt, sky**, &c.　Now if we exclude all
sc· words of various origins which are common to the standard
language and the dialects, it is a remarkable fact that the
English Dialect Dictionary contains 1,154 simple words
beginning with **sc· (sk·)**.

§ 162.　In this connexion it is important to remember that
the dialects spoken by the Scandinavian settlers had for a time
a life of their own side by side with the English dialects,
whilst the Scandinavians were still regarded by the English
as foreigners.　During this period of the existence of Scandinavian dialects spoken on English soil, owing to the inter-
course between the two nations, fresh loan-words were being
continually introduced into English, and then in the course
of time the two languages gradually became merged into one
which was chiefly English in form, but very rich in Scandinavian words.　This process was in a great measure brought
about by intermarriage between Scandinavian and English

families. That this was so is clearly seen by the large number of proper names of persons of Scandinavian origin which are found in late OE. and early ME. charters and documents, and by the large number of double forms with practically the same meaning, the one being Scandinavian and the other native English, as aȝe (awe) : eie *fear*, deilen : dęlen *to divide*, egg : eie (pl. eyren) *egg*, frā (frǭ) : fram *from*, garþ : ȝard *yard, garden*, grā : OE. grǣg, ME. grei *grey*, gayt : gāt, gǭt *goat*, heil : OE. hāl, ME. hāl, hǫl *sound, whole*, lagu : OE. ǣ *law*, lāten, lǭten : lęten, lęten (OE. lǣtan, lētan) *to let*, lǫupen : OE. hlēapan *to leap*, laus (lǫus) : OE. lēas *false, loose*, naut (nǫut) : OE. nēat *cattle*, scateren : schatern, skiften : schiften, sister : suster (OE. sweostor), swein : swān (swǭn) *servant*, NE. sky : heaven, trigg : OE. trēowe *fidelity*, þei : þā *those*, weik : OE. wāc *weak*, werre : worse, ępen : OE. wēpan *to cry*, &c.

§ 163. With these few preliminary remarks we shall now proceed to state the more important phonological criteria by which the Scandinavian element in ME. can easily be recognized, and shall, as a rule, only give such illustrative examples as are to be found in well-known ME. texts, such as the *Cursor Mundi* (1300), Richard Rolle de Hampole's *Pricke of Conscience* (about 1349), Barbour's *Bruce* (1375), the *Ormulum* (1200), *Genesis and Exodus* (about 1250), the *Lay of Havelok the Dane* (1300), Robert of Brunne's *Handlyng Synne* (1300-30), *Early English Alliterative Poems* (about 1350), &c. And it should be noted that the Scandinavian loan-words which came into ME. underwent all further sound-changes in common with the native words containing the same sounds. As Old Icelandic is the best representative of the Old Scandinavian languages the older illustrative examples are here taken from that language. When the OE. or ME. word comes first in the comparisons given in the following paragraphs, it means that the word is of native origin, but of Scandinavian origin when the O.Icel. word comes first.

§ 164. When a Scandinavian loan-word contained a short stem-vowel at the time it was borrowed we have no means of determining from the vowel alone whether the word was of Scandinavian or English origin, that is, the vowel fell together in sound with the corresponding OE. or early ME. vowel, as OE. **eall**, ME. **al(l)** = O.Icel. **all·r** *all*, OE. **dragan** = O.Icel. **draga** *to draw*, OE. **sealt**, ME. **salt** = O.Icel. **salt**, O.Icel. **taka** = OE. **tacan**, ME. **taken**, later **tāken**. O.Icel. **fela** = ME. **felen**, later **fēlen** *to conceal*, O.Icel. **geta** = ME. **gĕten** beside the native form **·ȝĕten** *to get*, O.Icel. **hnefi** = ME. **neve**, later **nĕve** *fist*, O.Icel. **ketill** = OE. **cietel**, ME. **ketel**, OE. **sendan** = O.Icel. **senda** *to send*. O.Icel. **skinn** = OE. **scinn**, ME. **skin**, O.Icel. **hitta** = ME. **hitten** *to hit*. O.Icel. **oddi** = ME. **odde** *odd*, OE. **open**, ME. **open**, later **ǫpen** = O.Icel. **opinn**, O.Icel. **rottinn** = ME. **roten** *rotten*. OE. **sum** = O.Icel. **sum·r** *some*, OE. **tunge** = O.Icel. **tunga** *tongue*. O.Icel. **flytja** = ME. **flitten**, **flütten** *to flit, migrate*, OE. **cynn** = O.Icel. **kyn** *kin, kindred*, O.Icel. **stytta** from older **stynta* = ME. **stinten**, **stenten**, **stünten** *to stint, stop*, see § 49, O.Icel. **syster** = ME. **sister**.

§ 165. From the examples of long vowels given below it will be seen that with the exception of Germanic **ǣ** (§ 52) we have no means of determining from the long vowel alone whether the word containing it is of Scandinavian or English origin, as OE. **dœ̄man**, **dēman**, ME. **dę̄men** = O.Icel. **dœ̄ma** *to judge*, OE. ME. **hēr** = O.Icel. **hēr** *here*, O.Icel. **sēr** = ME. **sę̄r** *separately*, OE. **bītan**, ·ME. **bīten** = O.Icel. **bīta** *to bite*, O.Icel. **tīþinde** = ME. **tīþende** *tidings, news*, O Icel. **þrīfa·sk** = ME. **þrīven** *to thrive*. OE. ME. **fōt** = O.Icel. **fōt·r** *foot*, O.Icel. **bōn** = ME. **bǫne** *request*, O.Icel. **rōt** = ME. **rǫte** *root*. OE. ME. **hūs** = O.Icel. **hūs** *house*, O.Icel. **būin·n** = ME. **boune** *ready*, O.Icel. **drūpa** = ME. **droupen** *to droop*. Pl. OE. **mȳs**, ME. **mīs**, **mēs**, **mūs** (§ 57)

= O.Icel. mȳss *mice*, O.Icel. brȳnn = ME. brīn *eyebrow*,
O.Icel. þrȳsta = ME. þrīsten, þrēsten, þrūsten *to thrust*.

§ 166. The treatment of Germanic ǣ is entirely different
in O.Icel. and OE. In O.Icel. it became ā, whereas in OE.
it became ē (= ME. ę̄) in the Anglian and Kentish dialects,
but remained in WS. Before nasals it became ō (= ME. ǭ)
in all the OE. dialects. In this case we have an excellent
test. If a ME. word is of Scandinavian origin it has ā, ǭ
(§ 51), if it is of English origin it has ę̄, ē̜ (§ 52), and ǭ
before nasals, as O.Icel. grā·r = ME. grā, grǭ beside OE.
grǣg, ME. grei *grey*, O.Icel. hār = ME. hāre, hǭre beside
OE. hǣr, hēr, ME. hę̄r, hē̜r *hair*, O.Icel. lāta = ME.
lāten, lǭten beside OE. lǣtan, lētan, ME. lę̄ten, lē̜ten
to let, O.Icel. rāþa = ME. rāþen, rǭþen beside OE. rǣdan
to counsel, O.Icel. vāpn = ME. wāpen, wǭpen beside OE.
wǣpen *weapon*, O.Icel. vǭrom from older *vārum = ME.
wāren, wǭren beside OE. wǣron *we were*, and similarly
bāren, bǭren *we bore*, gāven, gǭven *we gave*, OE. mōna =
ME. mǭne = O.Icel. māne *moon*. A similar distinction existed in ME. when the O.Icel. ā corresponded to OE. ēa,
of whatever origin, as O.Icel. fā·r = ME. fā, fǭ beside OE.
fēawe, ME. fę̄we *few*, O.Icel. flā = ME. flā(n), flǭ(n), beside
OE. flēan, ME. flę̄(n) *to flay*, O.Icel. slā = ME. slā(n), slǭ(n),
beside OE. slēan, ME. slę̄(n) *to slay*.

O.Icel. ār with ā from Germanic ai = ME. ār, ǭr beside
OE. ǣ from *airiz = ME. ę̄r *earlier, formerly, before*.

§ 167. A good test as to whether a ME. form is of Scandinavian or native English origin is to be found in the treatment of the Germanic diphthongs in the Scandinavian and
English languages, especially the diphthongs ai, au, and
the i-umlaut of the latter diphthong, as will be seen from the
table given below. It should be noted that in O.Icel. the
Germanic diphthong eu became a rising diphthong, viz
jū before f, p, g, k, and jō in all other positions. At the
time, however, when Scandinavian loan-words came into

English the diphthong from Germanic **eu** must have been a falling diphthong, because it had the same development in ME. as OE. **ēo**, that is, it became **ę̄**, so that no further notice of it will be taken here.

Prim. Germ.	ai	au	eu	
O.Icel.	ei	au	jō (jū)	ey
ME.	ei(ai)	ǫu	ę̄	ei(ai)
OE.	ā	ēa	ēo	īe
ME.	ā(ǭ)	ę̄	ę̄	ī, ū, ę̄

§ 168. O.Icel. ei : bleik·r = ME. bleik, blaik beside OE. blāc, ME. blāk, blǫk *bleak*, freista = ME. freisten *to ask*, geit = ME. geit, gait beside OE. gāt, ME. gāt, gǭt *goat*, heil(l) = ME. heil, hail beside OE. hāl, ME. hāl, hǫl *sound, whole*, heiþir·n = ME. heiþen, haiþen beside the OE. mutated form hǣþen, ME. hę̄þen *heathen*, leika = ME. leiken, laiken beside OE. lācan *to play*, leiþ·r = ME. leiþ, laiþ beside OE. lāþ, ME. lāþe, lǭþe *loathsome*, nei = ME. nai, nay beside OE. nā, ME. nā, nǭ *no, nay*, steik = ME. steike *steak*, þei·r, þeir(r)a, þeim = ME. þei, þeire, þeim, NE. they, their, them beside OE. þā *those*, þāra (þǣra), þǣm (þām), veik·r = ME. weik, waik beside OE. wāc, ME. wāke, wǭke *weak*.

NOTE.— The ei in the above and similar words became ai, also written ay, about 1300 (§ 107), and then in the dialects south of the Humber the ai became ę̄ before k about the end of the fourteenth century, as wę̄k beside older weik waik *weak*, and similarly blę̄k *bleak*, stę̄k *steak*.

§ 169. O.Icel. au : gaula = ME. gǫulèn, gaulen *to howl*, hlaupa = ME. lǫupen beside OE. hlēapan, ME. lę̄pen *to leap*, kaupa = ME. cǫupen beside OE. cēapian, ME. chę̄pen *to buy*, laus = ME. lǫus(e), lǭs *loose* beside OE. lēas, ME. lę̄s *false, untrue*, naut = ME. naut, nǭut beside OE. nēat, ME. nę̄te *cattle*, rauta = ME. rǫuten *to bellow*. Cp. §§ 113 note, 159.

§ 170. O. Icel. ey : leysa = ME. leisen, laisen beside OE. (Anglian) lēsan, ME. lẹsen *to loosen* (see § 66), neyta = ME. naiten *to make use of*, treysta = ME. treisten, traisten beside OE. *trȳstan, ME. trīsten, trūsten *to trust*.

§ 171. In order to keep together the various criteria by which Scandinavian loan-words can be recognized in OE. and ME. we shall also include here the consonants.

§ 172. Initial w disappeared in early Old Scandinavian before ö, ŭ and l, whence forms like ōepa = ME. ẹpen beside OE. wēpan, ME. wẹpen from *wōpjan *to weep*, ōkr = ME. ọker beside OE. wōcor *usury*, orm·r *snake* = ME. proper name Orm, NE. Ormsby beside OE. wurm, wyrm *snake, worm*, leita = ME. leiten, laiten *to seek, look for*, beside OE. wlātian *to gaze*.

§ 173. Germanic đ remained in Old Scandinavian, but became d in prehistoric OE. (*EOE. Gr.* §§ 113, 133), whence O. Icel. garð·r *enclosure, yard* = ME. garþ and many mod. n. dialects garth beside OE. geard, ME. ȝard, ȝerd *yard*, O. Icel. rāða = ME. rāþen, rọþen beside OE. rǣdan, rēdan, ME. rẹden, rẹden *to advise, counsel*, O. Icel. tiðinde = ME. tīþende, tīþinde beside ME. tīdende, tīdinde *tidings, news* : OE. tīd *time*.

§ 174. Old Scandinavian had no trace whatever of the palatalization of Germanic k when originally followed by a palatal vowel, whereas the k in this position became palatalized in prehistoric OE. (*EOE. Gr.* § 166), and then in late OE. or early ME. it became ass ibilated to tš, written ch, in all the dialects, see Hoops, *Wissenschaftliche Forschungsberichte*, pp. 78–9, but in other positions it remained both in OE. and ME. Examples are : O. Icel. bekkr = ME. bek beside OE. bece, ME. beche *brook*, O. Icel. kirkja = ME. kirke, mod. n. dialects kirk beside OE. cir(i)ce, ME. chir(e)che *church*, O. Icel. kirna = mod. n. dialects kirn beside ME. chirne *churn*, O. Icel. kista = mod. n. dialects kist beside OE. cest, cist, ME. cheste, chiste *chest*, O. Icel.

dīki = ME. dīke beside OE. dīc, ME. dīch, NE. dike
beside ditch, O.Icel. ketill = ME. ketel beside OE. cietel,
ME. chetel *kettle*. But O.Icel. kald‑r, early OE. ceald,
cald, ME. cāld, cǫld *cold* (see § 71), O.Icel. kalla, late OE.
ceallian, ME. callen *to call*, O.Icel. kenna, OE. cennan,
ME. kennen from *kannjan *to know, recognize*. See § 285.

§ 175. Initial, medial, and final sk is a good test, because
there can be no doubt that sk (sc) became sch in ME.
native words, see §161. Examples are: O.Icel. skel =
mod. n. dialects skel beside OE. sciell, ME. schelle *shell*,
O.Icel. skifta = ME. skiften, mod. n. dialects skift beside
OE. sciftan, ME. schiften *to shift*, O.Icel. aska = ME.
aske beside OE. asce, ME. asche *ashes*, fisk‑r = ME. fisk
(Orm pl. fisskess) beside OE. fisc, ME. fisch *fish*.

§ 176. The Germanic initial spirant ȝ became the explosive
g in the Old Scandinavian languages, and also during the
OE. period before guttural vowels, but remained in OE.
before palatal vowels (*EOE. Gr.* § 168), whence we have
O.Icel. g‑, but OE. and ME. g‑ beside ȝ‑, as O.Icel. gaf =
ME. gaf beside OE. geaf, ME. ȝaf, ȝef *he gave*, O.Icel.
gapa = ME. gāpen *to yawn, gape*, O.Icel. garn = ME. and
many mod. dialects garn beside OE. gearn *yarn*, O.Icel.
garð‑r *enclosure, yard* = ME. garþ beside OE. geard, ME.
ȝard, ȝerd *yard*, O.Icel. gat *hole, opening* = ME. gat, gāte
(cp. § 292) beside OE. geat, ME. ȝat, ȝet, and many mod.
dialects yat, yet *gate*, O.Icel. geta = ME. gēten *to get*,
beside OE. only in compounds, as forgietan, ME. forȝęten
to forget.

§177. Germanic medial ȝȝ, of whatever origin, became gg
in the prehistoric period of all the Germanic languages,
which in OE. became differentiated into palatal gg (written
cg) and guttural gg under the same conditions as those by
which Germanic k became differentiated into palatal and
guttural k (§ 280). The guttural gg remained in OE. and
ME., but palatal gg became assibilated to dž (written gg) in

late OE. or early ME., as OE. **dogga**, ME. **dogge** *dog*, but
OE. **licgan**, ME. **liggen** (=*lidžen) *to lie down*. Examples
are : O.Icel. **bryggja** = ME. **brigge** and mod. n. and Midl.
dialects **brig** beside OE. **brycg**, ME. **brigge**, **brügge** *bridge*,
O.Icel. **eggja** = ME. **eggen** *to egg on*, O.Icel. **hrygg·r** = ME.
and many mod. dialects **rig** beside OE. **hrycg**, ME. **rigge**,
rügge *ridge*, *back*, O.Icel. **liggja** = ME. **liggen** and many
mod. dialects **lig** beside OE. **licgan**, ME. **liggen** *to lie down*.

2. THE FRENCH ELEMENT IN ME.

§ 178. The French element which gained a permanent
footing in ME. was far greater in amount than the sum
total of all the other foreign elements, and it also differed
very materially in its nature from those elements. The
Scandinavian element consisted for the most part of everyday words, such as would be used by the common people,
whereas the French element was largely composed of words
representing a higher culture or state of civilization than
either the Scandinavian or the native element, such as mili-
tary, ecclesiastical, legal, hunting, and heraldic terms. This
is accounted for by the fact that the Anglo-Normans belonged
to the upper classes, whereas the Scandinavians belonged
chiefly to the yeoman and agricultural classes. Hence it
may be said that the French or Anglo-Norman element
penetrated from the higher to the lower classes, whereas the
Scandinavian element penetrated from the lower to the
upper classes, in so far as such words were permanently
incorporated into the standard language.

§ 179. As a result of the Norman Conquest French in
England had become the language of the Court, of the
nobility, of the clergy, and indeed of all who wished for
and sought advancement in Church or State. Robert of
Gloucester (1298) thus describes the important position of
French in the England of his day : ' Lo ! thus came England
into Normandy's hand and the Normans could then speak

nothing but their own tongue. They spoke French as they did at home, and taught their children to do likewise, so that men of high rank in the country, who are their descendants, keep to that same tongue, which they inherited from them, for unless a man knows French, he is little esteemed. But the lower ranks still keep to English, their own native tongue. I believe there is no country in all the world, save England only, that keeps not to its native speech. But one knows well, that it is good to be able to speak both, for the more knowledge a man has, the greater his worth,' see Morris and Skeat's *Specimens of Early English*, Part II, pp. 8–9. In the same volume (pp. 240–2) another interesting passage bearing on this subject is to be found in John of Trevisa's translation of Higden's *Polychronicon* (1387). He records how the English 'birth-tongue' has become 'impaired' by the admixture of too much French, for one reason because 'children in school, contrary to the usage and manner of all other nations, are compelled to neglect their own language and construe their lessons and hear things in French, and have done so, since the Normans came first into England'. But he goes on to tell us in an additional passage of his own authorship, that in the year of our Lord 1385 'in all the grammar schools of England, children neglect French, and construe and learn in English'.

§ 180. It has been estimated that the population of this country, including the Scandinavians, was about two millions at the time of the Norman Conquest, and that of these one-fourth were killed or otherwise disappeared during the Conqueror's reign, and that on the other hand at least 500,000 Frenchmen settled in England during his reign, so that there was for a time great danger lest the English language should be ousted by Norman-French. Had it not been for the strong infusion of Scandinavian settlers in England at this period, whose influence would tend towards the preservation of the kindred Germanic tongue, this danger would probably not have been averted.

§ 181. But the French element in ME. is not wholly Anglo-Norman, there was also a certain infusion of Central French, or, as it is sometimes termed, Parisian French. For some time Anglo-Norman prevailed, but gradually it came to be regarded as an inferior dialect of Old French, and already in the thirteenth century and onwards into the fourteenth century, the educated and upper classes began to learn and to speak Central French. And Anglo-Norman practically died out as a spoken language. This brought about the introduction of a large number of Central French words into the standard ME. of authors like Chaucer, Lydgate, &c. Nearly all the words introduced during the fifteenth century are from Central French. This admixture of the two French elements gave rise to many double forms in ME., the one being chiefly used by the lower and the other by the educated classes. And the difference between the forms manifested itself especially in the treatment of the vowels of unaccented syllables. Some of these differences are still reflected in the standard language and the dialects of the present day, as edjūkeit, edžūkeit : edikēt, -eət *educate*, fītšə : fiətə *feature*, kɒzn : kuzin *cousin*, væl·jū : valə vali *value*, &c.

§ 182. French was the language used in the Courts of Law until 1362, in which year it was decreed by an Act of Parliament that all pleadings in the Courts should henceforth be conducted in English, because, as is stated in the preamble to the Act, French was 'become much unknown in the realm'. But the mongrel French known as 'Law French' continued to exist for centuries later, and it was not finally abolished until 1731. The Proceedings in Parliament were recorded in French till 1483, when Richard III introduced a reform whereby the Statutes were for the first time drawn up in English. French or Latin was used at the

Universities, and it was not until 1349 that boys in schools began to learn Latin through the medium of English instead of French.

§ 183. The French element only found its way gradually into literature, and its influx was always much greater in the South than in the North, a difference still reflected in the modern English dialects. The Peterborough Chronicle, which was continued until 1154, contains only fourteen French words. The total number of French loan-words up to the end of the twelfth century amounts only to about a hundred. Between 1250 and 1350 hundreds of words were introduced, and then, after about the year 1400, the numbers began to decrease rapidly. As far as literature is concerned the period of greatest influx was between 1250 and 1400, the highest point being reached during the second half of the fourteenth century. Chaucer employed a far greater number of French words than any other author of his day. As an illustration of the French element in early ME. literature may be quoted the number of French words found in three works belonging to different dialects of the early part of the thirteenth century :—The *Ormulum* (about 1200), consisting of more than 20,000 lines, contains only about 20 ; Laȝamon's *Brut*, Text A (about 1203), consisting of 32,241 short lines, and based upon Wace's *Le Roman de Brut*, contains only 87 ; and the *Ancrcn Riwle* (about 1210), consisting of about 200 printed pages, contains 500. In conclusion it may be noted that French nouns and adjectives were generally taken over in their accusative forms (O.Fr. generally : nom. sing. -s, acc. sing. no s- ; nom. pl. no s-, acc. pl. -s). In the verbs the strong stem-form of the present sing. sometimes became the type for the whole of the inflexion, but sometimes the weak stem-form of the plural became the type, hence in ME. we often have side by side double forms, as destruien beside destroyen, pręven beside prǫven, see §§ 198, 202.

§ 184. Now that some account has been given of the
nature and amount of the French loan-words in ME. we will
proceed to look at the subject from a philological point of
view. Although it is true that after AN. and C.Fr. words
were introduced into English they underwent all further
changes in common with the native English words containing the same sounds, yet from a philological point of view
it is necessary to know not only how the words were pronounced at the time they were introduced, but also to
know what special phonological changes they underwent
at the time of their introduction. But this knowledge can
only be acquired by treating the subject in much the same
manner as the native element is generally treated in passing
from OE. to ME. By adopting this method of treatment
some light can be thrown upon many phonological points
connected with the native element in ME. By way of
illustration a few such points may be mentioned here:—

1. However early AN. words containing long ā were
introduced, they were not introduced early enough for the
long ā to fall together with OE. long ā in ME. except in
the northern dialects (§ 51). From this we can infer that
OE. long ā began to be rounded to ǭ at a very early period,
cp. ME. cāve, damāge, dāme beside bǭt *boat*, stǭn, tǭ *toe*.

2. The ME. ǭ from AN. o in open syllables fell together
with the OE. o in open syllables, as cǭte *coat*, rǭse *rose*
beside þrǭte (OE. þrote) *throat*, hǭpen (OE. hopian) *to hope*,
but not with the ME. ǭ from OE. ā, as in bǭt (OE. bāt)
boat, stǭn (OE. stān) *stone*. This is clearly proved by the
difference in the development of the two kinds of ǭ in
the modern dialects, kǫit, þrǫit beside buət, stuən (§ 51
note).

3. And similarly the modern dialects show that the ME.
ę̄ from older ei in AN. words (§ 205, 2) fell together with
the ME. ę̄ from OE. ǣ (= the i-umlaut of ā) and ēa (§§ 52,
63), but not with the ę̄ from OE. e in open syllables (§ 80).

4. The OE. ü-sound (written y) remained in the west Midland and southern dialects until the end of the fourteenth century and then became unrounded to i (§ 49, 3), but the ü in closed syllables of AN. words was never unrounded to i in the above dialects, but became u during the ME. period (§ 193), which shows that the two kinds of ü had not precisely the same pronunciation otherwise they would regularly have fallen together. And in like manner the OE. ü-sound (written ȳ) remained in the above dialects until the end of the fourteenth century, and then became unrounded to ī (§ 57, 3), but the ü, of whatever origin, in AN. words was never unrounded to ī; for it iu was substituted in all the dialects of England, see § 202.

§ 185. Before entering upon the history of the AN. simple vowels and diphthongs in ME. it will be useful to state here a few general principles concerning the vowel-system in general.

1. All the nasal vowels became denasalized and then these oral vowels generally had in ME. the same further development as the corresponding original oral vowels.

2. All final accented vowels were long or became long in ME.

3. All short vowels were lengthened in open syllables of dissyllabic forms.

4. Short vowels were lengthened in monosyllables before a single final consonant.

5. Short vowels were lengthened before a mute + liquid.

6. Short vowels were generally lengthened before st (§ 203).

7. Short accented vowels were lengthened before another vowel in dissyllabic words.

8. Vowels were short before consonant combinations other than a mute + liquid. They also remained short in open syllables of trisyllabic words.

The cause of the lengthening of the stem-vowel in type 4 was due to the inflected forms, just as in ME. native words

like cǭle (OE. col, gen. coles) *coal* (§ 81), &c. The stem-vowel
in words of types 5 and 6 was in reality generally in an
open syllable, because the following consonant combinations mostly belonged to the second syllable. There was
a tendency to shorten the vowel again in types 5 and 6,
especially when the final ·e ceased to be pronoūnced, as
propre, couple, double, trouble; arest, best beside bẹst
beast, forest, tempest, &c.

9. Instead of the AN. the O.Fr. vowel-system is sometimes
taken as the basis for treating the AN. element in ME.
When that is the case it should be remembered that several
of the O.Fr. diphthongs underwent changes in AN.; the
most important of the independent changes are given in the
following table:—

> O.Fr. ai, ǫi, üi, ie, ue
> AN.   ei, ui, ü, ẹ, ǒ

10. As a result of the AN. element in ME. two new
diphthongs were added to those already existing in the
native element, viz. ǫi and ui.

11. In dealing with the vowels we have to distinguish
between: (1) the vowels of accented syllables, (2) the vowels
of pretonic syllables, and (3) the vowels of post-tonic syllables
and unaccented syllables generally.

1. THE VOWELS OF ACCENTED SYLLABLES.

§ 186. The O.Fr. and AN. accented vowels in early
borrowed words, which became post-tonic in ME. through
shifting of the accent, remained for a time unchanged, and
then later became weakened down through loss of the new
secondary accent.

a. *The Short Vowels.*

§ 187. The short vowels generally remained before the
consonant combinations which had short vowels before them
in native words. They also remained in open syllables of

trisyllabic forms. The short nasalized vowels became de-nasalized and then generally had the same further development as the old oral vowels. Examples are :—

§ 188. a :, as balle, cacchen, calme, charge, charme, large, part, scarce; angle, blank, cancre, frank, janglen, cp. § 211.

§ 189. AN. ę and ẹ generally appear in ME. as ẹ, as accepten, castel, clerk, desert, detesten, dette *debt*, distresse, lettre, medlen, pressen, taverne, werre *war*, but cẹsen beside cessen *to cease*. The e was often lengthened before r + consonant, as pẹrche, sẹrchen, tẹrme beside perche, serchen, terme, see § 196. assenten, attempten, defenden, membre, menden, presence, silence. This e became i before nk at the same time e became i in native words, as enke, inke (O.Fr. enque), see § 132.

§ 190. i :, as consideren, deliveren, dische, epistle, finischen, punischen, resisten, riche; prince, simple, cp. § 199.

§ 191. o :, as apostle, cofre, fors *force*, loggen *to lodge*, ordre, propre, robben, rollen. But the o was often lengthened before r + consonant, see § 200.

§ 192. u : O.Fr. ǫ and u fell together in u in AN., and then the u generally remained in ME., as discuvren, purpre *purple*, purse, puschen (poschen) *to push*, turnen, turtle; with u = O.Fr. ǫ, as encumbren, numbre, summe, trumpe *trumpet*.

§ 193. AN. ü (written u) remained in early ME., but during the ME. period it became u, as juggen *to judge*, just, purgen *to purge*, sepulcre; humble.

b. *The Long Vowels.*

§ 194. All final accented vowels became long. Short vowels were lengthened in monosyllables before a single consonant. Short accented vowels were also lengthened before another vowel in dissyllabic words. All vowels were lengthened in open syllables of dissyllabic forms, and also before two consonants belonging to the second syllable.

§ 195. ā :, as blāme, cās *case*, cāve, debāte, escāpen, dāme, declāren, generāl, grāpe, lāke, pāle, pās ; fāble, mirācle, tāble ; āge (= *ā·dže), and similarly cāge, corāge, damāge, homāge, imāge ; grāce (= *grā·tse), chācen, plāce, trācen, see § 79 note 1. But the ă in AN. ·arie = C.Fr. ·aire from Lat. ·arium remained short in open syllables, and also generally in ME. verbs ending in ·arien, as adversarie, Februarie, necessarie ; carien, marien, tarien.

§ 196. O.Fr. ẹ̄, as bẹ̄k *beak*, condicionẹ̄l, eternẹ̄l, hostẹ̄l, nẹ̄t *neat*, prẹ̄chen, repẹ̄len, requẹ̄ren *to require*, wẹ̄re beside werre *war*, but O.Fr. e before r + consonant, as pẹ̄rcen (pẹrcen) *to pierce*, pẹ̄rle, rehẹ̄rsen *to rehearse*, sẹ̄rchen, tẹ̄rme, see §§ 63 note, 205.

§ 197. 1. ẹ̄ = O.Fr. e, as appẹ̄ren *to appear*, beautẹ̄ *beauty*, clẹ̄r *clear*, daungẹ̄r, frẹ̄re *brother*, pẹ̄r *peer*, pitẹ̄ *pity*, succẹ̄den. AN. ·ẹje, ·eie (= O.Fr. ·ẹ̄e from Lat. ·āta·) became ·eie (·ey) in ME. O.Fr. ·ẹ̄e also became ẹ̄ in forms introduced into ME., although the second e was preserved in writing, hence in ME. we often have double forms, as countreie and countrẹ̄, entreie and entrẹ̄, journeie and journẹ̄, valeie and valẹ̄ *valley*.

2. O.Fr. ie became ẹ̄ in AN. about 1150 and then the ẹ̄ remained in ME., sometimes written ie, as achẹ̄ven, fẹble, grẹ̄ven *to grieve*, manẹ̄re, matẹ̄re, nẹce *niece*, pẹce piece *piece*, preiẹre *prayer*, relẹ̄ven, rivẹ̄re, sẹ̄ge *siege* ; brẹf, chẹf, grẹf grief *grief*, meschẹf *mischief*, cp. § 50 ; contẹ̄nen, maintẹ̄nen, sustẹ̄nen. The verbs of this type were later remodelled after the analogy of verbs like ordeinen, see § 210.

§ 198. O.Fr. ue became ö in AN. and then the ö had the same further development in ME. as OE. ēo (§ 65), that is, it became unrounded to ẹ̄ in all the dialects except the west

Midland and the southern dialects, but in these latter dialects
it also became unrounded to ē about the end of the fourteenth
century. It was often written eo and in the west Midland
and southern dialects also oe, ue, o, and u, see § 65. Examples are: bēf *beef*, contrēven *to contrive*, dēl doel duel
sadness, mēven *to move*, pēple poeple people *pcople*, prēf
proof, prēven, reprēven. The verbal forms had in O.Fr.
ue in the first pers. singular and ǭ in the first pers. plural,
as muef, pl. mǭvons. In ME. the strong form of the
singular generally became the type for the whole inflexion,
but sometimes the weak form of the plural became the type,
hence in ME. we have side by side apprēven and apprǭven,
mēven and mǭven, prēven and prǭven, &c. The ē, ǭ
were shortened to e, o before an r in the following syllable,
as keveren, koveren *to cover*, &c.

§ 199. ī: as arrīven, brībe, companīe, crȳen, defȳen,
denȳen, delīt *delight*, desȳr, despīsen, devīsen, dīnen,
entīcen, justīse, malīce, mercȳ, strīven; gentīl, leisīr,
prȳs, strīf; bīble, tīgre; fīn *fine*, basīn, gardīn, cp. § 50.
The i also became ī before n + dental, as pīnte, but prince, &c.

§ 200. ǭ (= Lat. au, ǒ):, as clǭke, clǭsen, cǭte,
dispǭsen, nǭble, nǭte, repǭsen, reprǭchen, restǭren,
rǭbe, rǭse, suppǭsen, tresǭr; and also before r + consonant,
as fǫrce, fǫrge, pǫrk, pǫrt. Beside fǭl *fool*, pǭre (O.Fr.
povre) *poor*, trǭne *throne* we have fǭl, pǭre, trǭne. AN.
-orie (= C.Fr. -oire) became -ǭrie in ME., as glǭrie,
memǭrie, stǭrie, victǭrie.

§ 201. ū (= AN. u O.Fr. ǫ), as allowen, clamour,
creatour, culour, devouren, devout, doute *doubt*, flour
flower, goute, gracious, honour, houre, labour, poudre,
sermoun, spouse, tour *tower*, touchen, vouchen; before
r + consonant, as course, court, sours *source*; before mb, n,
nd, nt, nce, nge (= ndž), as abounden, acount, amount,
condicioun, count, encountren, līoun, mount, ounce,
pardoun, ploungen, prisoun, pronouncen, renoun, rēsoun

reason, round, soun *sound*, toumbe, but always uncle.
Cp. § 50.   The ū afterwards underwent shortening in
couple, double, ploungen, touchen, troublen.

§ 202. ŭ = 1. O.Fr. and AN. ü from Lat. ŭ.   The pure
ü-sound did 'not exist in any of the dialects of England at
the time the AN. words containing this sound were introduced.   There was a kind of ü-sound in the west Midland
and some of the southern dialects, but it was different from
the AN. sound, as is evidenced by the subsequent history of
the two sounds both in ME. and the modern dialects (cp.
§ 57).   For AN. ü was substituted what seemed to the
English ear the nearest equivalent, viz. iu, and this is also
the case in modern times when English people without
a knowledge of phonetics attempt to reproduce Modern
French ü.   In the older loan-words it was generally written
u, as duren, usen, vertu, and later also eu, ew, iu, yw
(cp. §§ 112, 116).   Examples are : accūsen, būgle, dūren,
creatūre, cūren, dūk *duke*, figūre, fortūne, mesūre, pūr,
rūde, rcfūsen, refūten, sūgre *sugar*, sūr, ūsen.

2. = O.Fr. üi (from Lat. ū, ŏ + i) became ü in AN.
for which iu was substituted in ME., written u (ui), eu, ew,
iu, iw, as fruit frut, pu pew puw *pew*, suit, cp. §§ 112, 116.
The verbal forms had in O.Fr. üi in the first pers. sing. and
ǫi in the first pers. plural.   In ME. the strong form of the
singular generally became the type for the whole of the
inflexion, but sometimes the weak form of the plural became
the type, hence in ME. we have side by side forms like
anuien and anoien, destruien and destroien, vuiden and
voiden.

§ 203. Before st we often have double forms just as in
native English words (cp. § 97), and one or other of the forms
became generalized, as chāste, hāste, tāsten, wāsten;
bęste, fęste *feast*, but arest, forest, tempest; Chrīst;
bǫsten, cǫste *coast*, hǫst, pǫst, rǫsten, tǫsten, but cost,
costen; crouste but later cruste; jŭst.

§ 204. In place of long vowel + a single consonant, we sometimes have a short vowel + double consonant, as chapelle : chapēle, passen : pās ; cessen : cēsen *to cease*, dette : dēte *debt*, lettre : lētre, plegge : plēge *pledge*, werre : wēre *war* ; quitte : quīte ; loggen : lōgen *to lodge*, proffren : prōfren ; copple (o = u) : couple ; süggre : sügre *sugar*, &c.

c. *The Diphthongs.*

ai, ei

§ 205. O.Fr. ai and ei fell together in ẹi in AN. and then the ei became ai in ME. at the same time as ei became ai in native words (§ 107). And then later the ai became ẹ before consonants, especially before liquids, dentals, and s, so that in ME. we often have ẹ beside ai, and ei.
Examples are :—

1. O.Fr. ai, as aiden, air, assaien *to test*, claimen, delai, gai, grain, lai *lay*, *song*, maire *mayor*, maistre, paien *to pay*, plain, rai, repairen, vain, waiten.

2. O.Fr. ei, as conveien, deceiven, despeir, displeien, heir, obeien, moneie, peine *pain*, preien *to pray*, receiven.

3. O.Fr. ai and ei, as decēven, dēs (deis) *table*, disēse, ēse (aise) *ease*, encrēsen, frēle (fraile) *frail*, grēse, mēre (maire), pēs (pais) *peace*, plēden, plēsen, recēt (receit) *receipt*, recēven (receiven), sēsen (saisen) *to seize*, trēten. See § 63 note.

ọi

§ 206. AN. ọi (= O.Fr. ọi from Lat. au + i) remained in ME., as chọis *choice*, clọistre, jọie, nọise, pọisen *to poise*, rejọisen. The ọi from older ei in C.Fr. loan-words also remained, as cọi, devọir, emplọyen, explọit, &c.

ui

§ 207. O.Fr. ọi, ui (from Lat. ō, u + i) = AN. ui which remained in ME. and also in NE. until the late sixteenth or

early seventeenth century, although it was generally written
oi (oy), as **acointen** *to acquaint*, **boilen, enointen, joint,
point, poisen** *to poison*, **soilen**, &c. Forms like **vǫice, mǫist**
were from Central French.

au

§ **208.** O.Fr. and AN. **au** from older **a+l** remained in
early ME., and then later it became **ā** before labials, as
assaut *assault*, **fauchon** *falchion*, **faute** *fault*, **heraud, paume,**
later **pāme** *palm of the hand*, **sauce, sauf** later **sāf** *safe*,
sauven later **sāven**, see § 213, 1.

ǫu

§ **209.** AN. **ǫu** (= O.Fr. **ieu**) remained in early ME. and
then became **iu** at the same time that **ǫu** in native words
became **iu**, written **u, eu, ew, iu, iw**, see § 112, as **adewe**
adieu, **Jew Jiw, reule rewle riule** *rule* ; and similarly
O.Fr. **ǫu** from older **ou**, as **corfew** *curfew*, **blew bliw** *blue*,
nevew *nephew*.

d. *The Formation of New Diphthongs.*

§ **210.** Palatal **lʲ** and **nʲ** generally became **il** and **in**, and
then the **i** combined with the preceding vowel to form
a diphthong or **ī** when the preceding vowel was **i**, as
assailen, aveilen, barain *barren*, **bataile, failen, fountaine, gainen, maille** *mail*, **montaine** *mountain*, **railen,
travail, vitaille** *victuals*. **atteinen, compleynen, feinen** *to
feign*, **feint, merveile** *marvel*, **ordeinen, peinten, reine** *reign*
restreinen, veile. And then the **ei** became **ai** at the same
time as **ei** in native words became **ai** (§ 107). **Coloigne**
Cologne. **ui** (written **oi**) from O.Fr. **ui**, as **boilen, joinen,
oile, soile, spoilen.** O.Fr. **üi** which became **ü** in AN. and
for which **iu** was substituted in ME., written **u, ui** (see § 202,
2), as **impugnen, Juil Jul** *July*, **Juin Jun** *June*. **benigne**
benīne, where -**ign** = -**īn**, and similarly **resīgnen, sīgne,**

vīgne ; perīl.　When the diphthongs in the above and similar examples lost their secondary accent during the M E. period they were generally weakened down to **e**, although the old spelling was generally preserved.

NOTE.—Palatal 1, n were often expressed by 1j (written lȝ, lȝh, ly), nj (written nȝ) in the Scottish dialects, as **batalȝe, ganȝe** beside **bataile, gaine;** and in late ME. they were also sometimes expressed by **1j, nj** (written li, ni) in the Southern dialects, as **talie, spaniel** beside **taile** *tally*, **spainel**, see JORDAN, *ME. Gr.* §§ 253, 256.

§ **211.** Between **a** and a nasal belonging to the same syllable a glide was developed in AN., which in ME. combined with the preceding vowel to form the diphthong **au**, before final **n**, before m + labial, and n + dental (= n + d, t or s, n + dž or tš), as **aungel, aunte, balaunce, braunche, chaumbre, chaunce, chaunge, daunce daunse, demaun·den, distaunce, exaumple, garlaunde, graunten, haunten, jaumbe, laumpe, paun, plesaunt, servaunt, slaundre, tauny, vaunten.**　And then later the **au** became **ā** before m + labial and n + dž or tš, see § 213, 1.

§ **212.** The **ā** which arose from the above **au** before n + dž or tš became **ai** in some parts of the western and northern areas about the end of the fourteenth century, as **chaynge** *change*, **raynge, straynge ; braynche** *branch*, **staynche** *to stanch.*

e. *Monophthongization.*

§ **213.** Before certain consonant combinations some of the diphthongs became monophthongs about the end of the thirteenth and early part of the fourteenth centuries :—

1. **au** became **ā** before labials, n + dž or tš, dž and tš, as **āngel, bāme** older **baum bawm** *balm*, **brānche, chāmbre, chāngen, jāmbe, lămpe** ; **fāchon** *falchion*, **gāgen, sāfe, săvage, sāven** *to save*, see §§ 208, 211.

2. **ai, ui** became **a, u** before **š** and s + consonant, as **abaschen** older **abaischen** *to abash*, **ascheler** (O.Fr.

aisselier) *ashlar,* māster older maister, casche (O.Fr.
caisse) ; buschel (O.Fr. buissel), cuschin older quischin
cushion, cruschen older cruischen *to crush.*

3. ęu became ę̄ before labials, as flę̄me older flęume
phlegm, rę̄me older ręume (reaume) *realm.*

f. *Vowel Contraction.*

§ 214. Vowel contraction took place partly in AN. and
partly in ME., especially when the second vowel or diphthong
was e, i, u, or ei, oi, as sę̄l (O.Fr. sëel) *seal,* vę̄l (O.Fr. vëel)
veal, chaine (O.Fr. chaëine), cǫin (O.Fr. cooin) *quince,*
brawn (O.Fr. braoun), mirour (O.Fr. mireür), sūr (O.Fr.
seür) *sure* ; O.Fr. third pers. sing. obeït *he obeys,* pl.
obeïssent, whence ME. obeien beside obeischen, and
similarly abaischen *to abash,* traien beside traischen *to
betray,* rejǫischen *to rejoice.*

Contraction also took place when intervocalic i-consonant
disappeared, as dę̄n (O.Fr. deien) *dean,* lę̄l (O.Fr. leiel)
loyal, mę̄n (O.Fr. mcien) *mean, middle.*

2. The Vowels of Pretonic Syllables.

§ 215. The O.Fr. and AN. pretonic vowels and diphthongs
which became tonic (accented) through the shifting of the
accent generally remained in ME. The short vowels were,
however, generally lengthened before a following vowel and
in open syllables of early borrowed words, but remained
short in later borrowed words.

a. *The Simple Vowels.*

§ 216. a, ā, au :, as amorous, baroun, bataile, carpenter,
chapę̄le, chariot, gardīn, manę̄re, palais, ravenous,
taverne, travaien. ă·miable, ă·precock *apricot,* băcoun,
bāsīn *basin,* flāvour, grācious, māsoun *mason,* nācioun
nation, nātūre *nature,* pācient, see § 79 note 1. AN. ă was

denasalized to a before nd, nt, and ng, as **anguische,
language, mantel, standard.** In other positions it had the
same development as in accented syllables (§ 211), as **auncieat,
brandischen** beside **braundischen, chaumpion, chauncel,
daungēr, raunsoun** *ransom.*

§ **217. e, ẹ :,** as **lessoun, mercī, metal, nevew, perīl**
beside **peril, plesaunt, present, secounde; aventūre,
engīn, gentīl, plentẹ, tempeste.** **lẹsīr, plẹsir, rẹsĭn** *grape,*
rẹsoun *reason,* see § 63 note. Before **r** + consonant we
have **e** later **a** (§ 129), as **gerlaund, merchaunt, merveile,
persoune, sermoun,** later **garlaund,** &c.

§ **218. i, ī :,** as **citẹ, diner, finischen, pitẹ, scriptūre,
vinẹgre.** **gīaunt** *giant,* **līoun, squīer.** **pīlot, īvorie.**

§ **219. o :,** as **comoun, folie** *folly,* **foreste, fortūne,
gobelet, honouren, office, solas** *solace,* **torment.**

§ **220. u, ū** (written **ou, ow**), as **buteler, butoun** *button,*
culour, glutoun, mutoun, sudain, supere. **coward,
dowere doure** *dowry,* **powere, towaile** *towel;* **bountẹ,
counseil, countrẹ, fountaine, mountaine.**

§ **221. ü, ǖ.** **ü** remained in early ME., but became **u**
during the ME. period (cp. § 125), and **iu** was substituted for
ü (cp. § 202), as **duchesse, juggement, punischen, studien**
to study. **cruel crewel, humilitẹ, humour, suretẹ, usage.**

b. *The Diphthongs.*

§ **222.** The pretonic diphthongs generally had the same
development in ME. as the tonic (accented) diphthongs
except that **ei** underwent weakening in medial syllables.

§ **223. ai** was generally monophthongized to **ẹ,** but forms
with **ai** also occur in ME., as **fẹtüre** and **faitüre** *feature,*
rẹsoun and **raisoun, sẹsoun** and **saisoun,** see §§ 63 note,
205; the **ai** remained before old palatal **1,** as **tailour** *tailor,*
see § 210.

§ **224. ei :,** as **leisīr** *leisure,* **preiẹre** *prayer,* **veiäge** (O.Fr.
voiäge) *voyage.* . **curtesie** beside older **curteisle, orisoun**

beside older **oreisoun, venisoun** beside older **veneisoun** (O.Fr. **venoison**).

§ 225. ǫi :, as **jǫious**.

§ 226. **ui** (written **oi**):, as **oinoun** *onion*, **poisoun** *poison*.

§ 227. O.Fr. **üi** = AN. **ü**, for which the **iu**-sound was substituted in ME. (§ 202, 2), as **nuisaunce**.

§ 228. **au** :, as **auter** *altar*, **faucon** *falcon*, **saumoun** *salmon*, **sauvāge** (see § 213, 1).

§ 229. **eau, ęu** became **iu** (see § 112), as **beautę̄ beutę̄ bewtę̄** *beauty* ; **fewaile** *fuel*, **jewel** *jewel*.

3. The Vowels of Post-tonic and Unaccented Syllables generally.

§ 230. The vowel in post-tonic syllables was always ·**e**, as in **chapę̄le, faute, justise, madāme, natūre, reine** *reign*. The final ·**e** in these and similar words disappeared in pronunciation earlier in ME. than the ·**e** in words of English origin (cp. §§ 141–2). This was especially the case after **st**, **ce** (= **s**) and after vowels, as **bę̄st(e), tempest(e), plāc(e), foli(e)** *folly*, **maladi(e), prei(e)** *prey*. In this respect Chaucer was behind the spoken language of his time. In his poetry the final ·**e** was preserved in pronunciation, and he never allowed words ending in ·**ce** (= **s**) to rhyme with those ending in ·**s** nor those ending in ·**ye** (·**ie**) with those ending in ·**y**.

For the weakening down of long vowels and diphthongs which were accented in O.Fr. and AN., but became unaccented in ME. through the shifting of the principal accent, see §§ 186, 210.

§ 231. Initial **e**· disappeared before **s** + tenuis, as **Spaine, spȳen, staat** beside **estaat, stüdien, scāpen** beside **escāpen, squirel** (O Fr. **escurel**). Initial vowels also often disappeared before other consonants, as **menden** beside **amenden, prentȳs** beside **aprentȳs, pistīl** beside **epistīl**.

Initial prefixes often disappeared, as **fenden** beside **defenden,** **steinen** beside **desteinen** *to stain,* **sport** beside **disport,** **saumple** beside **ensaumple,** &c.

§ **232.** Medial vowels often disappeared between consonants, as **chimneie** beside **chimeneie** *chimney,* **kerchẹf** beside **keverchẹf, nortūre** beside **noritūre, pantrie** beside **panetrie** *pantry,* **palfrei** beside **palefrei,** &c., cp. § **154.**

CHAPTER VI

THE ME. DEVELOPMENT OF THE OE. CONSONANT-SYSTEM

§ **233.** OE. had the following consonant-system :—

		Labial.	Inter-dental.	Dental.	Guttu-ral.	Pala-tal.
Explosives	voiceless	p, pp		t, tt	c, cc	c, cc
	voiced	b, bb		d, dd	g, gg	g, cg
Spirants	voiceless	f, ff	þ, þþ	s, ss	h, hh	h, hh
	voiced	f	þ	s	g	g
Nasals		m, mm		n, nn	n	n
Liquids				l, ll; r, rr		
Semi-vowel	w					

To these must be added the aspirate **h,** and **x.** The double consonants were pronounced long as in Modern Italian and Swedish, thus **habban** = **hab-ban** *to have,* **swimman** = **swim-man** *to swim.* On the doubling of consonants in late ME., see § **12,** and *ENE. Gr.* §§ 53–4.

§ **234.** Many of the changes which the OE. consonant-system underwent in ME. were not sound-changes, but merely orthographical changes due to the influence of the Anglo-Norman system of orthography. Most of these changes have been stated in §§ **13–20,** and others will be dealt with in the treatment of the separate consonants.

The sound-changes which the OE. consonants underwent in ME. were insignificant compared with the vowel-changes. In fact the consonants have changed comparatively little in the whole history of the language, whereas the vowels have been continuously on the change and still are so. It may therefore be said that the consonants in a language like English merely form, as it were, the framework of the language, and that the vowels are the clockwork or living organism. This is quite different from a language like French where the consonants equally with the vowels have undergone great and radical changes in passing from popular Latin to the French of the present day.

§ 235. Before entering upon the history of the individual consonants in ME., it will be well to treat here several consonant-changes which are best dealt with collectively, viz. the voicing and unvoicing of consonants, the vocalization of consonants, assimilation, metathesis, the loss of consonants, and the development of glide consonants.

1. The Voicing of Consonants.

§ 236. The initial voiceless spirants f, s, þ became the voiced spirants v, z, ð in late OE. or early ME. in Kentish and the southern, especially the south-western dialects, as **vader, vat, vlesch, vrend; zaule zǫule, zinne zenne zünne** *sin*, **ðat ðet, ðing**. The modern dialects show that this voicing of the initial voiceless spirants must have taken place at an early period, because it is almost exclusively confined to native words, hence the change must have taken place before the great influx of Anglo-Norman words into these dialects. The use of the initial voiced for the voiceless spirants is now obsolete in Ken., Sur., Sus., and obsolescent in s. Pem., Hamp., and the I. W., but it is still in general use in east Hrf., parts of Glo., west Brks., Wil., Som., and Dev. These modern dialects help to throw some light upon the standard NE. voiced ð (written **th**) in pronouns and the adverbs related to them. There is no indication either in ME. or NE. to show when the **þ·** became voiced in such words, but the dialects of Sus., Ken., and s. Pem. show that it must have taken place pretty early, because in these dialects the **þ·** has become **d·**, although the forms with **d·** are now obsolescent in the two latter counties. Examples are : **deə** *their, there*, **dem, den**, **di** *the*, **dis**. These forms with **d·** show that the voicing of the **þ·** in pronominal and adverbial forms was older than the voicing of it in the other OE. words beginning with **þ**. See *ED. Gr.* §§ 278, 310, 320.

§ 237. In simple words the voiceless spirants **f, s, þ** became voiced between voiced sounds in early OE., although they were always retained in writing, and this rule was also preserved in ME., see *EOE. Gr.* § 139. Final **·s** and **·þ** became voiced after vowels during the ME. period in un-accented syllables, although the **·s, ·þ** (**·th**) were retained in writing. And similarly in unaccented words like **his, is, was**.

2. The Unvoicing of Consonants.

§ 238. In early OE. the voiced spirants **v** (written **f**), **ʒ** became voiceless **f, χ** before voiceless sounds and finally, and this rule was also preserved in early ME., see §§ 266, 308, and *EOE. Gr.* § 140. When final **·e** disappeared at an early period (§ 139) **z, v** and **ð** became unvoiced to **s, f** and **þ**, as **bōþę, erþę, froþę**, northern dialects **rīs** *to rise*, **gif** *to give*, **luf** *to love*, beside older **rīse(n), give(n), luve(n)**.

The **g** in the combination **ŋg** became **k** (written **c**) before voiceless consonants in OE., but the **g** was generally restored through association with forms where the **g** was regular, as **strencþ** beside **strengþ** with **g** restored from **strang** *strong* (cp. *EOE. Gr.* § 140), whence such ME. double forms as **lenkþ, strenkþ** beside **lengþ, strengþ**, and forms with **ŋk** are still common in many of the modern dialects, see Index

to *ED. Gr.* There was also a tendency for final ŋg to become
ŋk in some of the ME. dialects, especially in the north-west
Midland, as in *Sir Gawain and the Green Knight*: ȝonk(e)
young, rynk *ring*, þink *thing*, &c., and such forms are still
common in some of the dialects of this area, see *ED. Gr.* § 274.

§ 239. In early OE. d became t before and after voiceless
consonants. When two dentals thus came together, they
became tt which were simplified to t finally and after consonants (*EOE. Gr.* § 140). This rule also remained as
a characteristic feature of the southern dialects in the ME.
period, as bintst beside older bīndest *thou bindest*, bitst
beside older bidest *thou prayest*, bint from *bindþ, older
bīndeþ *he binds*, bit from *bidþ, older bideþ *he prays*, &c.
And in like manner the d also became t in the pp. of
trisyllabic weak verbs after the loss of the ·e· in the final
syllable, as punischt, witnest beside older punisched,
witnessed, see § 155. In ME. as in the modern dialects
(cp. *ED. Gr.* §§ 303-4) there was a tendency to unvoice d to
t in final unaccented syllables. This was especially the case
in the preterite and past participle in the Scottish and west
Midland dialects. For the unvoicing of d to t in the preterite
and past participle of verbal stems ending in ·ld, ·nd, and ·rd,
see § 270. And in the west Midland dialects d also became
t finally after l, n, r in monosyllables, as bẹrt *beard*, felt
field, pret. helt *held*, lont *land*, wint *wind*, &c.; the t in
these and similar words has been preserved in many of the
dialects of this area down to the present day, see *ED. Gr.*
§ 302.

3. THE VOCALIZATION OF CONSONANTS.

§ 240. The prefix ȝe· became i· through the intermediate
stages ī·, ȝi·, which remained initially (also written y·), as
iwis ywis (OE. gewiss) *certain*, iclad yclad *clothed*, but
disappeared medially through the intermediate stage ·e·, as
neighbour, older nehhebour (OE. nēahgebūr), see § 153.

Medial palatal ʒ became i between r and a following vowel, as burie(n) birie(n) (OE. byr(i)gan) *to bury*, murie mirie (OE. myr(i)ge) *pleasant*, terie(n) (OE. tergan) *to annoy*, and similarly in French words, carie(n), contrarie, marie(n), studie(n). Palatal ʒ became vocalized to i after vowels and then combined with a preceding vowel to form a diphthong of the i-type, see §§ 105, 299.

§ 241. When w came to stand finally after consonants it became vocalized to u, as pl. ʒarwe (OE. gearwe) from which was formed a new sing. ʒaru *ready*, and similarly holu *hollow*, naru *narrow*, &c., see § 134 (a). Postvocalic old w became vocalized to u, and then combined with the preceding vowel to form a diphthong of the u-type, as chẹwen (OE. cēowan) *to chew*, knǫwen (OE. cnāwan) *to know*, schẹwen (OE. scēawian, later sceáwian) *to show*, beside northern chẹu (chẹu), knau, schẹu, see §§ 110, 2, 111. And in like manner w from OE. and early ME. guttural ʒ became vocalized to u after a guttural vowel and then combined with the preceding vowel to form a diphthong of the u-type, see §§ 105, 298.

§ 242. v was vocalized to u (generally written w) when it stood or came to stand before a consonant through the loss of a medial unaccented vowel (§ 153), as awkward from older *avkward, *avuk-, pl. chaules (OE. cēaflas) from which was formed a new singular chaul *cheek*, crawlen (ON. krafla) *to crawl*, ẹwte older evete (OE. efete) *newt*, pl. hawkes (OE. hafocas) from which a new singular hawk was formed, nauger older naveger (OE. nafogār) *auger*.

4. Assimilation.

§ 243. Partial or total assimilation of dentals took place in unaccented particles, as and tat = and þat, atte = at þe, þatte = þat þe, and similarly with þū *thou* after verbal forms with simplification of the tt, as artū *art thou?*, wiltū *wilt*

thou ? ; these and similar forms are still a characteristic
feature of the Modern northern and north Midland dialects,
see *ED. Gr.* § 404. ln and nl became ll, as elle older elne
(OE. eln) *ell*, mille older milne (OE. myln), ellevẹn(e) beside
older enleven (OE. en(d)leofan) *eleven*. fm became mm, as
lemman (OE. lēofman) *sweetheart*, wimman (OE. wimman
beside wīfman) *woman*. n became m before f and p, as com·
fort (O.Fr. confort), hemp (OE. henep), noumpere (O.Fr.
nonper) *umpire*. pf became ff, as chaffare (OE. *cēapfaru)
trade.

5. METATHESIS.

§ 244. The metathesis of r was common in QE., especially
in the Northumbrian dialect. Already at that period antevocalic r often became postvocalic when a short vowel was
followed by n, nn, s or s + consonant (*EOE. Gr.* § 143).
ME. examples are : bird (OE. brid), briȝt (OE. beorht)
bright, forst beside frost (OE. forst beside frost), hors (OE.
hros), þirde (OE. þridda) ; asken beside axen = OE.
āscian beside āxian *to ask*.

6. THE LOSS OF CONSONANTS.

§ 245. Postconsonantal w disappeared before back-rounded
vowels, as alsọ, ase (OE. ealswā), sọ (OE. swā), soche
suche beside swich (OE. swylc), sord beside sword, sọte
beside swọte *sweet* adv., suster (OE. sweostor, § 38) *sister*,
tọ beside twọ (OE. twā), þong beside þwong, họ beside
whọ (OE. hwā). It also disappeared in certain verbal forms
with the negative prefix, as nas (OE. næs = ne wæs) *was
not*, nille (OE. nille = ne wille) *will not*, and similarly niste
I knew not, nọt *I know not*, nolde *I would not*, &c.

§ 246. l disappeared in the Midland and southern dialects
before and after ch = OE. palatal c, as ẹch (OE. ǣlc) *each*,
muche moche, miche (OE. mycel) *great*, suche soche,
siche, swich (OE. swylc), which whuch (OE. hwylc),

beside northern **ilk, mikel, swilk, quilk.** It also disappeared in the unaccented particle **ase** beside the accented form **alsǫ** (OE. **ealswā**).

§ 247. Final **-n** disappeared early in dissyllabic and trisyllabic nouns and adjectives in the Midland and southern dialects, but was often or generally restored again from the inflected forms, as **kinręde, kindred** (OE. **cyn·ræden**), **ēve** beside **ęven** *evening*, **maide(n)**. It had disappeared in Northumbrian during the OE. period in words of more than one syllable. This law was fairly well preserved in the infinitive, the present and preterite plural subjunctive, the weak declension of nouns and adjectives, numerals and adverbs, but in strong nouns and adjectives including the past participles of strong verbs, the final **-n** was generally reintroduced into the nom. singular from the inflected forms. It was also mostly reintroduced into the pret. indicative plural through the influence of the past participle, which itself was a new formation.

In early ME. the final **-n** disappeared in unaccented syllables except in the pp. of strong verbs in the northern and north Midland dialects. In the other Midland dialects it was mostly retained, especially in the present plural of the indicative, the infinitive, and the past participle of strong verbs. It was retained in the southern dialects in the weak declension of nouns and adjectives, whereas in the Kentish dialect it disappeared at an early period in the past participle of strong verbs, see § 147. Final **-n** disappeared in the indefinite article and the possessive pronouns when the next word began with a consonant, as **ā, ǫ** **þing** (OE. **ān**), **nǫ** **þing** (OE. **nān**) **mī fader** (OE. **mīn**). When the next word began with a vowel the **-n** was run on to it, as **mī nęm** (OE. **mīn ēam**) *my uncle*.

§ 248. Final **b** disappeared after **m** in the northern dialects about the beginning of the fourteenth century, as **dum** *dumb*, **lam** *lamb*. **f** disappeared in O.Fr. before final **-s**, as nom. sing. **baillis** beside acc. **baillif**, whence ME. **bailli** beside **baillif, joli** beside **jolif, pensi** beside **pensif** *thoughtful*. The forms **baily** and **pensy** are still very common in the modern dialects. **v** from older **f** also disappeared before consonants, as **hẹd** beside older **hẹved** (OE. **hēafod**) *head*, **lādi** from older **lavdie, lavedie** (OE. **hlæfdige**) *lady*, **larke** from older **laverke** (§ 88), **lọrd** from older **lọverd** (OE. **hlāford, -ard**) *lord*. The common forms **þar** *I need*, **þarst, þar**, beside **þarf, þarft, þarf** were due to association with **dar** *I dare*, **darst, dar**.

§ **249.** **t** disappeared before **st**, between **s** and **s** or **m**, as **best** (OE. **bet(e)st**), **laste** (OE. **latost**) *last*, **Wessex** (OE. **West-Seaxan**), **blosme** (OE **blōstma** beside **blōsma**) *blossom*. **d** disappeared before **s**, as **answere** (OE. **andswaru**), **gospel** beside older **godspel, gossib** beside older **godsib**. **þ** disappeared at the end of the first element of compounds, as **Norfolk** (OE. **Norþ-folc**), **Sussex** (OE. **Sūþ-seaxan**), **wurschipe** beside older **wurþschipe** *worship*. It also disappeared in the medial combinations -**þn**-, -**þr**- with lengthening of the preceding vowel, as **hĕn** (ON. **heþan**) *hence*, **sĭn, sĕn** (OE. **siþþan, sioþþan**) *since*, **þĕn** (ON. **þeþan**) *thence*, **whĕr** *whether*, see § 76.

§ **250.** Intervocalic **k** disappeared in the preterite and past participle **māde, mād** (maad) for older **mākede, māked**. From the pret. and pp. was then formed a new present **mā(n)** in the northern and north Midland dialects, after the analogy of which was also formed a new present **tā(n)** for **tāken**, see § 79 note 1. Final -**ch** disappeared in unaccented words and syllables in late ME., as **I** beside **ich**, -**ly** beside older -**liche**, as in **hevenly** beside **hevenliche**. Initial **h**- disappeared before **l, n, r**, but these combinations were often written **lh, nh, rh** in early ME., especially in Kentish, as **lẹpen** (OE. **hlẹapan**) *to leap*, **lauʒen** (Anglian **hlæhha(n)**) *to laugh*, **neien** (OE. **hnægan**) *to neigh*, **nute** (OE. **hnutu**) *nut*, **rāven** (OE. **hræfn**), **ring** (OE. **hring**).

7. The Development of Glide Consonants in ME.

§ 251. Glide consonants were developed, especially in the neighbourhood of nasals and s.

A b was developed between m·l, m·r, as bremble (OE. brēmel, gen. brēmles) *bramble*, schamble (OE. sceamol, gen. sceam(o)les), þimble (OE. þȳmel, gen. þȳmles), slumbren (OE. slŭmerian), and also after m in croumbe (OE. crūma) *crumb*, þoumbe (OE. þūma) *thumb*. A p was developed between m·n, m·t, as nempnen (OE. nemnan) *to name*, empti (OE. ǣmtig), and in French words like autumpne *autumn*, dampnen *to damn*, solempne *solemn*, tempten *to attempt*.

A d was developed between l·r, n·r, as alder (OE. alr, alor) *alder*, þe alderbeste (OE. ealra betsta) *the best of all*, and similarly alderfirst, alderlast; kindred (OE. cyn·rǣden), þunder (OE. þunor, gen. þun(o)res). jaundice beside jaunice (AN. jaunisse). A final ·t was developed after n in AN. words, as auncient (O.Fr. ancien), and similarly fesaunt, tiraunt, ribant (riband) beside riban *ribbon*. A t was developed between s and n in glistnen (OE. glisnian), listnen (OE. hlysnan) *to listen*, and after final ·s, as aȝainest beside older aȝaines, bihẹ̄ste (OE. behǣs) *vow, promise*, hẹ̄st (OE. hǣs) *command*.

The Semivowels.

w

§ 252. OE. Ƿ was still used occasionally until the thirteenth century, but in early ME. w was generally written uu, more rarely vv, and in northern manuscripts u after dentals and s. In late northern manuscripts it was often written v. w was introduced from the AN. alphabet in the thirteenth century, and OE. cw came to be written qu.

§ **253.** OE. **w** remained initially before vowels, and generally also initially before and after consonants, as **warm** (OE. **wearm**), **weder** (OE. **weder**) *weather*, **wlank** (OE. **wlanc**) *proud*, **wrīten** (OE. **wrītan**), **twelf** (OE. **twelf**), and similarly **was, water, wēpen** *to weep*, **wīde, winter, wischen, wolf, wounde, wunder**, and similarly in AN. words, as **waiten, wāsten, werre** *war*. &c.; **wlite** *face, form*, **wrecche** *wretched*; **dwellen, swimmen, twig; quēne** (OE. **cwēn**) *queen, woman*, **quik** (OE. **cwic**).

It also remained medially after consonants, as **wid(e)we** (OE. **wid(e)we**) *widow*, **medwe** beside **mēde** (OE. gen. **mǣdwe** beside nom. **mǣd**) *meadow*, and similarly **holwe** *hollow*, **schadwe, swalwe**. For the vocalization and loss of **w** see §§ 241, 245.

§ **254.** AN. **w** (= O.Fr. **gu**, later **g**, in words of Germanic origin) remained in ME., as **rewarden, wāge, waiten, wāsten, werre** *war*.

The O.Fr. combination **qu** = **kw** remained in ME. before **a, e, i**, but became **k** (c) before **o, u**, as **equal, qualitēe, quarter, questioun**; but **cǫi, likour**.

Germanic j

§ **255.** Germanic initial **j** had become a palatal spirant like the **y** in NE. **yet, you** in the oldest period of the language. This explains why it was written **g** in OE., and ȝ, later **y**, in ME., see *EOE. Gr.* §§ 150–1. The OE. sound remained initially in ME., as ȝě (OE. gě) *ye*, ȝēr ȝēr (OE. gēar, gēr) *year*, and similarly ȝet ȝit *yet*, ȝif *if*, ȝok ȝǫke *yoke*, ȝong *young*, ȝouþe *youth*. See § 240.

The Liquids.

l

§ **256.** OE. and AN. **l** generally remained in all positions of the word, as **loud** (OE. **hlūd**), **fallen** (OE. **feallan**), **āle** (OE. **ealu**), **clēne** (OE. **clǣne**), **all** (OE. **eall**), **dēl** (OE. **dǣl**),

and similarly lamb, lępen, litel, loven ; fillen, sellen,
tellen, wolle ; blọd, flesch, folk, glad, helpen, milk,
nędle, silver, sọule, stęlen ; foul, full, sadel ; labour,
langāge ; blāmen, calme, delai, failen, tāble ; crüel. For
the loss of 1 see § 246.

r

§ 257. OE. and AN. r generally remained in all positions
of the word, as roum (OE. rūm), bringen (OE. bringan),
bęren (OE. beran), hard (OE. heard), sterre (OE. steorra)
star, fader (OE. fæder), and similarly ręd *red*, rein *rain*,
rīden ; arm, bāre, erþe *earth*, ferre *far*, grēne, spręden,
stręm *stream*, trę, word, wrīten ; better, fȳr *fire*, mọder ;
rāge, round ; chaumbre, fǫrce, grāce, natüre, trouble ;
pür. For the metathesis of r see § 244.

THE NASALS.

m

§ 258. OE. and AN. m generally remained in ME., as
mọder (OE. mōdor) *mother*, clīmben (OE. climban), nāme
(OE. nama), roum (OE. rūm), and similarly māken, man,
mīn, mouþ ; cọmb, cumen, swimmen, tīme ; bọsem,
botem, brọm, faþem, helm, worm ; maladie, moneie ;
chaumbre, damāge, lampe.

§ 259. Final ·m, when an element of inflexion, became ·n
in late OE., as dat. pl. dagon, giefon, sunon beside older
dagum, giefum, sunum ; dat. sing. and pl. gōdon beside
older gōdum. This change of final ·m to ·n was due to the
levelling out of the ·n in the n·stems into the dative plural,
and from which it was then extended analogically to the
other stems. The ·n disappeared at an early period in ME.
(cp. § 147). The old inflexional ending with ·m was preserved in the ME. isolated form whīlom, the dat. pl. of OE.
hwīl *time*, used adverbially.

n

§ 260. OE. and AN. dental n generally remained, as nāme (OE. nama), biginnen (OE. beginnan), sune (OE. sunu) *son*, stǫn *stone*, and similarly nēdle, niȝt; gnawen *to gnaw*, grēne, henne, hound, knē, land, quēne, senden, sunne *sun*; chin, toun; natūre, nǫble, nǫise; aunte, chaunce, point; baroun, vain. For the loss of final ·n see §§ 147, 247.

ŋ

§ 261. OE. and AN. guttural ŋ (written n) remained, as bringen (OE. bringan), singen, pret. pl. sungen (OE. singan, sungon), tunge (OE. tunge), and similarly drinken, finger, king, lang long, þanken; anguische, frank, langāge, &c.

§ 262. OE. palatal ŋc (§ 286) and ŋg (§ 294) became ntš (written nch) and ndž (written ng), as benche (OE. benc), finch (OE. finc), þenchen (OE. þencan) *to think*; sengen singen (OE. sengean) *to singe*.

§ 263. In many dialects the OE. palatal combinations eŋc, eŋg became ein before d, t, þ with i to indicate the palatal nature of the n, the ei then later became e, as pret. meinde (OE. mengde) *he mixed*, dreinte (OE. drencte) *he drowned*, and similarly bleinte *he deceived*, seinde *he singed*, sleinde *he slung*, &c., leinten, later lenten (OE. lengten, lencten) *spring*, *Lent*, leinþe, lenþe (OE. lengþu), streinþe, strenþe (OE. strengþu). The forms lenþ strenþ are still the usual forms in all the dialects of Scotland and the northern counties. Cp. §§ 238, 295.

The Labials.

p

§ 264. OE. and AN. p generally remained in all positions of the word, as paþ (OE. pæþ), slēpen slēpen (OE. slǣpan, slēpan), dēp (OE. dēop), and similarly peni, pleien *to play*,

pound, pręst, proud; cuppe, harpe, helpen, lippe,
spęken, steppen, wępen *to weep*; pret. halp, schip; part,
plęsen *to please*, present; lampe, purple, spāce.

b

§ 265. OE. and AN. b generally remained in all positions
of the word, as bęren (OE. beran), bręken (OE. brecan),
ribbe (OE. ribb), web (OE. webb), and similarly baþ,
bīnden, blak, bǭn, bringen; clīmben, clubbe, ebbe,
webbe *female weaver*; cǭmb, doumb *dumb*, gossib; bęst,
blāmen, boilen; chaumbre, labour, membre, tāble.

ME. hăven *to have*, hęven *to raise, heave*, liven beside
OE. habban, hebban, libban were new formations made
from the present second and third pers. singular hafast,
hafaþ, &c.

f

§ 263. OE. medial and final f had a twofold origin and
a twofold pronunciation, see *EOE. Gr.* §§ 157–8.

1. Medially in combination with voiceless sounds, and
finally, it was pronounced like NE. f, and corresponded to
Germanic ƀ and f, as wīf (= OHG. wīb, NHG. weib), wulf
(= OHG. wolf).

2. Medially between voiced sounds it was pronounced like
the v in NE. vine, five, and corresponded to Germanic ƀ
and f, as giefan (OHG. geban), pl. wulfas (OHG. wolfa).
In early ME. the OE. voiced f was generally written u
(rarely v). In the Scottish and northern dialects w was
sometimes written for v in AN. words, as wertu, trawail

1. OE. Voiceless f.

§ 267. OE. initial and final f, and f in combination with
voiceless sounds, remained, as fader (OE. fæder), dęf (OE.
dēaf) *deaf*, fif (OE. fīf) *five*, after (OE. æfter), and similarly

ferre *far*, fīnden, flȳen *to fly*, folk, frḗsen *to freeze*, full ;
calf, lḗf *leaf*, turf, twelf ; gift, offren ; also in AN. words,
as fāce, frut (fruit) ; brḗf *brief*, strīf. Forms like fīve beside fīf, grāve beside OE. græf, twelve beside older twelf
were new formations from the inflected forms. For the
voicing of initial f in Kentish and the southern dialects see
§ 236.

2. OE. Medial f = v.

§ 268. OE. medial f = v generally remained, as drīven
(OE. drīfan), havest, haveþ (OE. hafast, hafaþ), and
similarly bḗver, given (ȝiven), heven, knāve, loven,
rāven, seven, sterven *to die*, wḗven ; also in AN. words,
as valour, verai ; availen, avengen, serven. f from older
v disappeared in the unaccented forms hast, haþ beside the
accented forms havest, haveþ. For other examples of the
loss of v see § 248. For the unvoicing of v see § 238, and
for the vocalization of v to u (generally written w) see
§ 242.

The Dentals.

t

§ 269. OE. and AN. t generally remained in all positions
of the word, as tāle (OE. talu), tunge (OE. tunge), bīten
(OE. bītan), setten (OE. settan), what (OE. hwæt), and
similarly tāken, tellen, tīme, toun, trē, twig ; better,
ḗten, fiȝten *to fight*, herte, resten, sitten, swḗte, preterites
like grette *he greeted*, kepte, slepte ; fǭt, mǭst, niȝt *night* ;
tāble, tempest ; douten *to doubt*, straunge ; delīt *delight*.

Note.—1. c, z (also occasionally ȝ) were sometimes written for
ts, as blecen (Orm blettsenn, OE. bletsian) *to bless*, milze,
Orm millce (OE. milts) *mercy*.

2. In late ME. th was sometimes written for t in French words,
as autour (O.Fr. auteur) later authour, tḗme (O.Fr. tesme) later
thḗme, trǭne (O.Fr. trone) later thrǭne.

d

270. OE. and AN. d generally remained in all positions of the word, as dai (OE. dæg), drinken (OE. drincan), bidden (OE. biddan), bīnden (OE. bindan), fader (OE. fæder), dẹ̄d (OE. dēad), and similarly dẹ̄p, doṳʒter *daughter*, dwellen; bodi, bladder, fīnden, fọ̄lden, sadel, þunder, weder *weather*, wīlde; bed, fẹ̄ld, god, hard, land, ọ̄ld, word; dāme, daungẹ̄r; maladie, pardoun; round. But single d between a vowel and a following vocalic r (written er) began to become ð in native words from the beginning of the fifteenth century, as father, gather(en), wether *weather*, from older fader, gaderen, weder, see *ENE. Gr.* § 230. The t in the preterite and pp. of verbal stems ending in ·l, ·ll, ·ld, ·rd, ·m, ·n, ·nd was due to the analogy of preterites and past participles like kepte, kept; mette, met; kiste, kist, where the t was regular, as bilte (OE. bylde), bilt; dwelte, dwelt; felte, felt; girte, girt; dremte, dremt; blente, blent *blended*, sente, sent. For the unvoicing of d see § 239.

þ

§ 271. OE. þ (ð) had a twofold pronunciation, see *EOE. Gr.* § 139.

1. Initially, medially when doubled, and finally it was pronounced like the th in NE. thin.

2. Medially between voiced sounds it was pronounced like the th in NE. then.

In the fourteenth century th gradually came to be used beside þ, but the þ continued to be written beside th, especially initially, throughout the ME. period. In the best manuscripts of the *Canterbury Tales* th is generally used (cp. § 20).

1. Voiceless þ.

§ 272. OE. voiceless þ generally remained, as þing (OE. þing), þrẹ̄d þrẹ̄d (OE. þrǣd) *thread*, kiþþe (OE. cȳþþu) *kindred*, dēþ (OE. dēaþ) *death*, and similarly þanken, þenken þinken, þorn; wraþþe; baþ, mouþ, tōþ. The pret. quod beside quoþ had d from the old plural. For the voicing of initial þ in the Kentish and southern dialects see § 236, and of final ·þ in unaccented syllables, see § 237.

§ 273. þ became t after voiceless spirants, as drouȝte (OE. drūgoþ) *drought*, heiȝte (OE. hīehþu) *height*, leste (OE. þȳ læs þe) *lest*, nosterl beside older nosþyrl *nostril*, siȝte (OE. gesihþ) *sight*, þefte (OE. þēofþ, þīefþ) *theft*.

2. Voiced þ.

§ 274. OE. voiced þ generally remained, as brōþer (OE. brōþor), leþer (OE. leþer) *leather*, and similarly bāþen, biquẹ̄þen, blīþe, faþem, hẹ̄þen *heathen*, ōþer, sẹ̄þen *to seethe*, &c. The pret. coude beside couþe *could* was a new formation after the analogy of the other preterites in ·de. For the unvoicing of þ see § 238.

§ 275. þ became d before and after liquids, as aforden beside older aforþen (OE. geforþian), burdene beside older burþene (OE. byrþenn), and similarly fiddle, murdren *to murder*.

The Sibilant s.

§ 276. OE. s had a twofold pronunciation, see *EOE. Gr.* § 139.

1. It was voiceless initially, medially when doubled, and in combination with voiceless consonants, and finally. In ME. the letter c was sometimes used for s initially and in AN. words both initially and medially (cp. § 24). sc was also sometimes written for ss, as blescen bliscen = blessen *to bless*. The OE. final ·s which in ME. became voiced after voiced sounds in unaccented syllables (§ 237) was sometimes written ȝ, as heggeȝ *hedges*.

2. It was voiced (= z) medially between voiced sounds. In early ME. voiced s was only occasionally written z, but the z became more common in late ME.

1. Voiceless s.

§ 277. OE. and AN. voiceless s generally remained,. as senden (OE. sendan), spęken (OE. specan, older sprecan), fist (OE. fȳst), kissen (OE. cyssan), hous (OE. hūs), and similarly sand, singen, slępen, smal, sonne *sun*, standen, strong, swęte *sweet*; asken, asse; hors, mous, was; sāven, cęsen *to cease*, spāce, stout; deceiven, hǫst, passen; cās *case*, pęs *peace*. For the voicing of initial s· in the Kentish and southern dialects, and of final ·s in un-accented syllables, see §§ 236-7.

NOTE.—Initial sl· was sometimes written scl·, as sclępen, sclain, sclender beside slępen, slain, slender.

§ 278. AN. ·(i)ss· became ·(i)sch· in ME., as punischen (O.Fr. punir : puniss·), and similarly anguische, cherischen, finischen, perischen, &c.   See § 289 note.

2. Voiced s.

§ 279. OE. and AN. voiced s remained, as fręsen (OE. frēosan) *to freeze*, rīsen (OE. rīsan), and similarly bęsme *besom*, chęsen *to choose*, rǫse; desīr, plęsen, prisoun, visāge, visiten, &c., cp. § 18.   For the unvoicing of z (written s) see § 238.

The Gutturals.

k

§ 280. Germanic k became differentiated into a guttural and a palatal k in OE., generally written c in both cases. For the cause of this differentiation see *EOE. Gr.* § 166.

1. OE. Guttural c.

§ 281. OE. guttural c remained in ME., and was generally written c before guttural vowels and l, r, and k before palatal vowels, n, and finally, and cw was generally written qu (§ 14), as **kichene** (OE. cycene), **kissen** (OE. cyssan), **cōl** (OE. cōl) *cool*, **corn** (OE. corn), **cumen** (OE. cuman), **bāken** (OE. bacan), **sinken** (OE. sincan), **spēken** (OE. specan, older sprecan), **blak** (OE. blæc), **bǭk** (OE. bōc), and similarly **biquēþen, can, keie** *key*, **kēne, kēpen, king, clēne, clīmben, knē, knǫwen, cǭld, cǭmb, craft, crēpen, quēne, cou** *cow*, **cuppe**; **brēken, drinken, māken**; **stikke sticke, þikke þicke** (see § 14); **bak, dark, folk, milk, work**; also written **c** in AN. words, as **cacchen** *to catch*, **colour, commoun, doctour, escāpen**, &c.

OE. Palatal c.

282. There is still some difference of opinion among scholars about what was the normal development of the OE. palatal **c** in ME. Some scholars assume that it became assibilated to **tš** in the Midland and southern dialects some time during the OE. period, but that in the northern dialects the palatalization was given up and that consequently no assibilation took place. They explain the **tš**-forms in the northern dialects as being importations from the other dialects, and conversely the **k**-forms in the Midland and southern dialects as being importations from the northern dialects. This explanation can hardly be the correct one, because the **tš**-forms in the oldest records of the northern dialects are so numerous, and such common everyday words, that they cannot all have been importations from the other dialects, especially at such an early period. Other scholars assume that OE. palatal **c** became assibilated to **tš** in all the dialects (but see § 284), and that the **k**-forms in ME. and standard NE. are either Scandinavian words (cp. § 174) or are due to Scandinavian influence caused by the Scandinavian element of the population substituting the **k**-sound for the **tš** with which they were unfamiliar, and that then some of these **k**-forms gradually spread beyond the Scandinavian area. This explanation is probably the correct one. It is also possible that forms like þenken (OE. þencan) *to think*, þinken (OE. þyncan) *to seem*, sēken (OE. sēcan) *to seek*, beside þenchen, þinchen, sēchen were new formations from the early OE. syncopated forms like þencþ, þyncþ, sēcþ (see *EOE. Gr.* § 319) with regular change from the palatal to the guttural c.

§ 283. In some southern texts ch was written for OE. palatal c in all positions as far back as the twelfth century. In the early ME. period the tš was written ch, and medially when doubled cch. Later it was written tch medially and finally. Examples are:—chęwen (OE. cēowan) *to chew*, chīld (OE. cild), chin (OE. cinn), chicken (OE. cīcen, gen. cīcnes), fecchen (OE. feccean beside fetian), tęchen (OE. tǣcan) *to teach*, birche (OE. birce), and similarly chęke, chęp, cheris *çherry*, chęse, chīden, chile; bęche *becch*, kichene, strecchen, chirche, crucche, hevenliche, spęche, wicche *witch*, wrecche; dich, pich.

NOTE.—In kerven (OE. ceorfan) *to carve* the k of the pret. pl. and pp. was levelled out into the present.

§ 284. Assibilation did not take place initially in the Anglian area before ME. ǎ from early OE. (Anglian) æ = WS. ea, as caf (Angl. cæf) : chaf (WS. ceaf) *chaff*, and similarly calf : chalf, cāld cǫld : chāld chęld *cold* (§ 71), calk : chalk.

§ 285. In a number of words k- and ch-forms exist side by side. The k-forms occur chiefly, but not exclusively, in the ME. period in those areas where Scandinavian influence was greatest, as ic ik : ich (OE. ic) *I*, ilk : ęch (OE. ǣlc) *each*, līk : līche (OE. līc) *like*, mikel : miche muche (OE. mycel), sęken : sęchen (OE. sēcan), swilk : siche suche swich (OE. swylc), þenken : þenchen (OE. þencan) *to think*, þinken : þinchen (OE. þyncan) *to seem*, quilk : which (OE. hwylc), wirken : wirchen (OE. wyrcan) *to work* (cp. § 282). For further examples see § 174.

In AN. words we also sometimes have **k·** and **ch·** side by side, because in the dialects of north Normandy and Picardy the **k·** remained unassibilated, as **calengen : chalengen** *to challenge*, **calice : chalice, catel : chatel** *property*.

§ **286.** Palatal ŋc became ntš (written nch), as **benche** (OE. benc), **þenchen** (OE. þencan) *to think*, and similarly **finch, þinchen** *to seem*, **wenche**, see § **262**.

§ **287.** In many dialects the palatal combination ·eŋc· became ·ein· before **t**, with **i** to indicate the palatal nature of the combination, as **dreinte** (OE. drencte) *he drowned*, **leinten** later **lenten** (OE. lengten, lencten) *spring, Lent*, see § **263**.

§ **288.** AN. **ch** (= tš) remained in ME., as **chaumbre, charge, chaunce; achẹven, prẹchen** *to preach*, **touchen,** &c.

sc

§ **289.** In the oldest period of the language **sc**, like **k**, was guttural or palatal according as it was originally followed by a guttural or a palatal vowel (*EOE. Gr.* § 167), but some time during the OE. period the guttural **sc** became palatal, except in loan-words. **sc** became **š** in late OE. or early ME. In early ME. it was generally written **sch** or sometimes **sh** as in the *Ormulum*, also medially and finally **ssh, sch,** later **sh,** in the *Cursor Mundi* **sc,** and in Kentish **ss**. Examples are:—**schaft** (OE. sceaft), **schẹld** (OE. scield), **schilling** (OE. scilling), **waschen** (OE. wascan), **fisch** (OE. fisc), and similarly **schāde, schal, scharp, schẹwen** *to show*, **schīnen, schort; asche, wischen; englisch, flesch**. West Midland and south-western dialects **aschen** (OE. āscian, āxian, § 244) beside **asken** with later metathesis again of **ks = x** in the other dialects, and similarly **tusch** beside **tusk =** OE. **tusc** beside **tux**. For **sc** in loan-words see §§ **161, 175**.

Note.—In the northern dialects the **š**, of whatever origin, became **s** in unaccented syllables, as **felasip** *fellowship*, **inglis**

English, and similarly in AN. words, as **blemis** *blemish*, **finis** *to finish*, &c. (cp. § 278). It also became s in unaccented words, as **sal** *shall*, **suld** *should*, which are still the usual—now accented—forms in the modern northern dialects, see *ED. Gr.* § 337.

g, ʒ

§ 290. Germanic ʒ became **g** after ŋ during the prim. Germanic period. ʒj and ʒn became **gg** in West Germanic. Germanic ʒ remained a spirant in all other positions in the oldest period of OE. Germanic initial and medial ʒ became differentiated in prehistoric OE. into a guttural and a palatal voiced spirant under the same conditions as those by which Germanic **k** became differentiated into a guttural and a palatal explosive, see *EOE. Gr.* § 168.

§ 291. Initial guttural ʒ remained in the oldest period of the language, but had become the voiced explosive **g** before the end of the OE. period. And then the **g** remained in ME. (cp. § 16), as **gaderen** (OE. **gaderian**) *to gather*, **gāte** (OE. pl. **gatu**), **glad** (OE. **glæd**), **gọ̄d** (OE. **gōd**), **ground** (OE. **grund**), and similarly **gilden**, **gilt** *guilt*, **glọ̄f** *glove*, **god**, **gǭn gān** *to go*, **gọ̄s**, **gnawen**, **gras**. AN. **g** remained in ME. both initially and medially, as **gai**, **grāce**, **tīgre**, **vigour**.

§ 292. OE. initial palatal ʒ remained a spirant (= the **y** in NE. **yet, yon**) in ME., and was written ʒ later **y**, as ʒ**af** (OE. **geaf**) *he gave*, ʒ**ard**, ʒ**erd** (OE. **geard**), ʒ**ę̄lden** (OE. **gieldan**) *to recompense*, and similarly ʒ**ellen**, ʒ**elwe** *yellow*, ʒ**ernen**, ʒ**esterdai**, **forʒę̆ten forʒiten**. In OE. the guttural and palatal ʒ often existed side by side in different forms of the same word, and then at a later period one or other of the forms became generalized, as OE. pl. **gatu** beside sing. **geat**, whence ME. **gāte** beside ʒ**at**, ʒ**et** (cp. § 176). And similarly ME. **biginnen** had its **g** from the preterite and past participle. In a few words the English and Scandinavian forms existed side by side in ME., as **forʒę̆ten forʒiten** (OE. **forgietan**) beside **gę̆ten** (ON. **geta**), and similarly ӡĕven, ӡiven beside **given**, northern **gif, ӡift** beside **gift**, see § 176.

§ **293.** Initial ӡi· became i· (later written **y·**) through the intermediate stage ī·, as **icchen**, older ӡicchen (OE. **gicc(e)an**) *to itch*, **if** beside older ӡif. And similarly the OE. prefix **ge·** became ӡi· and then later i· (**y·**), see § **240**, as **iwis ywis** (OE. **gewiss**) *certain*, inǫuӡ ynǫuӡ (OE. **genōg, genōh**) *enough*, and in past participles, as **islain, iclad.** This prefix of the pp. generally disappeared in the northern dialects and often also in the Midland.

§ **294.** The g in the combination ŋg remained guttural or became palatal in OE. according as it was originally followed by a guttural or a palatal vowel or **j** (*EOE. Gr.* § 168).

OE. guttural ŋg (written **ng**) remained in ME., as **bringen** (OE. **bringan**), **hunger** (OE. **hungor**), **lang long** (OE. **lang, long**), and similarly **England, finger, singen, tonge tunge; king, ring, þing.**

OE. palatal ŋg became assibilated to ndž (written **ng**) in late OE. or early ME., as **crengen** (OE. ***creng(e)an**) *to crinӡe*, **sengen singen** (OE. **seng(e)an**) *to singe*.

§ **295.** In many dialects the OE. palatal combination ·eŋg· became ·ein· before d, þ with i to denote the palatal nature of the n. The ei then later became e, as pret. **meinde** (OE. **mengde**) *he mixed*, **leinþe** later **lenþe** (OE. **lengþu**) *length*, **streinþe** later **strenþe** (OE. **strengþu**) *strength*, see §§ **238, 263.**

§ **296.** West Germanic **gg** became differentiated into guttural **gg** and palatal **gg** in OE. under the same conditions as those by which Germanic k became differentiated into a guttural and palatal explosive.

OE. guttural **gg** remained in ME., as **dogge** (OE. **dogga**), and similarly **frogge, hogge, stagge,** and also in ON. loanwords like **draggen** *to drag, draw*, **haggen** *to hew*. **waggen** *to wag, shake*, &c.

OE. palatal **gg (written cg,** often also **cge, cgi)** became

assibilated to dž in late OE. or early ME., and was written
gge later dge, as brigge (OE. brycg), cuggele (OE. cycgel),
and similarly egge, hegge, migge, rigge, wegge. The
southern dialects had the regular forms in the verbs, as
biggen büggen beggen (OE. bycgan) *to buy*, leggen (OE.
lecg(e)an) *to lay*, and similarly liggen *to lie down*, seggen
ziggen (Ken.) *to say*, but bȳen *to buy*, leien *to lay*, lȳen *to
lie down*, seien sai *to say*, in the Midland and northern
dialects were new formations from the second and third pers.
sing. of the present.

NOTE.—There is both in ME. and in the modern dialects of the
northern, Midland and eastern counties a number of words with
the explosive g where we should regularly expect dž, as brig,
fligd *fledged*, lig *to lie down*, rig *back*, *ridge*, seg *sedge*. The g in
these words is no doubt due to Scandinavian influence as the
forms only occur in those areas where that influence was strong,
cp. § 235.

§ 297. The dž (written j, g initially and g, gg medially)
remained in AN. words, as cāge, chargen; generāl,
joinen, juge, juggen, plege plegge.

§ 298. OE. medial guttural ʒ (written g) remained in early
ME. after guttural vowels and liquids, but became vocalized
to u·consonant (written w) before the end of the twelfth
century except in Kentish where the change did not take
place until about 1400, and then the w combined with a
preceding guttural vowel to form a diphthong of the u·type,
but ū (written ou, ow) if the preceding vowel was ŭ, as
draȝen, drawen (OE. dragan) *to draw*, haȝe, hawe (OE.
hagu) *haw*, see § 110, 3 ; āȝen, awe, ǫwen (OE. āgan) *to
possess*, see § 110, 4 and § 113, 3 ; bǫȝe, bǫue bǫwe (OE.
boga) *bow*, pl. trǫȝes, trǫwes (OE. trogas) *troughs*, see
§ 113, 2 ; pl. bǭȝes, bǫwes (OE. bōgas) *boughs*, drǭȝen,
drǫwen (OE. drōgon) *they drew*, see § 114, 2 (*b*) ; fuȝel, fūel,
fou(e)l (OE. fugol) *bird*, *fowl*, see § 122, 5 ; būȝen, būen,
bouen bowen (OE. būgan) *to bend*, see § 122, 6 ; belǫwes

(OE. pl. belgas) *bellows* (cp. § 152, 2), berȝen, berwen (OE.
beorgan) *to protect* ; folȝen, folwen (OE. folgian) *to follow*,
halȝen, halwen (OE. hālgian) *to hallow*, morȝen, morwe(n)
(OE. morgen) *morning, morrow*, sorȝe, sorwe (OE. sorh,
sorg, gen. sorge) *sorrow*, swelȝen, swelwen, swolwen
(OE. swelgan) *to swallow*, wirȝen, wirwen (OE. wyrgan)
to strangle.

§ 299. The vocalization of palatal ȝ to i-consonant took
place already in late OE. after palatal vowels finally and
before consonants, and in early ME. also medially between
vowels, and then the i-consonant combined with a preceding
palatal vowel to form a diphthong of the i-type, but ī if the
preceding vowel was ĭ, as mai (OE. mæg, later mæi) *he may*,
maȝen, main (OE. mægen) *power*, saide (OE. sægde) *he
said*, see § 106 ; wei (OE. weg, later wei) *way*, pleȝen,
pleien (OE. plegian) *to play*, see § 107, 1 ; clei (OE. clǣg)
clay, pret. pl. leien (OE. lǣgon) *they lay*, see § 107, 5 ;
dēȝen, deien, dīen (late OE. dēgian) *to dye*, ēȝe, eie, ȳe
(late OE. ēge) *eye*, flēȝen, fleien, flȳen (late OE. flēgan,
earlier flēogan) *to fly*, see §§ 107, 6, 108 ; stiȝele, stīle (OE.
stigel) *style*, see § 122, 1 ; stīȝen, stīen (OE. stīgan) *to
ascend*, see § 122, 2.

For the vocalization of OE. final ·ig in unaccented
syllables and of g between r and a following vowel see
§§ 138, 240.

h

§ 300. OE. initial h (except in the combination hw) was
an aspirate like the h in NE. hand, but with a strong
emission of breath between the h and the following vowel or
consonant.   Initial hw was pronounced χw, like the wh in
many modern Scottish dialects.   In all other positions h,
including hh, was a guttural or a palatal spirant according
as it was originally followed by a guttural or a palatal vowel
or j, cp. *EOE. Gr.* §§ 166, 174.

§ 301. OE. initial **h** remained in ME. before accented vowels, as **hous** (OE. **hūs**), **hęlen** (OE. **hǣlan**) *to heal*, and similarly **hām hǫm** *home*, **hand hond, hard, hāre** *hare*, **helpen, herte** *heart*, **hound**. But before unaccented vowels it often disappeared, especially in pronominal forms, as **em, im, it** beside accented **hem** *them*, **him, hit**; and in unaccented forms it was sometimes wrongly inserted, as **hart, his =** **art** (v.), **is**. This indicates that the **h.** either had a very weak articulation or had ceased to be pronounced.

§ 302. AN. initial **h** was not pronounced, and accordingly it was often omitted in the writing of such loan-words as **habit abit, hāste āste, heire eire** *heir*, **honest onest, honour onour, houre oure** *hour*.

§ 303. OE. **hw** came to be written **qu, qv, quh, qw, qwh** in the northern dialects, especially the Scottish, and **wh** in the Midland and southern dialects (cp. § 17). This difference in the spelling indicates that the χ in χ**w** was pronounced with greater force in the northern than in the other dialects, and it is also attested by the modern dialects which have χ**w** in the former, but **w** in the latter, see *ED. Gr.* § 240. Examples are : **what : quat qvat quhat** (OE. **hwæt**), **whǫ whǫ : quā qvā quhā** (OE. **hwā**), and similarly **while, white**, &c.

§ 304. Initial **h.** disappeared before **l, n, r**, but these combinations were often written **lh, nh, rh** in early ME., especially in Kentish, as **lępen** (OE. **hlēapan**) *to leap*, **nute** (OE. **hnutu**) *nut*, **ring** (OE. **hring**), and similarly **ladder, lauȝen** *to laugh*, **lid, lǫf** *loaf*, **lot, neien** *to neigh*, **rāven**, &c.

§ 305. Medial and final **hs** (= χ**s**) had become **ks** (written **x**) in the oldest period of the language, as **waxen** (OE. **weaxan**, Goth. **wahsjan**) *to grow*, **six** (OE. **siex, six**, Goth. **saíhs**) *six*, and similarly **flax, fox, oxe**, &c.

§ 306. Intervocalic **h** (= Germanic χ) disappeared in the prehistoric period of the language (*EOE. Gr.* § 144). OE.

medial **hh** was simplified to **h** in ME. and was written ȝ, ȝh, gh, hȝ, &c., as lauȝen laughen (Anglian **hlæhha(n)**) beside liȝhen lihȝen leihȝen (early WS. **hliehhan**, later **hlihhan, hlyhhan**) *to laugh*, coȝuen coughen (OE. **cohhettan**) *to cough*.

§ 307. The **h** in the OE. combination **ht** was guttural or palatal according as it was preceded by a guttural or a palatal vowel, and this distinction was generally preserved in ME., see §§ 107, 4 ; 110, 5, 6 ; 113, 4, 5.   In ME. the **ht** was generally written ȝt, ȝht, ght, rarely ct.   Examples are : doȝuter doughter (OE. **dohtor**) *daughter*, pp. foȝuten foȝhten (OE. **fohten**) *fought*, pret. boȝuȝte boȝughte *he bought*, pp. boȝuȝt boȝught (OE. **bohte, boht**), and similarly broȝuȝte, broȝuȝt; soȝuȝte, soȝuȝt ; wroȝuȝte, wroȝuȝt.   auȝt aught, aȝt aght (OE. **āht**) *aught, anything*, pret. teiȝte teighte (OE. **tæhte**) beside tauȝte, taȝte, Orm tahhte (OE. **tāhte**) *he taught*, pret. fauȝt, faȝt (late Anglian **fæht**) beside feiȝt (late WS. **feht**) *he fought*, auȝte aughte, aȝte aghte (late Anglian **æhta**) beside eiȝte eighte (late WS. **ehta**) *eight*, and similarly lauȝter laughter, slauȝter slaughter, strauȝte straughte *he stretched*. feiȝten feighten older fehten beside fiȝten (Orm **fihhten**) *to fight*. For examples of late OE. i + ht see § 46.

NOTE.—The palatal spirantal element began to disappear in pronunciation from about the end of the fourteenth century in the south Midland and southern dialects, and the guttural spirantal element began to disappear or become f in these dialects during the fifteenth century.

§ 308. OE. postvocalic final -**h**, which was guttural or palatal according as it was preceded by a guttural or a palatal vowel, generally remained in ME. and was written **h, ȝ, ȝh, gh**, and occasionally **c, g**, see §§ 107, 4 ; 109 ; 110, 5 ; 113, 4 ; and 114, 115.   Examples are : dāȝ dāgh, doȝuȝ dough (OE. **dāh, dāg**) *dough*, pret. sauȝ saugh, saȝ sagh (late Anglian **sæh**) beside seiȝ seigh (late WS. **seh**) *he saw*. troȝuȝ trough

(OE. **troh, trog**) *trough*.　**bọuȝ bọugh** later **bọuȝ bọugh**
(OE. **bōh**) *bough* (§ 114, 2), and similarly **inọuȝ inọugh**,
plọuȝ plọugh, **þọuȝ þọugh** *though*.　**heiȝ heigh** beside **hīȝ**
hīgh (late OE. **hēh**) *high*, **þeiȝ þeigh** beside **þīȝ þīgh** (late OE.
þēh) *thigh*.　ME. **fẹ̄** *cattle, money* beside **feh feiȝ** (OE. **feoh**,
gen. **fēos**) was a new formation from the inflected forms
where intervocalic **h** regularly disappeared (*EOE. Gr.* § 144),
and similarly **schọ̄** (OE. **scōh**, gen. **scōs**) *shoe*.

§ 309.　OE. final -**h** after liquids generally remained in
ME., as **þurh þurȝ** (OE. **þurh**) *through*, cp. § 241.　Forms
like **holu** *hollow* beside **holȝ** (OE. **holh**, gen. **holwes**) were
new formations from the inflected forms, and similarly with
forms like **sẹ̄le** (OE. **seolh**, gen. **sēoles**) *a seal* (cp. § 134 (*a*)).

ACCIDENCE

CHAPTER VII

THE DECLENSION OF NOUNS

§ 310. ME. nouns have two numbers : singular and plural ; three genders : masculine, feminine, and neuter ; four cases : nominative, accusative, genitive, and dative. The vocative is like the nominative, as in OE.

§ 311. In ME. as in OE. nouns are divided into two great classes, according as the stem originally ended in a vowel or a consonant. Nouns whose stems originally ended in a vowel belong to the vocalic or so-called strong declension. Those whose stems originally ended in -n belong to the so-called weak or n-declension. All other consonantal stems are generally put together under the general heading 'Minor Declensions'.

§ 312. In OE. nouns whose stems originally ended in a vowel are subdivided into four declensions. The first or a-declension comprises masculine and neuter nouns only, and includes pure a-stems, ja-stems, and wa-stems. The second or ō-declension contains feminine nouns only, and includes pure ō-stems, jō-stems, and wō-stems. The third or i-declension comprises masculine, feminine, and neuter nouns. The fourth or u-declension comprises masculine and feminine nouns only. The neuter nouns of the a-declension had the same case-endings in the singular and plural as the masculine, except that the nominative and accusative plural of the neuter nouns ended in -u (-o) or had no ending, and the masculine nouns ended in -as. In the plural the genitive had the ending -a (-en-a) and the dative the ending -um in all four declensions (see § 259).

§ **313.** These declensions underwent such radical changes
in passing from OE. to ME. that in ME. it is no longer
practicable to classify the strong declension of nouns according to the vowels in which the stems originally ended. We
shall therefore adopt the plan of subdividing it into three
declensions according to the gender of the nouns in OE.,
viz. (1) the declension of masculine nouns, (2) the declension
of neuter nouns, and (3) the declension of feminine nouns.
The chief cause of the breaking up of the OE. system of the
declension of nouns was that in passing from OE. to ME. all
the OE. vowels of the case-endings were weakened to e
(§ 134). The result of this weakening of all vowels to e was
that many different case-endings fell together, and that in
some instances different declensions fell entirely together,
e.g. the feminine ō- and u-declensions, the declension of the
masculine and feminine weak nouns.

§ **314.** With this weakening of all the vowels to e is also
closely connected the loss of grammatical gender in nouns,
which was partly due to the breaking up of the old declensions themselves, and partly to the weakening or loss of the
inflexional endings in the definite article, the demonstrative
pronouns, and the adjectives. It was in a great measure due
to the changes which these latter parts of speech underwent
in late OE. and early ME. that grammatical gender had
become lost in all the dialects by about the end of the
fourteenth century ; cp. the opposite process in MHG. and
NHG., where grammatical gender has been mainly preserved
through the preservation of the inflexional endings in these
parts of speech. This loss of grammatical gender did not
take place concurrently in all the dialects. The process
began much earlier in the northern than in the other dialects.
Even in the OE. period both the gender and declension of
nouns fluctuated considerably in the Northumbrian as compared with the other dialects. It had almost entirely disappeared in the Midland dialects by the end of the twelfth or

early part of the thirteenth century, in the south-western dialects by the middle of the thirteenth century, and in the south-eastern dialects, including Kentish, in the latter part of the fourteenth century.

§ 315. One of the most characteristic differences between OE. and ME. is the breaking up of the old system of declensions, the substitution of natural for grammatical gender, and the gradual spreading of the endings of the genitive singular and of the nominative and accusative plural of the old masculine **a**-declension to the types of nouns which did not regularly have these endings in OE., viz. to the **ō**-stems, the feminine and neuter **i**-stems, the **u**-stems, the **n**-stems, most of the other old consonant stems, and the plural of the old neuter **a**-stems. Some of these changes began to take place during the late OE. period, especially in Northumbrian. Even at that early period the plural ending -**as** of the masculine **a**- and **i**-declensions was often extended to the neuter **a**-stems, the masculine short **u**-stems, and the masculine nouns belonging to the 'Minor Declensions', and in late Northumbrian it also began to be extended to the feminine **ō**- and **i**-stems as well as to the **n**-stems after the loss of the final -**n** in the tenth century. In late OE. the plural ending in -**en** (-**an**) was sometimes even extended to old strong nouns. This was especially common in the southern dialects.

§ 316. This gradual extension of the s-plural was continued during the ME. period until it eventually became general for all classes of nouns except a few old neuter **a**-stems (§ 331), and mutated plurals like **fēt, men** (§ 346), but this radical change in the formation of the plural did not take place at the same pace in all the dialects. In the northern and north Midland dialects it had spread to all classes of nouns by the end of the twelfth century. In the south Midland dialects it had become the general rule from about 1250 for strong nouns of all genders, and often also for weak nouns. Many weak nouns, however, preserved the old plural ending in -n, which was also sometimes extended to the strong nouns, but by the time of Chaucer the s-plural had with few exceptions been extended to all classes of nouns. In the southern dialects the history of the formation of the plural was somewhat different from that in the other dialects. The neuter nouns of the a-declension took the plural ending -es in early ME., but strong feminines and the masculine short i- and u-stems gradually took the n-plural after the analogy of the weak nouns. During the thirteenth century the reverse process set in, and from then onwards the s-plural gradually encroached upon the n-plural and through the loss of the final -e-n towards the end of the fourteenth century it rapidly gained ground until in the fifteenth century it became general for all classes of nouns.

§ 317. In OE. the a- and the masculine and neuter i-stems regularly had the ending -es in the genitive singular, but the ō- and feminine i-stems had -e, the u-stems -a, and the n-stems -an, which became weakened down to -e, -en in early ME. (§ 134). Parallel with the gradual extension of the s-plural to all classes of nouns also went that of the genitive ending -es, but genitives without -(e)s in those types of nouns which did not have it in OE. are occasionally found throughout the ME. period, and a few such genitives are still preserved in NE., as **Friday, Lady day** beside **Thursday, the Lord's day**. The e in -es was generally written, but not pronounced after secondary accented syllables of trisyllabic forms, as **felawęs, housbondęs, bodięs, lādięs**, &c.

§ 318. During the ME. period the preposition **of** came to be used before the nominative and accusative singular to express the genitival relationship, and similarly the preposition **to** to express the dative.

§ 319. The nominative and accusative plural were always alike in OE. and so also in ME. In OE. the genitive plural of all strong nouns, of whatever gender, ended in -a (= ME.

-e), except the pure ō-stems which had -ena (= ME. -ene)
beside -a. The genitive plural of weak nouns ended in -ena
(= ME. -ene). And the dative plural of all nouns, of whatever gender and declension, ended in -um, late OE. -un, -on,
-an (= ME. -en), see § 259. The endings -ene and -en
remained for a time in ME. in those nouns which had the
weak ending -en (= OE. -an) in the nominative and accusative
plural. But in those nouns where -(e)s had come to be used
for the nominative and accusative plural, the -(e)s was
gradually extended to the genitive and dative, that is to say
the nominative and accusative came to be used for the
genitive and dative.

§ 320. Trisyllabic inflected forms with -el-, -en-, -er-
generally syncopated the medial -e-, as **foules, apples,
wintres, fingres, fadres, mōdres** (cp. § 102). But when
the medial -el-, -en-, -er- were preceded by m, v, þ the
medial -e- was retained in writing, but not in pronunciation, as **hameres, develes, hevenes, brōþeres**. All nouns
ending in f, s, þ changed these to v, z (written s), and ð
(written þ) in the inflected forms. Original medial double
consonants were generally simplified when they came to
stand finally, as gen. **hilles, mannes, pottes** beside nom.
hil, man, pot. With rare exceptions the Anglo-Norman
nouns were inflected in ME. like the native English nouns
which in OE. belonged to the masculine a-declension, that
is, the genitive singular ended in -es, the dative in -e, and
the plural in -es.

A. THE VOCALIC or STRONG DECLENSION

1. Masculine Nouns.

§ 321. To this declension belong: (*a*) the OE. masculine
a-, ja-, and **wa**-stems ; (*b*) the OE. masculine i-stems ; and
(*c*) the OE. masculine u-stems. In OE. the nominative and
accusative singular of the a-stems, the **ja**-stems with an

original short stem-syllable, and the long i- and u-stems generally ended in a consonant, as **stān** *stone*, **dæg** *day*, **mearh** *horse*, **scōh** *shoe*; **hyll** *hill*, **mycg** *midge*; **dǣl** *part*, **giest** *guest*, **wyrm** *worm*; **fēld** *field*, **sumor** *summer*; but the nominative and accusative singular of the ja-stems with an original long stem-syllable, the short i- and u-stems ended in a vowel, as **ende** *end*, **drincere** *drinker*; **wine** *friend*, **stede** *place*; **sunu** *son*, **wudu** *wood*. This difference in the ending of the nominative and accusative singular was regularly preserved in nearly all the nouns in ME.

§ 322. In passing from OE. to ME. the following changes took place in the nom. and acc. singular: nouns like **dæg** came to end in a diphthong, as **dai** (pl. **daies** beside **dawes**), **wei** (OE. **weg**), which also sometimes took -e from the inflected forms, as **daie** (**daye**), **weie** (**weye**, *Ormulum* **weȝȝe**). Nouns of the type **mearh**, **scōh**, **mycg** came to end in a vowel through having been remodelled after the analogy of the inflected forms, as **mēre** (OE. **mearh**, gen. **mēares**), **schǭ** (OE. **scōh**, gen. **scōs**), **migge** (OE. **mycg**, gen. **mycges**). In late ME. a mute -e was sometimes added to monosyllables ending in a single consonant and containing a long vowel in order to indicate that the preceding vowel was long, as **stǭne** *stone*, **strēme** *stream*, beside **stǭn**, **strēm** (§ 11). Final -u was weakened to -e (§ 134).

§ 323. ME. nouns ending in a consonant; and generally also those ending in a diphthong, took -es (also sometimes written -us, -is, -ys, see § 134) in the gen. singular, as **stǫnes**, **daies** beside **dais**, and those ending in a vowel took -s, as **schǭs**, **sēs** *seas*. In early ME. the dat. singular ended in -e (§ 141). This -e was retained when the nom. and acc. ended in -e, but when they did not end in -e they came to be used for the dative also, as nom. acc. and dat. sing. **stǫn**, **schǭ**, **dai**. Trisyllabic forms containing medial -el-, -en-, -er- generally syncopated the medial -e-, as gen. **apples**, **fingres** beside nom. **appel**, **finger** (cp. § 102).

§ **324.** Through the weakening of the OE. ending ·as to ·es in ME. the ending of the nom. and acc. plural came to be lǐke that of the gen. singular. The OE. gen. plural ending ·a and the dat. ending ·um (= late OE. ·un, ·on, ·an, § 259) were weakened to ·e and ·en which remained in the transition period, but already in early ME. they were supplanted by the nominative and accusative. and thus all cases of the plural came to be alike.

§ **325.** st**ǭn** *stone*, **engel** *angel*, **ende** *end*, and **sone** *son* will serve as models for the nouns belonging to this declension.

§ **326.**

		ME.	OE.	ME.	OE.
Sing. Nom.	Acc.	stǭn	stān	engel	engel
	Gen.	stǭnes	stānes	engles	engles
	Dat.	stǭn(e)	stāne	engle	engle
Plural Nom.	Acc.	stǭnes	stānas	engles	englas
	Gen.	stǭnes	stāna	engles	engla
	Dat.	stǭnes	stānum	engles	englum

§ **327.** Like st**ǭn** are declined a large number of nouns, as **arm, bǭt, brǭm, cǫmb, craft, dǭm, fisch, gǭst** *ghost*, **hail, hǫm, hound, king, nail, rein** *rain*, **rǭp, roum** *room*, **schaft, stǭl, storm, swan, trǫuȝh, wind,** &c. ; and similarly old long wa·stems, as **snǫw, dęw**; old long i·stems, as **dęl, dint, gest, fliȝt, pliȝt, wurm**; old long u·stems, as **fęld, fǭrd, þorn,** &c. Nouns ending in a voiceless spirant changed it to the corresponding voiced spirant in the inflected forms. as **þęf** *thief*, **mouþ**, gen. **þęves, mouþes**, and similarly **lǭf** *loaf*, **knīf, staf, wolf, ǭþ** *oath*, **paþ**. Medial double consonants were simplified when they came to stand finally, as gen. **briddes, hilles, pittes, walles**, beside nom. **brid**, &c.

§ **328.** Like **engel** are declined nouns ending in ·el, ·en, ·er, as **appel, crādel, girdel, hunger, sadel, þimbel, þunder**. But when the ·el, ·en, ·er were preceded by **m** or **v** the medial · was written in the inflected forms, but was not pronounced, as gen. hamęres, hevęnes, dat. hamęre, hevęne: nom. hamer, heven.

§ 329.

		ME.	OE.	ME.	OE.
Sing. Nom.	Acc.	ende	ende	sone	sunu
	Gen.	endes	endes	sones	suna
	Dat.	ende	ende	sone	suna
Plural Nom.	Acc.	endes	endas	sones	suna
	Gen.	endes	enda	sones	suna
	Dat.	endes	endum	sones	sunum

And similarly męre māre *horse*, sęle *seal* (animal); old ja-stems like migge *midge*, rigge *back*, wegge *wedge*; herde *shepherd*, whęte; bākere, drinkere, fischere; old short i-stems, as bile *bill*, bite, dęne *valley*, stiche; old short u-stems, as męde *mead*, spite *spit*, 'veru', wode wude *wood*.

§ 330. Nouns ending in a vowel other than -e had simply -s in the gen. singular and in the plural, and no -e in the dat. singular, as flę *flea*, gen. flęs, dat. flę, pl. flęs, and similarly schǫ *shoe*, sę *sea*, peni (inflected penięs, penes). dai and wei were also similarly inflected, as dais, dat. sing dai.

2. NEUTER NOUNS.

§ 331. To this declension belong: (a) the OE. neuter a-, ja-, and wa-stems, and (b) the OE. neuter i-stems. These stems were inflected in OE. exactly like the corresponding masculine stems except in the nom. and acc. plural. In OE. the nom. and acc. plural of neuter stems ended either in -u or had no ending (*EOE. Gr.* § 188), whereas the masculine stems ended in -as (= ME. -es). Therefore in treating the neuter nouns it is only necessary to take into consideration the formation of the plural.

1. When the singular ended in a consonant the plural was generally formed by adding -es after the analogy of the old masculine a-declension, as word, pl. wordes, and similarly

bak, barn, bōn, bōrd, horn, land, nest, schip, werk; lēf
leaf, pl. lēves, and similarly baþ, hous, līf, &c.; water, pl.
watres, and similarly tōken, wonder, but pl. maidens
never maidnes in Chaucer; ja-stems, as bed, pl. beddes,
and similarly bil, den, kin, net, rib, web; long i-stems, as
flěsch, pl. flęsches, and similarly flēs *fleece*, hilt, &c.

Monosyllabic nouns with a long stem-syllable denoting
collectivity, weight, measure, and time generally remained
uninflected in the plural just as in OE., as dēr *deer*, folk,
nēt *cattle*, pound, schēp, swīn, ȝēr ȝēr *year*, &c., cp. NE.
deer, sheep, swine, five-pound note. This rule practically
agrees with that in the modern dialects. In all the modern
dialects nouns denoting collectivity, time, space, weight,
measure, and number when immediately preceded by a
cardinal number generally remain unchanged in the plural,
see *ED. Gr.* § 382.

2. When the singular ended in a vowel or a diphthong in
ME. the plural took -s after the analogy of the corresponding
old masculine nouns, as cǫle *coal*, pl. cǫles, and similarly
dāle, gāte, hǫle, ȝǫke (§ 103), fē (OE. feoh, gen. fēos)
cattle; old long ja-stems, as ěrende *errand*, flicche, stęle
steel; old wa-stems, as męle *meal, flour*, tēre *tar*; knē, trē,
strēę beside straw (OE. strēa beside gen. *strawes); short
i-stems, as sive *sieve*, spēre *spear*, &c.

3. Feminine Nouns.

§ 332. To this declension belong: (*a*) the OE. ō-, jō-, and
wō-stems; (*b*) the OE. feminine i-stems; and (*c*) the OE.
feminine u-stems. After the OE. final vowels had been
weakened to -e the following changes took place in the types
of nouns belonging to this declension: In the ō- and jō-stems
which in OE. ended in a consonant the -e of the oblique
cases was levelled out into the nominative, as bǫte *advan-
tage*, sǫule, henne = OE. bōt, sāwol, henn. In the wō-

stems we have double forms in ME. according as the old nominative or accusative singular became generalized, as short **wō**-stems **schāde** (= OE. nom. **sceadu**) beside **schadwe** (= OE. acc. **sceadwe**), **sine** (= OE. nom. **sinu, sionu**) beside **sinewe** (= OE. acc. **sinwe**) *sinew* ; long **wō**-stems, as **mę̄de** with **·e** from the inflected forms (= OE. nom. **mǣd**) beside **medwe medewe** (= OE. acc. **mǣdwe**) *meadow.* In the i-stems the **·e** of the gen. and dat. was levelled out into the nom. and accusative, as **quę̄ne** (= OE. nom. acc. **cwēn**, gen. and dat. **cwēne**). In the long u-stems the **·e** (= OE. **·a**) of the gen. and dat. was not levelled out into the nom. and accusative, as nom. acc. **hand, flọ̄r, quern** = OE. **hand, flōr, cweorn** *hand-mill.* The **·e** of the oblique cases was also not levelled out into the nominative or respectively into the nominative and accusative of other stems ending in **·ing** (**·ung**), **·st**, **·ȝt**, as **lerning, fist, miȝt** = OE. **leornung, fȳst, miht.** With the exception of the types of nouns just mentioned, all the other types belonging to this declension regularly have **·e** from older **·u** in the nominative, as **tāle** (= OE. **talu**), **love** (= OE. **lufu**), &c.

§ 333. In early Northumbrian, and then later also in WS. and Kentish, the acc. sing. of the i-stems often had **·e** after the analogy of the **ō**-stems. The genitive ending **·(e)s** of the strong masc. and neut. nouns was gradually extended to the feminine, but throughout the ME. period forms without **·s** are sometimes found. Feminine nouns denoting animate objects generally had the ending **·(e)s**, whereas abstract nouns and nouns denoting inanimate objects mostly or often had simply **·e**. The nom. and acc. of those nouns which in ME. ended in a consonant came to be used for the dative at an early period, as **hand, lerning, fist**, &c. Chaucer has the dat. **honde** beside **hond**. The plural ending of the OE. masculine **a·** and i-declensions was gradually extended to the strong feminines. The strong feminines had begun to take the **s·**plural in Northumbrian already in the late OE. period,

as **saules, dēdes,** &c. The strong feminines regularly
formed their plural in -(e)s in Chaucer, but the southern
dialects of the fourteenth century mostly had -en after the
analogy of the n-declension. Later on, however, the plural
in these dialects also took the ending -(e)s. See §§ 315–17.

§ 334. **tāle** *number, tale,* **whīle** *time,* **quẹne** *queen,* and
hand will serve as models for the nouns belonging to this
declension.

§ 335.

Sing.	ME.	OE.	ME.	OE.	ME.	OE.
Nom.	tāle	talu	whīle	hwīl	quẹne	cwēn
Acc.	tāle	tale	whīle	hwīle	quẹne	cwēn
Gen.	tāle(s)	tale	whīle(s)	hwīle	quẹne(s)	cwēne
Dat.	tāle	tale	whīle	hwīle	quẹne	cwēne
Plural						
Nom. Acc.	tāles	tala, -e	whīles	hwīla, -e	quẹnes	cwēne, -a
Gen.	tāles	tala, -ena	whīles	hwīla, -ena	quẹnes	cwēna
Dat.	tāles	talum (§ 259)	whīles	hwīlum	quẹnes	cwēnum

§ 336. Like **tāle** are declined the OE. ō-stems with a short
stem-syllable, as **cāre,** love, **schāme, wrāke** *vengeance* ;
the OE. abstract nouns in -þu, as **lengþe, strengþe** ; the
OE. wō-stems with a short stem-syllable, as **schāde
(schadwe), sine (sinewe)** ; and the OE. short u-stems, as
dore dure, nọse.

§ 337. Like **whīle** are declined the OE. ō-stems which did
not have -u in the nom. singular, as **fetere, feþere, glọve,
lọre, nẹdle, netele, sorwe, sọule, wounde** ; the OE. jō-
stems, as **brigge** *bridge,* **cribbe, egge** *edge,* **helle, henne,
sibbe** *relationship,* **sille, sinne** ; **blisse, hīnde** *doe,* **họlinesse,
reste** ; the OE. long wō-stems, **mẹde (medwe), stọwe.**

§ 338. Like **quẹne** are declined the OE. feminine i-stems,
as **benche, brīde, dẹde, hīde, hīve, nẹde** *need,* **spẹde**
success, **tīde.**

§ 339.

			ME.	OE.
Sing.	Nom.	Acc.	hand	hand
		Gen.	hande(s)	handa
		Dat.	hand(e)	handa
Plural	Nom.	Acc.	handes	handa
		Gen.	handes	handa
		Dat.	handes	handum (§ 259)

§ 340. Like hand hond are declined the OE. feminine long u-stems, as flōr, quern *hand-mill*; the OE. abstract nouns in -ung (-ing) and nouns ending in -st, -ht, as blessing, ēvening, lerning, fist, miȝt. The plural hend *hands*, which was common in the northern dialects, was of ON. origin (O.Icel. hend-r).

B. THE WEAK OR N-DECLENSION

§ 341. This declension contained in OE. masculine, feminine, and neuter nouns. It contained a large number of masculine and feminine nouns, but only three neuter nouns all of which denote parts of the body, viz. ēage *eye*, ēare *ear*, and wange *cheek*. The only distinction between the masculines and the feminines in OE. was that the nominative singular of the former ended in -a, and that of the latter in -e. After the -a had been weakened to -e in the nom. singular of the masculines the two classes of nouns had the same endings in all cases of the singular and plural. So that the early ME. case-endings were :—

	ME.	OE.
Sing. Nom.	-e	-a, -e
Acc. Gen. Dat.	-en	-an
Plural Nom. Acc.	-en	-an
Gen.	-ene	-ena
Dat.	-en	-um (§ 259)

The following changes took place:—The -e of the nom.

singular supplanted the ·en (= OE. ·an) of the oblique cases
of the singular, and then later ·s was added for the gen.
singular. The singular thus fell together with the old
masculine, feminine, and neuter strong nouns whose nom.
singular ended in ·e in ME. The extension of ·(e)s from the
old strong masculines and neuters of the a· and i·declensions
to the nouns of this declension took place earlier in the
masculines than in the feminines. And in the masculines
it took place earlier in nouns denoting animate objects than
in those denoting inanimate objects. In Chaucer the old
feminines generally have ·(e)s in the gen. singular, but
forms like gen. lādy, sonne, widwe also occur. The old
·en plurals remained much longer in the southern and
Kentish dialects than in the Midland and northern. In the
former dialects the ·en plural was often extended to nouns
which were strong in OE. and even also to Anglo-Norman
words. This was especially common with the gen. plural
ending ·ene (= OE. ·ena) of the OE. ō and n·declensions.
On the other hand the ·en plural was supplanted by the
·(e)s plural at an early period in the northern and north
Midland dialects. For the approximate dates at which the
change from the weak to the strong declension took place in
the separate dialects, see § 316.

§ 342. The three OE. neuter nouns ēage, ēare, wange =
ME. ę̄ʒe, eye, ȳe (§ 107, 6), ę̄re, wange (wonge) were inflected in ME. like the old masculine and feminine weak
nouns. The old masculine and feminine contracted weak
nouns were inflected in ME. just like the uncontracted nouns,
as flę̄ (OE. flēa) *flea*, pl. flę̄s, flę̄n, and similarly fǭ *foe,* rǭ
roe; bę̄ (OE. bēo) *bee*, pl. bę̄s, bę̄n, and similarly slǭ *sloe,*
tǭ *toe.*

§ 343. Examples of OE. masculine nouns which belong
to this declension in ME. are: āpe, asse, bę̄re, bǫwe
(OE. boga) *bow,* bukke, dogge, fǭle, frogge, hǎre, lippe,
mǭne, nǎme, oxe, sterre *star*, þoumbe *thumb*, &c. And

of feminine nouns : asche, belle, bladdre, chẹke, chirche, cuppe, harpe, herte, moþþe, oule, pīpe, sonne, swalwe, tonge tunge, þrọte, widewe, wolle *wool*. lādi older lavdie, lavedie (OE. hlǣfdige) lost its final -e at an early period, cp. Orm's laffdiȝ (§ 154), and similarly pley (OE. plega).

§ 344. Only a small number of the old plurals in -en are found in Chaucer, as họsen, oxen ; in a few words he has weak and strong forms side by side, as aschen, bẹẹn, flẹẹn, fọọn, tọọn beside asches, bẹẹs, flẹẹs, fọọs, tọọs, and in the old strong noun schọọn beside schọọs.

C. THE MINOR DECLENSIONS

§ 345. The nouns belonging to these categories are all old consonant stems, and include nouns belonging to all genders. In treating their history in ME. we shall follow the same order as in the *EOE. Gr.* §§ 255–67.

1. Monosyllabic Consonant Stems.

a. Masculine.

§ 346. The nouns of this type had umlaut in the dat. singular and the nom. acc. plural, otherwise the case-endings were the same as in the OE. masculine a-declension. In ME. a new dat. singular in -e without umlaut was formed after the analogy of nouns like stọn, as fọte beside OE. fēt. The OE. umlauted form of the nom. acc. plural remained and also came to be used for the dative, to which was then added the ending -es to form a new genitive, as nom. acc. dat. fẹt, gen. fẹtes beside OE. nom. acc. fēt, gen. fōta, dat. fōtum, and similarly man, gen. mannes, pl. men ; wim(m)an wum(m)an wom(m)an, pl. wim(m)en, &c. ; tọþ, pl. tẹþ.

b. Feminine.

§ 347. The nouns of this type had umlaut in the dat. singular, and many also had it in the genitive, as dat. sing.

bēc, hnyte, gen. bēc beside bōce, hnute. These cases
were remodelled in ME. after the analogy of the old
a-declension, as nom. acc. bǫk, note nute *nut*, gen. bǫkes,
notes, dat. bǫke, note. In OE. the nom. acc. plural had
umlaut, as bēc, hnyte, otherwise the case-endings of the
plural were the same as in the a-declension. Of the OE.
nouns which belonged to this type five preserved the
umlaut in the nom. acc. plural in ME., and these cases also
came to be used for the old genitive and dative, as nom. acc.
gen. dat. gēs beside OE. nom. acc. gēs, gen. gōsa, dat.
gōsum; and similarly lous, pl. līs; mous, pl. mīs; brēch
(OE. brēc beside sing. brōc) *trousers*; cou, pl. kī kȳ beside
kȳn kīen with ·n, ·en from the weak declension. In all
the other nouns a new plural in ·es was formed from the
singular after the analogy of nouns like stǫn, pl. stǫnes, as
nom. acc. gen. dat. bǫkes, beside OE. nom. acc. bēc, gen.
bōca, dat. bōcum; and similarly burȝ buruȝ *borough*, pl.
burȝes burwes; furȝ furuȝ *furrow*, pl. furȝes furwes;
gǫtes beside gēt *goats*; nite, pl. nites; niȝt, pl. niȝtes beside niȝt *nights*; note, pl. notes *nuts*; ǫk, pl. ǫkes *oaks*;
turf, pl. turves.

c. *Neuter*.

§ 348. The only noun belonging to this type in OE. was
scrūd *garment*. Already in OE. it had come to be declined
like the long neuter a-stems except that the dat. singular
was scrȳd beside scrūde. In ME. it was declined like an
ordinary old neuter a-stem with dat. in ·(e) and plural in
·es, as schroud, pl. schroudes.

2. Stems in ·þ.

§ 349. Of the four OE. nouns belonging to this type only
two were preserved in ME., viz. mǫneþ (OE. mōnaþ), and
āle *ale* (OE. ealu, gen. and dat. ealoþ). In OE. mōnaþ
was declined like a masc. a-stem except that the nom. acc.

plural was **mōnaþ**. In ME. a new plural in **·es** was formed after the analogy of nouns like **stǫnes**, as **mǭn(e)þes** beside the uninflected form **mǭneþ**. **āle** remained uninflected in ME.

3. STEMS IN ·r.

§ 350. To this type belong the nouns of relationship : fader (OE. fæder), brōþer (OE. brōþor), mǫder (OE. mōdor), dǫuӡter (OE. dohtor), suster soster (OE. sweostor), sister (ON. syster).

The plural of **fæder** was inflected like a masculine **a**·stem. The nom. acc. pl. **fæderas** regularly became **fadres fadęres** in ME. and was then used for the gen. and dat. also. In OE. the sing. was **fæder** in all cases, but the gen. had **fæderes** beside **fæder**, and similarly in ME. nom. acc. dat. **fader**, gen. **fader** beside **fadres**.

The uninflected forms **brōþer, mǫder, dǫuӡter** of the nom. acc. and gen. singular came to be used for the old umlauted forms **brēþer, mēder, dehter** of the dat. singular, so that the singular of these nouns generally remained un-inflected in ME., but sometimes, however, a gen. **brōþęres, mǫdres, dǫuӡtres** is also found.

The OE. nom. acc. pl. **mōdor, dohtor** regularly became **mǫder, dǫuӡter** in ME., and were then used for the old gen. and dative, but beside these forms there also occur plurals in **·es** after the analogy of **fadres**, &c., and in **·en** after the analogy of the weak declension, as **mǫdres, mǫdren ; dǫuӡtres, dǫuӡtren**. **brōþer** also has three plural forms all of which are new formations, viz. **brēþer** formed after the analogy of words like **tǭþ**, pl. **tēþ ; brōþęres** formed after the analogy of words like **fader, pl. fadres ; and brēþęren** formed from **brēþer** with **·en** from the weak declension.

suster soster (OE. **sweostor**), **sister** (ON. **syster**) remained uninflected in the singular just as in OE. This word like **mǫder** has also three plural forms in ME., viz.

suster, soster, sister, and the plural forms in ·en, ·es, as **sustren, sustres.**

4. MASCULINE STEMS IN ·nd.

§ 351. OE. had several nouns of this type of which only two were preserved in ME., viz. **frę̄nd** *friend* (OE. **frēond**) and **fę̄nd** *enemy, fiend* (OE. **fēond**), see § 73.   In OE. the dat. sing. and nom. acc. pl. had umlauted beside unumlauted forms, as dat. sing. **frīend** beside **frēonde,** pl. **frīend** beside **frēondas,** otherwise the nouns of this type were inflected like masculine **a**-stems.   In ME. the umlauted form of the dat. singulaı disappeared, so that the singular was inflected just like an old masculine **a**-stem.   In early ME. the umlauted plural form **frę̄nd** (OE. **frīend**) was preserved, and then later the ·es plural **frę̄ndes** (OE. **frēondas**) became generalized for all cases, and similarly with **fę̄nd.**

5. NEUTER STEMS IN ·os, ·es.

§ 352. This declension originally contained a large number of nouns, all of which, with the exception of six, passed over into other declensions in the prehistoric period of the language.   The six nouns which remained are: **cealf** *calf,* **cild** *child,* **ǣg** *egg,* **lamb** *lamb,* **speld** *splinter,* and the pl. **brēadru** *crumbs,* the last two of which disappeared in ME.

The singular of **cealf, cild, ǣg,** and **lamb** was inflected in OE. like an **a**-stem, and similarly also in ME.   In OE. the plural of these nouns was **cealfru, ǣgru, lambru,** and **cild** beside **cildru.**   The ending ·ru regularly became ·re in ME., to which was added ·n in the southern dialects after the analogy of the weak declension, as **calvren, eiren, lombren, children** beside **childer.**   In the northern dialects we also have **children** beside **childer,** but in the other words a new plural in ·es was formed direct from the singular, as **calves, lambes, egges** from ON. **egg,** and then the ·es plural gradually spread to all the dialects.

CHAPTER VIII

ADJECTIVES

1. THE DECLENSION OF ADJECTIVES

a. THE STRONG DECLENSION.

§ 353. In OE. the strong declension is divided into pure **a-**, **ō-**stems, **ja-**, **jō-**stems, and **wā-**, **wō-**stems like the corresponding nouns. The original **i-** and **u-**stems passed over almost entirely into this declension in prehistoric OE. In OE. the declension of the **ja-**, **jō-**stems and **wa-**, **wō-**stems only differed from that of the pure **a-**, **ō-**stems in the masc. and fem. nom. singular and the neuter nom. acc. singular, and even here the **ja-**, **jō-**stems with an original short stem-syllable and the **wa-**, **wō-**stems with a long stem-syllable were declined like pure **a-**, **ō-**stems, see *EOE. Gr.* §§ 270, 279, 284. The ending of the nom. singular of the various types was accordingly in OE. :—

	Masc.	*Neut.*	*Fem.*
Pure **a-**, **ō-**stems or stems declined like them	—	—	—, ·u (·o)
ja-, **jō-**stems or stems declined like them	·e	·e	·u (·o)
Short **wa-**, **wō-**stems	·u (·o)	·u (·o)	·u (·o)

After the ending ·u (·o) had been weakened to ·e (§ 134 (*a*)), the masc. neut. and fem. singular of the adjectives of these types ended in a consonant or in **e-**, as short **a-**, **ō-**stems : **glad** (OE. masc. and neut. **glæd**, fem. **gladu, ·o**), and similarly **blak, smal,** &c. ; long **a-**, **ō-**stems and long **wa-**, **wō-**stems : **brǭd** *broad* (OE. masc. neut. and fem. **brād**), and similarly **cǭld, dẹ̄d** *dead,* **dẹ̄f** *deaf,* **hard, lang** (long)**, rẹ̄d** *red,* **riȝt, wīs ; slǫw** (OE. **slāw** with ·w from the inflected forms) ; pl. **fęwe** (OE. **fēawe** *few*) ; **ja-**, **jō-**stems : **clẹ̄ne**

(OE. masc. and neut. **clǣne**, fem. **clǣnu**, ·o), and similarly
blīþe, grēne, kēne, newe, rīpe, þinne, &c.; **frē** (OE. **frēo**
free); short **wa·, wō·**-stems: **narwe** (OE. masc. neut. and
fem. **nearu**, gen. masc. and neut. **nearwes**) with **w** from
the old inflected forms, and similarly **falewe** (**fāle**) *fallow*,
ʒelwe (**ʒelowe**) *yellow*, &c.

A certain number of OE. adjectives with a short stem-
syllable came to end in ·e in ME. through the levelling out
of the inflected forms, as **bāre** beside **bar** (OE. **bær**, gen.
bares), and similarly **lāte, smāle** beside **lat, smal**, see
§ 103. And as OE. final ·ig was weakened to ·i in ME. all
the adjectives of this type also ended in a vowel in ME., as
hevi (OE. **hefig**), and similarly **blǫdi, hǫli**, &c., see § 138.

§ 354. The OE. endings of the oblique cases were :—

		Masc.	*Neut.*	*Fem.*
Sing.	Acc.	·ne	= Nom.	·e
	Gen.	·es	·es	·re
	Dat.	·um	·um	·re
Plural Nom.	Acc.	·e	—, ·u (·o)	·a, ·e
	Gen.	·ra	·ra	·ra
	Dat.	·um	·um	·um

In late OE. and early ME. the endings ·um (see § 259),
·u (·o), ·a, and ·ra were regularly weakened to ·en, ·e, ·re
(§ 134). A few of the old case-endings are occasionally found
in early ME., viz. the ending of the acc. masc. singular ·ne,
the gen. and dat. fem. singular ·e (·ere), and a few isolated
forms of the gen. plural were still preserved in Chaucer, as
oure aller cok, alderbest, alderwerst, alderfirst, see
§ 148. Apart from these isolated forms of the gen. plural,
the form of the masc. nom. singular had become generalized
for the whole of the singular, and the form of the nom. acc.
plural had become generalized for the whole of the plural
before the end of the first half of the thirteenth century.
We accordingly arrive at the following scheme for the

inflexion of strong adjectives in what might be termed standard ME. :—

(*a*) Monosyllabic adjectives ending in a consonant remained uninflected throughout the singular, and had ·e throughout the plural, as **brǫd, gǫd, glad,** pl. **brǫde, gǫde, glade.**

(*b*) Adjectives which ended in a vowel in OE. or which came to end in a vowel in ME. (§ 140) remained uninflected throughout the singular and plural.

(*c*) Dissyllabic adjectives including past participles ending in a consonant remained uninflected throughout the singular and plural through loss of the old final ·e in the plural, as **bitter, litel, bounden, cursed,** &c., see § 142.

The Anglo-Norman adjectives were generally inflected like the native English adjectives.

b. THE WEAK DECLENSION.

§ 355. In OE. the weak declension of adjectives had the same case-endings as the weak declension of nouns except that the gen. plural had the strong ending ·**ra** beside the weak ending ·**ena**. The nom. singular of the masculine ended in ·**a**, and that of the feminine and neuter in ·**e**, as **gōda, gōde; clǣna, clǣne; nearwa, nearwe.** Through the weakening of the final ·a to ·e the nom. singular came to be alike for all genders in ME.

§ 356. The endings of the oblique cases were :—

		Masc.	*Neut.*	*Fem.*
Sing.	Acc.	·an	·e	·an
	Gen.	·an	·an	·an
	Dat.	·an	·an	·an
Plural Nom.	Acc.	·an	·an	·an
	Gen.	·ena	·ena	·ena
	Dat.	·um	·um	·um

In late OE. and early ME. the endings ·**an, ·ena, um** (see § 259) were regularly weakened to ·**en, ·ene,** and even these

two endings had ceased to be in use after about the beginning
of the thirteenth century. In ordinary standard ME. the
only distinction preserved between the old strong and weak
declensions of adjectives is in the singular of monosyllabic
adjectives ending in a consonant, as strong sing. gǫd,
pl. gǫde ; weak sing. gǫde, pl. gǫde. In all the other types
of adjectives there was no longer any distinction between the
strong and weak declensions.

2. THE COMPARISON OF ADJECTIVES

§ 357. In OE. the comparative and superlative belonged
to the weak declension except that the neuter nom. acc.
singular had the strong beside the weak form in the superlative, but in ME. they ceased to be inflected at an early
period, cp. § 154. In OE. the comparative had or had not
umlaut in the stem-syllable according as the ending -ra
corresponded to Germanic -izõ or -ōzõ, and similarly in the
superlative ·est = Germanic ·ist· beside ·ost = Germanic
·ōst·, see *EOE. Gr.* § 291, as

eald *old*	ieldra	ieldest
geong *young*	giengra⎫ gingra ⎬	giengest⎫ gingest ⎬
grēat *great*	grīetra	grīetest
lang *long*	lengra	lengest
but earm *poor*	earmra	earmost
glæd *glad*	glædra	gladost
lēof *dear*	lēofra	lēofost

The ·ra and ·ost regularly became ·re (·ere) and ·est in late
OE. and early ME. (§§ 148, 149), so that in ME. the comparative was generally formed by means of ·re (·ere), later
·(e)r, and the superlative by ·(e)st, as

hard	harder	hardest
fair	fairer	fairest
clẽne	clẽner	clẽnest

§ **358.** Only a small number of OE. adjectives had umlaut in the comparative and superlative, and even some of these did not have it in ME. The most important ME. examples are :—

grȩ̄t	gretter (OE. grīetra)	grettest
lang (long)	lenger	lengest beside longest
nei3, ni3 *near*	nȩ̄re (OE. nēahra) ⎫ nerre (OE. nēarra) ⎭	next (OE. nīehst) nĕst (Angl. nēst)
ō̧ld	elder	eldest
strang (strong)	strenger	strengest

Note.—The usual ME. comparative and superlative of 3ung *young* were 3ungre, -er, 3ungest formed direct from the positive, but beside these there were also the regular forms 3ingre (OE. gingra), 3ingest (OE. gingest) from which a new positive 3ing was formed, and which was common throughout the ME. period.

§ **359.** Long vowels were regularly shortened in the comparative (§ 90), and then the short vowel was often extended to the superlative, and sometimes even to the positive, as

grȩ̄t	gretter	grettest
hō̧t	hotter	hottest
lāte	latter	last
stīf	stiffer	stiffest

In later ME. the comparative and superlative were generally formed direct from the positive, as grȩ̄ter, grȩ̄test beside older gretter, grettest; and similarly ō̧lder, ō̧ldest beside elder, eldest; lāter, lātest beside latter, last (§ 249); &c.

§ **360.** Anglo-Norman monosyllabic and dissyllabic adjectives also formed their comparative in **-er** and superlative in **-est,** but adjectives of more than two syllables generally formed their comparative and superlative by prefixing **mō̧re, mō̧st** to the positive.

§ **361.** A certain number of adjectives in ME. as in OE. and NE. form their comparatives and superlatives from a different root than the positive:—

gǭd	better	best (§ 249)
ēvel, ill, badde	werse, wurse	werst, wurst (§ 123)
muche(l), mikel	mǫre (māre)	mēst (mǭst, māst)
litel, līte	lasse, lesse	lēst(e)

§ **362.** In a certain number of OE. words the comparative was originally formed from an adverb or a preposition, with a superlative in ·um·, ·uma. The simple superlative suffix was preserved in OE. **forma** = Goth. **fruma**, ME. **þe forme** *the first*, from which was formed in ME. the new comparative **former**. In prehistoric OE., as in Gothic, to ·um· was added the ordinary superlative suffix ·ist· which gave rise to the double superlative suffix ·umist·, as Goth. **frumists** *first*, **hindumists** *hindmost*. In OE. ·umist· regularly became ·ymist·, later ·imest·, ·emest·, ·mest·, as **inne** *within*, **innera, innemest**. In ME. the ending ·mest came to be associated with **mēst**, later **mǫst (māst)** with ǭ (ā) from the old comparative, whence such ME. forms as **formēst, formǫst, formāst**, beside **formest**, and similarly **inmǫst** (**innermǫst**), **souþmǫst, ŭtmǫst** (**uttermǫst**), &c.

3. NUMERALS

a. CARDINAL NUMERALS.

§ **363.** Apart from the regular phonological changes the cardinal numerals also underwent other changes in passing from OE. to ME. The following are the most important changes to be noted:—

ǭn (northern ān), but ǭ (northern ā) before words beginning with a consonant, was used as a numeral; and the early shortened form **an** (§ 101), but **a** before words beginning with a consonant, was used as the indefinite article (§ 247).

twǭ, twǭ, tǭ (northern tuā) = OE. fem. and neut. twā, came to be used also for the masculine; and similarly twein(e), tweie (= OE. masc. twēgen) came to be used also for the feminine and neuter.

þrē̦ = OE. fem. and neut. þrīo, þrēo, came to be used also for the masculine.

In OE. the cardinals 4 to 19 generally remained uninflected when they stood before a noun, whereas, if they stood after a noun or were used as nouns, they were inflected as follows: nom. acc. masc. and fem. ·e, neut. ·u (·o), gen. ·a, dat. ·um. The inflexional ending ·e was also preserved in ME., especially when the numerals stood after the noun or were used alone, whence the ME. double forms fīve, sevene, &c., beside fīf, seven, &c.

The regular OE. forms used for expressing the decades 70 to 120, as hundseofontig, hundeahtatig, hundnigontig, hundtēontig, hundendleofantig, hundtwelftig were supplanted by the new formations seventi, &c., hundred and ten, hundred and twenti. The form hund, which along with the units was used to express the hundreds 200 to 900, was gradually supplanted by hundred. In OE. the decades, hundred (hund), and þūsend were nouns and governed the genitive case. In ME. they were almost exclusively used as adjectives.

§ 364. The ME. cardinals are: ǭn, ǭ (northern ān, ā), twǭ, twǭ, tǭ (northern tuā), tweine, tweie; þrē̦; fǫur(e), fǫwre (cp. § 112 note 2); fīf, fīve; six(e), sex(e) (Angl. sex); seven(e); eiȝte, auȝte (northern aȝt(e)), see §§ 107, 4, 110, 5; niȝen(e), nīne; tḗne beside the shortened form ten (§ 92); ellevẹn(e), elevẹn(e), enleven (cp. § 243); twelf, twelve; þrettḗne, þrittḗne; fǫurtḗne; fiftḗne; sixtḗne; seven-tḗne; eiȝtetḗne; niȝentḗne, nīnetḗne; twenti, þretti (þritti), fǫurti, fifti, sixti, seventi, eiȝteti (eiȝti), niȝenti (nīn(e)ti), hundred beside hundreþ (ON. hundraþ), þousend.

b. Ordinal Numerals.

§ 365. In passing from OE. to ME. some of the ordinals underwent analogical changes besides the regular phonological changes. From about the end of the thirteenth century onwards the French form **secounde** was used beside the English form ōþer. Several of the ordinals were new formations formed direct from the corresponding ME. cardinals, as sevenþe, nīnþe, tĕnþe, þrettĕnþe (þrittĕnþe), &c., beside the regular forms seveþe (OE. seofoþa), niȝeþe (OE. nigoþa), tēþe (OE. tēoþa), þrettēþe þrittēþe (OE. þrēotēoþa), &c. Besides these new formations there were also others ending in -de which were partly or entirely due to ON. influence, as sevende (O.Nth. seofunda, siofunda, O.Icel. sjaunde), niȝende, nīnde (O.Icel. nīonde), tĕnde (O.Icel. tīonde, tīunde), þrettĕnde, þrittĕnde (O.Icel. þrettānde), &c. hundred and þousend had no ordinal forms in ME. just as in OE.

§ 366. The ME. ordinals are: first, fürst, ferst, verst (OE. fyrest), ōþer (secounde), þridde (þirde), fourþe (ferþe, firþe), fifte, sixte, seveþe (sevenþe, sevende), eiȝteþe (eȝtende, northern aȝtand), niȝeþe (niȝende, nīnde, nīnþe), tēþe (tĕnþe, tĕnde), ellefte (ellevende), twelfte, þrettēþe (þrittēþe, þrettĕnþe, þrittĕnde), and similarly fourtēþe, fiftēþe, sixtēþe, seventēþe, &c., twentiþe, þrittiþe, &c.

c. Other Numerals.

§ 367. The ME. multiplicative numeral adjectives were formed from the cardinals and the suffix -fọld (= OE. -feald), ọnfọld beside the loan-word simple, twọ-, twọ-fọld beside the loan-word double, þrēfọld, &c., fẹlefọld, manifọld.

§ 368. Adverbial multiplicatives are: ọnes, ānes, ẹnes (OE. gen. ǣnes), twīes, þrīes. The remaining multiplicatives were expressed by sīþe, tīmes, as fīf sīþe (OE. fīf sīþum), tīmes, &c., fẹlesīþe, mani sīþe.

§ 369. For the first, second, third, &c., time, were expressed by sīþe, tīme and the ordinals just as in OE., as þe þridde sīþe (OE. þriddan sīþe).

§ 370. The distributive numerals were expressed by bǐ along with a cardinal, or by two cardinals connected by and, as ǭn and ǭn, þrē and þrē ; bǐ þrē, bǐ twelve, &c.

CHAPTER IX

PRONOUNS

1. PERSONAL

§ 371. The old accusative forms mec, þec, ūsic and ēowic of the first and second persons singular and plural had been supplanted by the old dative forms mě, þě, ūs, ēow already in late OE., so that the old datives were used to express both cases in ME. also. And in ME. the old accusative forms of the masculine and feminine and the old accusative plural forms of the third person were also supplanted by the old dative forms. The old genitives (OE. mīn, þīn, pl. ūre, ēower; his, hiere (hire), pl. hiera, hira, heora) lost their genitival meaning in fairly early ME. except in isolated phrases like ūre nǭn *nonc of us*, ūre aller *of all of us*. The old genitival meaning came to be expressed by the preposition of and the dative of the personal pronouns. The old dual forms nom. wit, ȝit ; acc. dat. unc, inc ; gen. uncer, incer occur in Laȝamon, *Ormulum, Genesis and Exodus, Havelok*, and *The Owl and the Nightingale*, but gradually disappeared in the latter half of the thirteenth century.

a. THE FIRST AND SECOND PERSONS.

§ 372. Singular: Nom. accented form : northern ik, ic, Midland and southern ich (§ 295), but also ic until the beginning of the thirteenth century. The unaccented form

i began to be used in the northern and Midland dialects
from the twelfth century onwards.   At this early period i
only occurred when the next word began with a consonant,
but the i gradually came to be used also when the next word
began with a vowel, and by about 1400 it had become the
only form used in these dialects.   Chaucer generally has i
both for the accented and unaccented form.   He rarely used
ich.   From i was formed at a later period a new accented
form ī (= NE. ai), but the old unaccented form i has been
preserved in many modern dialects in interrogative and
subordinate sentences.   The form ich was in use throughout
the ME. period in the southern and south-western dialects.
The forms ich (uch, utchy) along with contracted forms
ch'am, &c., were formerly used in the modern dialects of
Dor., Som., and Dev., and these forms are still used by old
people in a small district of Som. close to Yeovil on the
borders of Dor.   Contracted forms were also common in the
Elizabethan dramatists in the speech of rustics, as in *King
Lear* chill *I will*, chud *I would*.   Accusative and dative
mĕ.

Nom. þū (þou) beside the unaccented form þŭ, which became
tou (tŭ) when attached enclitically to a verb, as hastou, ·tŭ
hast thou, wiltou, tŭ *wilt thou* (cp. § 243).   This form with t·
has also been regularly preserved in interrogative and subordinate sentences in many of the modern dialects.   Thou
in its various dialect forms is still in general use in most of
the modern dialects of England, but not in Scotland, to express
familiarity or contempt, but it cannot be used to a superior
without conveying the idea of impertinence.   Accusative
and dative þĕ.   From the thirteenth century onwards ȝĕ (yĕ)
began to be used for þou as the pronoun of respect in
addressing a superior, and in the form ī (generally written
ee) it has survived in most of the south Midland and
southern dialects down to the present day.   During the
fourteenth century you also came to be used for both þou

and þē, and then in the fifteenth century ye also came to be
used for the acc. þē and you.

Plural : nom. wĕ, acc. and dat. ūs (ous) beside the unaccented form ŭs (= NE. us); nom. ȝĕ (OE. gĕ), also
written ȝee, ye(e), ȝhe, yhe, &c., acc. and dat. ȝou (ȝow)
you (for numerous variant spellings see *N. E. D.* s. v.) from
OE. eów older éow (§ 112 note 1).

b. The Third Person.

§ 373. Masculine Singular : nom. hĕ beside the unaccented
forms ha, a, rarely e (still preserved in the modern dialects
in the form ə). The dat. him had supplanted the old acc.
hin(e) in the northern and Midland dialects by about 1150,
and in the southern dialects in the early part of the fourteenth
century. But in the south Midland and southern dialects it
must have remained in colloquial use throughout the ME.
period, as is evidenced by the modern dialects of this area.
en, un (= ən), the unaccented form of OE. hine, is still in
general use in the modern dialects of the south Midland,
southern, and south-western counties as the unaccented
form of 'im. It is also used of inanimate objects and in
West Som. of feminine animals though never of women.
Dative him.

§ 374. The Neuter Singular: Nom. Acc. hit (OE. hit)
beside the unaccented form it (§ 301). it began to appear
so early as the twelfth century, and in the fifteenth century
supplanted the old accented form in the standard language.
hit is still used in the modern dialects of Scotland and
Northumberland. Dative him, which was never used for
the accusative.

§ 375. The Feminine Singular: The nom. had several
forms in ME. which arose partly from OE. hio (hēo), Anglian
hīe *she*, and partly from the OE. feminine demonstrative
sīo (sēo), Anglian sīe *the, that*.

Although not expressed in writing, late OE. must have had double forms of hīo (hēo), hīe according as the stress remained on the first element of the diphthongs or was shifted on to the second element, as hío (héo), híe beside hjó (hjó), hjé. In late OE. hío only occurred in Kentish, where it also became a rising diphthong in early ME. (§ 67). The héo regularly became hę in late OE. or early ME. (§ 65), and also in early ME. the forms hjó, hjé became differentiated into hǭ, ȝhǭ (also written ȝo, ȝeo, hyo, &c.) and hę, ȝhę (also written ȝe, ge, ghe, hye, &c.) according as the j element entirely disappeared or united with the aspirate h to form a kind of spirant. So that apart from the sh-forms which will be dealt with below early ME. had the four forms hę, hǭ, ȝhę, ȝhǭ (cp. § 65 note). hę (Ken. hǐ, § 67) beside the unaccented form ha occurs in the south Midland (but see below) and southern dialects, especially the south-western, until the middle of the fifteenth century, and was then gradually supplanted by schę in literary records. The change in these dialects was probably due to the fact that the masculine and feminine had regularly fallen together in hę. But it must have remained in colloquial use, because in many of the dialects of the eastern, southern, and south-western counties ǐ (generally written he) is still used of feminine objects. hǭ beside the unaccented forms ha, a occurs throughout the ME. period in the west Midland dialects and also in parts of the south-western area, as is evidenced by the modern dialects which regularly have ǔ (generally written hoo) in the west Midland area. In the west Midland dialect of the fourteenth century there also occurs the form hue which is a direct descendant of OE. hēo, see § 65. The ME. forms ȝhę, ȝhǭ (Orm ȝhǭ) occur so far north as the east Midland dialect, but not in the northern dialects.

The late OE. simple demonstrative sīo (sēo), Anglian sīe must have had the double forms séo, síe beside sjó, sjé just like the above héo, híe beside hjó, hjé. The sjé,

sjǒ́ then regularly became in early ME. schę̄ (also written
sge, shee, sse, se, &c.) and schǭ (also written sco,
sso, &c.).   The type schę̄ was of east Midland origin, and
the earliest record of it occurs in the form scǣ in the
OE. Chronicle (Laud MS.) of about the middle of the twelfth
century.   It is not recorded elsewhere until about a hundred
years later when we find it written sge, sche, she in *Gen.
& Ex.*   From about 1250 it had become fully established in
the east Midland dialects.   From here it first spread to the
south Midland dialects where it had become the general form
by the middle of the fourteenth century, and by that time it
had also begun to spread to the west Midland dialects, but
it never became the colloquial form in the southern dialects
during the ME. period.   The type schǭ was of north
Midland and northern origin, and is first found in literary
records towards the end of the thirteenth century.   The
regular descendant of schǭ is still preserved in the form
shŭ, unaccented shə, in many of the northern and north
Midland dialects from Cum. to Der.

The OE. acc. hīe began to be supplanted by the dat. hiere,
hire so early as the tenth century, and by the time of the
early ME. period the hīe had been supplanted by hire, hir ;
here, her in all the dialects except Kentish where it
lingered on into the early part of the fourteenth century.

§ 376. The Plural : In early ME. the OE. acc. hīe, hī was
supplanted by the dative hem beside the unaccented forms
ham, hom (= OE. him, hiom, heom) in the northern and
Midland dialects, but the old form hĭ lingered on in the
southern and south-eastern dialects until about the middle
of the fourteenth century.   From this hĭ was formed in the
late twelfth century a new acc. plural (also used as acc. fem.
singular) hise (his, hes) beside the unaccented forms is (es)
which were often attached enclitically to a preceding word.
These forms remained in these dialects until about the end
of the fourteenth century, and then became obsolete.

The ordinary ME. plural forms are partly of native and partly of Scandinavian origin. In the east Midland dialects the native nom. pl. hĭ, he had begun to be supplanted by the Scandinavian form þei (ON. þeir) in the twelfth century, and þei (written þeȝȝ) is the only form found in the *Ormulum* (1200). By the early part of the fourteenth century it had become general in this dialect. It had also become general in the south Midland dialects before the middle of the fourteenth century, in the west Midland dialects by the second half of the fourteenth century, and in the southern dialects, including Kentish, during the fifteenth century. In the northern dialects þai (þei) is the only form even in the oldest ME. records. The substitution of the Scandinavian dat. form þeim for the early ME. native form hem did not take place concurrently with that of þei for hĭ in the various dialects. Orm has dat. and acc. þeȝȝm beside hemm, but in the other east Midland texts þeim does not occur until the fifteenth century. It had become general in the Midland and southern dialects from about 1500. In the northern dialects þaim (þam) was general in the oldest ME. records. In all the modern dialects the accented form is ðem, but in the dialects of England the unaccented form is əm (= OE. heom), and similarly in colloquial standard NE.

2. REFLEXIVE

§ 377. When the personal pronouns were used reflexively in OE. the word self (declined strong and weak) was often added to emphasize them, as ic self beside ic selfa, acc. mec selfne, gen. mīn selfes, dat. mē selfum ; or with the dative of the personal pronoun prefixed to the nominative self, as ic mē self, pl. wē ūs selfe, and similarly in early ME. From the early part of the thirteenth century new forms began to appear. In the first and second persons singular the form self came to be regarded as a noun and then the possessive pronoun was substituted for the dative of the

personal pronoun, as mī self, þī self beside older mě self,
þě self, and then in the early part of the fourteenth century
this new formation was extended to the plural also, as our(e)
self(e), selve(n), ʒọur(e) self(e), selve(n) beside older wě ūs
selve(n), ʒě ʒọu selve(n). And then towards the end of the
fifteenth century the present s-plurals ourselves, yọurselves
came into existence and eventually became the standard
forms. This change in the formation of the reflexive
pronouns did not take place in the third person so early
as in the first and second persons. his selve(n), þeir(e)
selve(n), þair(e) selve(n) beside hem selve(n), þem selve(n)
did not begin to appear until the first half of the fourteenth
century. All these new formations of the third person
disappeared in the standard language about the end of
the fifteenth century, but have remained in the dialects down
to the present day. The s-plural themselves came into
existence about 1500 and during the first half of the sixteenth
century became the standard form. From the form alone it
cannot be determined whether the hire in ME. hire self and
the her in NE. herself represent the old dat. acc. or the old
possessive.

In ME. as in OE. the reflexive pronouns were often also
expressed simply by the acc. dat. forms of the personal
pronouns as is very often the case in the modern dialects, as
And for bonnie Annie Laurie I'd lay me down and dee.

3. POSSESSIVE

§ 378. The OE. possessive pronouns mīn, þīn, sīn *his, her,
its* were declined in the singular and plural, all genders, like
an ordinary strong adjective. Instead of sīn, which was
mostly used in poetry, the genitive of the personal pronouns
was generally used (masc. and neut. his, fem. hiere, hire).
sīn did not survive in ME. The other possessive pronouns
were expressed by the genitive of the personal pronouns, as
ūre beside ūser which did not survive in ME. ; ēower ;

hiera, hira, hiora, heora.   OE. ūre was declined like an
ordinary strong adjective, see *EOE. Gr.* § 308.   The old dual
forms **uncer, incer** disappeared in the thirteenth century.

§ **379.** In ME. we have to distinguish between the conjunctive and disjunctive use of the possessive pronouns :—

a. CONJUNCTIVE.

The conjunctive forms were: singular **mīn, þīn** before
a following word beginning with a vowel, and **mī, þī** when
the next word began with a consonant (cp. § 247).   The
plural forms were **mīne, þīne.**   From **mī, þī** were formed in
the southern dialects of the twelfth century the fem. dat.
sing. **mīre, þīre** after the analogy of forms like **hire, ūre**
(oure), and similarly the fem. dat. form **ǭre** from **ǭ** *one.*   **his**
with a plural form **hise.**   Beside **his** the form **hit** was used
in the west Midland dialects of the fourteenth century, and
similarly **it** in the Elizabethan dramatists, and in the modern
northern and most of the Midland dialects, where in standard
NE. we use **its.**   The old neut. possessive **his** has been
preserved in the modern Hampshire dialects.   **hir(e), her(e)**
her, **our(e), ȝour(e).**   To express **their** the northern dialects
had **þair(e)** (ON. **þeir(r)a**) in the earliest ME. records, also
written **þaier, þeir** beside the unaccented forms **þer(e),**
þar(e), and **þeȝȝre** beside **heore** also occurs in the *Ormulum*
of the east Midland dialect.   The usual forms in the Midland
and southern dialects were **her(e), hir(e)** with their variants
hor(e), har(e), hur(e), &c.   By the latter half of the fifteenth
century **þeir (þair)** had spread to all the dialects.

b. DISJUNCTIVE.

In OE. and early ME. the disjunctive and the conjunctive
possessive pronouns were alike in form.   The differentiation
in form first began to appear in the northern dialects towards
the end of the thirteenth century, and had gradually spread
to all the other dialects by about 1500, although in some

southern writers the old forms are found until well on into the seventeenth century.

The disjunctive forms were mīn, þīn, pl. mīne, þīne ; his. The possessive pronouns ending in ·r(e) took a new genitive ending ·es, as hires heres *hers*, ūres oures, ӡoures, heres (þaires, þeires) *theirs*. These new formations began to appear in the northern dialects towards the end of the thirteenth century, whence they gradually spread to the Midland dialects in the latter part of the fourteenth century. In the southern dialects the usual forms throughout the ME. period were : hir(e) her(e) *hers*, our(e), ӡour(e), her(e) *theirs*. Besides the above forms the southern and Midland dialects had forms ending in ·n which began to be formed after the analogy of mīn, þīn from about the middle of the fourteenth century, as hisen (hisn, hizzen, hysene), hiren (hern, huron) *hers*, ouren (ourn), ӡouren (ӡourn), hiren (heren, hern) *theirs*, and in the Midland, eastern, southern, and south-western dialects all the disjunctive pronouns including theirn end in ·n right down to the present day.

4. DEMONSTRATIVE

§ 380. The OE. demonstrative sĕ̄, þæt, sīo (sēo) was used to express the definite article *the* and the demonstrative *that*, and was declined as follows : —

SING.	*Masc.*	*Neut.*	*Fem.*
Nom.	sĕ̄	þæt	sīo, sēo
Acc.	þone	þæt	þā
Gen.	þæs	þæs	þǣre
Dat.	þǣm, þām	þǣm, þām	þǣre
Instr.		þȳ, þon	

PLUR. ALL GENDERS.

Nom. Acc.	þā
Gen.	þāra, þǣra
Dat.	þǣm, þām

The late OE. weakened inflected forms were for the most
part preserved in early ME. The inflected forms of the
singular began to be lost from about the middle of the twelfth
century. · This loss of inflexion began much earlier in the
northern and Midland than in the southern and Kentish
dialects. In fact it was only in these latter dialects that the
inflected forms were preserved for any length of time in ME.
The s-form of the nom. masc. and fem. singular had begun
to take þ· from the oblique forms in late OE., and by about
the middle of the thirteenth century it had disappeared in
all the dialects except Kentish where the masc. **ze,** and fem.
zy remained until about a century later. In the northern
and east Midland dialects the uninflected nom. masc. and
fem. form þĕ had come to be simply *the* by about 1150, and
almost everywhere else by about 1300. The neuter **þat**
(south-eastern dialects **þet**) remained with the meaning
the for some time longer before words beginning with
a vowel, but by about 1200 (e. g. in the *Ormulum*) it had
begun to be used more definitely with the meaning *that* as
opposed to *this* than with the meaning *the*. Inflected forms
of some of the oblique cases lingered on in the southern
dialects until about 1400.

§ **381.** The early ME. inflected forms were :—
Singular: Besides þĕ the masc. nom. sĕ (Ken. zĕ) also
occurs, and the fem. nom. **se, si, syo** (Ken. **zy**) beside þēo,
and the old acc. þǭ, þa, þæ used for the nom. in the
thirteenth century. Accusative masc. þan(e), þon(e), þen(e);
fem. þǭ, þa beside the old nom. þeo, þīe. Genitive masc.
and neut. þæs, þas, þes (Orm þess), þeos (Laȝamon, 1205) ;
fem. þer(e), þar(e); Dative masc. and neut. þæn, þen, þon,
þan, Ken. also þo in the first half of the fourteenth century;
fem. þer(e), þar(e), Laȝamon also þære. But beside these
inflected forms the uninflected form þē had come to be used
in early ME. as the definite article for all cases and genders
of the singular except in a few isolated phrases like **atte**

nāle (OE. æt þǣm ealoþ), for þe nǫnes = for þen ǫnes
found in Chaucer, &c. þī *therefore, because* = the OE. instrumental neuter þȳ remained in use until about the middle
of the thirteenth century, also in the compound forþī *because,
for this reason, therefore* until the end of the fourteenth
century, and in the weakened form þe before comparatives
until the present day. þon = OE. þon in the compound
forþon *therefore* remained until the middle of the fifteenth
century, and in the northern dialects until the end of the
eighteenth century.

þat (þet) remained longer as the neuter of the definite
article in the southern than in the Midland and northern
dialects. þat for all genders with the plural þā = OE. þā
had come to be used exclusively as a demonstrative in the
Ormulum (1200), and then about 1300 þās = OE. þās, which
was properly the plural of the OE. word for *this*, began to be
used in the northern dialects of England as the plural of þat.
þǭs (§ 51) corresponding to the northern þās did not become
common as the plural of þat in the Midland and southern
dialects until the latter part of the fifteenth century. The
old ending of the OE. neuter form of the definite article
survives in tone = OE. þæt ān, and toðer = OE. þæt ōþer
in all the modern dialects.

Plural : The early ME. inflected forms of the plural
were :—Nom. acc. þā in the northern dialects and þǭ in the
dialects south of the Humber (§ 51). Genitive þar(e), þer(e).
Dative þan, þon, þen. These gen. and dat. forms disappeared in the first half of the thirteenth century. As in
the singular (see above) so also in the plural the uninflected
form þě came to be used at an early period as the definite
article for all cases and genders of the plural just as in
Chaucer, &c. And then the northern þǎ and the Midland
and southern þǭ came to be used only as the plural of the
demonstrative þat just as in Chaucer, &c. The regular
descendants (ðē, ᵹeə, iə) of ME. þā *those* have remained in

the dialects of Scotland and in some of the northern counties
of England down to the present day. þǭs with the meaning
those began to be used in the Midland and southern dialects
from about 1475, and by about 1550 had completely supplanted the form þǭ. It is a remarkable fact that **those** is
not used in genuine dialect speech in any of the modern
dialects. For the various ways in which it is expressed see
ED. Gr. § 420.

§ **382.** The OE. forms for *this*, plural *these* were : masc.
þěs, neut. þis, fem. þīos (þēos), plural þās. This pronoun
was declined as follows :—

Sing.	*Masc.*	*Neut.*	*Fem.*
Nom.	þěs	þis	þīos, þēos
Acc.	þisne	þis	þās
Gen.	þis(s)es	þis(s)es	þisse
Dat.	þis(s)um	þis(s)um	þisse
Instr.		þȳs, þīs	

PLUR. ALL GENDERS.

Nom. Acc.	þās
Gen.	þissa
Dat.	þis(s)um

The medial ·ss· was often simplified to ·s·. In the dat.
sing. and pl. Anglian has þios(s)um, þeos(s)um with
u·umlaut beside þis(s)um. Fem gen. and dat. sing. þisse
from older *þisre, gen. pl. þissa from older *þisra ; in
late OE. there also occur þissere, þissera with ·re, ·ra
from the simple demonstrative, beside þisre, þisra with
syncope of the medial vowel and simplification of the ss,
see *EOE. Gr.* § 310.

The late OE. weakened inflected forms were for the most
part preserved until about the middle of the twelfth century,

but by the end of the century the neuter nom. acc. sing. þis
had come to be used in the east Midland dialect (*Ormulum*)
and doubtless also in the north Midland and northern
dialects for all cases and genders of the singular, by the
fourteenth century it had spread to the south Midland
dialects (Chaucer, &c.), and by the fifteenth century to all the
dialects.

§ 383. The early ME. inflected forms were :—

Singular: Nom. masc. þĕs beside the new forms þus,
þeos; fem. þeos, þies, þyos, þas (Laȝamon), þues (§ 65).
Already at this early period the nom. masc. came to be used
for the feminine, as þies (§ 9), and the fem. for the masculine,
as þeos, þus. The old masc. þēs, and fem. þeos, þues
were preserved in the southern dialects until the middle
of the fourteenth century. Accusative masc. þisne, þesne,
þusne (Laȝamon); fem. þās, þes. Genitive masc. and neut.
þisses, þesses, þisis; fem. þisse, þissere. Dative masc.
and neut. þissen, þisse, þisen, þise; þisse beside the new
form þusse. The instrumental neut. (OE. þȳs, þīs *like this,
thus*) seems not to have been common in ME. as it only
occurs sporadically between 1375 and the end of the sixteenth
century, see *N. E. D.*

Plural: Old inflected forms of the gen. and dat. are only
found in the southern dialects, and even there the gen.
þissere disappeared about the end of the twelfth century,
and the dat. þis(s)en, þesse(n) is not found so late as 1340
except in the *Ayenbite*. As we have already seen (§ 381) the
old nom. acc. pl. þās, þǭs = OE. þās *these* came to be used
at an early period for the plural of þat with the meaning
those. Before this change in function took place the plural,
irrespective of gender, had often come to be expressed by the
masc. nom. sing. þĕs and the neut. nom. acc. þis before the
end of the twelfth century, and in some of the south-western
dialects by þūs or þōs (OE. þēos, § 65) in the thirteenth
century, but side by side with these singular forms the new

plurals þēse, þise, þūse or þōse were formed by adding ·e
to the singular after the analogy of the adjectival plural in
·e. It should be noted that the ē in þēs, þēse can represent
both the ē in OE. þēs and the OE. ēo in the fem. þēos
(§ 65), so that the forms þēs, þēse may be partly of feminine
origin. þēs, þēse seem to occur earliest in the Midland
dialects, and then to have spread to the northern dialects,
and by about 1500 to all the dialects. From the fourteenth
century onwards the northern dialects also had þir (? from
ON. þeir) as well as the variants þire, þeir(e), þair, þier,
þer(e), þar(e), which has remained in the dialects of
Scotland and the northern counties of England down to the
present day. þis, þise (Orm, &c., þise) were special Midland
forms, and remained in these dialects until about 1500, by
which time they had been supplanted by þēsę (Chaucer has
þisę beside þēsę, generally spelt þes). þūs or þōs, þūse
or þōse occur in some of the south-western dialects from
the thirteenth until well on into the fifteenth century, and
were then supplanted by þēsę.

NOTE.—The precise quality of the ē in ME. þēse is uncertain.
The ordinary ME. spelling may represent ē or ę̄. In the sixteenth
century it was often spelt þeis which points to ę̄, and the pronunciation of the various forms for *these* in many of the modern
dialects also presupposes a late OE. form þǣs which according to
the *N. E. D.* did exist.

§ 384. Other ME. demonstrative pronouns are :—

In OE. ilca *same* only occurred in combination with the
definite article, as sē̆ ilca, þæt, sēo ilce *the same*, and was
inflected like a weak adjective. In ME. we have þe ilke,
þat ilke, þis ilke *the same* ; þe ilke was often contracted into
þilke ; self, which in OE. and early ME. was inflected
according to the strong or weak declension of adjectives ;
ʒon, pl. ʒone ; ʒond is also used as a demonstrative *that* in
the *Ormulum*.

5. RELATIVE

§ 385. A relative pronoun proper did not exist in the oldest periods of any of the Germanic languages, and for that reason it was expressed in various ways in the separate languages. In OE. it was expressed by the relative particle þe alone or in combination with the personal or the simple demonstrative pronoun, and for the third person also by the simple demonstrative pronoun alone, see *EOE. Gr.* § 312.

þe alone was also used in early ME., especially in the southern dialects, but it had gone out of general use by about 1250, after which date it is only found sporadically. The combination of the simple demonstrative pronoun with þe for expressing the relative pronoun died out about 1100. From the twelfth century onwards the uninflected old demonstrative neuter þat came to be used for the singular and plural of all genders, but for þat the ON. form at was used in the northern and some of the north Midland dialects in the oldest ME. records, and it is the usual form in the dialects of this area down to the present day. In order to indicate more clearly the gender and case of the antecedent to the relative it became common in the fourteenth century to add the personal pronoun of the third person to the þat, as þat . . . he (sche) = *who*; þat . . . it = *which*; þat . . . his = *whose*; þat . . . him = *whom*, &c. ; and similarly with which, as which . . . his = *whose*, &c. These and similar constructions continued in general use until the end of the fifteenth century, and then became obsolete in the sixteenth century. which (plural which(e)), referring both to persons and things, and the oblique cases whǭs, whǭm of the interrogative pronoun whǭ whǭ, also came to be used as relatives at an early period. In later ME. the definite article þe was often added in front of which after the analogy of French usage, as þe which = lequel, and similarly also sometimes with þat. **What,** referring to things and rarely to personal pronouns or sentences, began to be used as a relative in the early part of the thirteenth century.

6. INTERROGATIVE

§ 386. The OE. simple interrogative pronoun had no independent form for the feminine, and was declined in the singular only, as

	Masc. Fem.	*Neut.*
Nom.	hwă	hwæt
Acc.	hwone	hwæt
Gen.	hwæs	hwæs
Dat.	hwǣm, hwām	hwǣm, hwām
Instr.		hwȳ, hwī

The old acc. form **hwone** disappeared in early ME., and its place was taken by the dative **whǫm whọm,** northern **quām quhām.** The ME. gen. **whǫs whọs,** northern **quās quhās** with ǫ (ọ), ā from the nominative and dative. The old instrumental was preserved in **whī whȳ** *why.* **which** (northern **quilk**), OE. **hwelc, hwilc, hwylc;** ME. pl. **whiche, whichę.**

7. INDEFINITE

§ 387. The more important ME. indefinite pronouns are :—**auȝt** (OE. **āwiht**) *anything, aught,* **nauȝt** (OE. **nāwiht**) *nothing, naught,* **auþer** (OE. **āhwæþer, āwþer**) *one of two,* **nauþer** (OE. **nāhwæþer, nāwþer**) *neither of two,* **ęch,** northern **ilk** (OE. **ælc**) *each,* **eni, ani** (OE. **ænig**) *any,* see § 92, 2, **eiþer,** Orm **eȝȝþerr** (OE. **æghwæþer**) *each of two,* **neiþer** *neither of two,* **man** (pl **men,** unaccented form **me**) *one,* **nǫn,** northern **nān** *none,* but **nǫ, nā** when the next word begins with a vowel; **ǫuȝt** (OE. **ōwiht** later **ōht, oht**) *anything, aught,* see § 113, 5, **nǫuȝt** (OE. **nōwiht**) *nothing, naught,* **ǫuþer** (OE. **ōhwæþer, ōwþer**) *one of two,* **nǫuþer** (OE. **nōhwæþer, nōwþer**) *neither of two,* **sum som** (pl. **sume some**) *some one,*

swich, siche, suche, northern **swilk suilk** (OE. **swylc**) *such,* beside northern **slik** (ON. **slīkr**) *such.*

CHAPTER X

VERBS

§ **388.** In treating the history of the verbs from OE. to the end of the ME. period we shall generally follow the same order as that adopted in the *EOE. Gr.* §§ 316–95.

The ME., like the OE. verb, has the following independent forms : one voice (active), two numbers, three persons, two tenses (present and preterite), two complete moods (indicative and subjunctive), besides an imperative which is only used in the present tense ; one verbal noun (the present infinitive), a present participle with active meaning, and one verbal adjective (the past participle).

§ **389.** ME. verbs like the OE. are divided into two great classes :—Strong and Weak. The strong verbs form their preterite and past participle by means of ablaut (*EOE. Gr.* § 103). The weak verbs form their preterite by the addition of a syllable containing a dental (OE. ·de, ·te) and their past participle by means of a dental suffix (OE. ·d, ·t). Besides these two great classes of strong and weak verbs, there are a few others, which will be treated under the general heading of *Minor Groups.*

§ **390.** The chief characteristic differences between the OE. and ME. verbal forms are :—(*a*) the weakening of the OE. vowels **a** and **o** to **e** in medial and final syllables, and the gradual loss of many of the old verbal endings ; (*b*) the numerous levellings and analogical formations which took place, especially in the preterite both of strong and weak verbs ; (*c*) many of the OE. strong verbs became weak in ME. either in the preterite or past participle or in both.

ME. VERBAL ENDINGS

a. THE PRESENT.

§ 391. The normal ME. endings of the present are:—

Indic.	S. and Ken.	E.M.	W.M.	N.
Sing.	·e, (e)st, ·(e)þ	·e, ·est, ·eþ	·e, ·es(t), ·es	·e, ·es, ·es
Pl.	·eþ	·en	·en (·es)	·es

Subj. Sing. ·e, pl. ·en in all the dialects.   OE. sing. ·e, pl. ·en.

Imper. Sing. —, ·e, pl. M. and S. ·eþ, N. ·es.

Pres. Part. M. ·ende (but south-west Midland inde), S. ·inde (later ·inge, ·ing), N. ·and(e), § 138.

Inf. ·en (OE. ·an).

The east Midland dialects often have ·es for ·eþ in the third pers. sing. from the northern dialects, and similarly ·es for ·est, ·eþ in the west Midland dialects. For the northern ending ·is and the west Midland endings ·us, ·ust, ·uþ see § 134. The OE. West Saxon syncopated and contracted forms of the second and third persons singular were generally preserved in the ME. southern dialects, as bintst, bint, rīst, rīst; sitst, sit; stantst, stant, see § 239. The ending ·eþ of the third pers. singular and plural has been preserved in the form ·ð among the older generation of dialect speakers in Somersetshire and Devonshire. The Midland plural ending ·en of the pres. indicative was a new formation from the endings of the present subjunctive and preterite indicative. This plural ending in ·en has been preserved in many of the modern Midland dialects. In the OE. period the Northumbrian dialect had ·es beside ·est in the second pers. singular, ·es beside ·eþ in the third pers. singular, and ·as beside ·aþ in the plural. In early ME. the endings with ·t and ·þ gradually disappeared, and then later ·es was extended to the first pers. singular, so that

eventually the whole of the singular and plural ended in ·es.
The northern plural ending ·es spread at an early period to
the west Midland dialects bordering on the northern. In the
modern Scottish, northern, and most of the north Midland
dialects all persons singular and plural take ·s, ·z (or ·əz)
when not immediately preceded or followed by their proper
pronoun, that is, when the subject is a noun, an interrogative or relative pronoun, or when the verb and the subject
are separated by a clause. Through the ME. weakening of
the OE. endings the present of all classes of weak verbs fell
together except in the southern and Kentish dialects which
had the endings ·ie in the first pers. singular, ·ieþ in the
plural and ·ien in the inf. of the verbs which in OE. belonged
to class II, and verbs of the type **werian** *to defend*, belonging to class I (*EOE. Gr.* §§ 370, 380). In the modern
south-western dialects, especially those of Dor., Som., and
Dev., the old ending ·i, generally written y, has been preserved in intransitive verbs. In the plural of the imperative
the west Midland dialects often have ·es from the northern
dialects. This also occurs occasionally in the east Midland
dialects. From about the end of the thirteenth century the
southern dialects have the ending ·inge (·ing) beside ·inde in
the present participle, which was due to the influence of the
old endings ·inge, ·ing (OE. ·ung, ·ing) of the verbal noun.
In Chaucer the present participle regularly ends in ·ing(e).
The OE. ending ·anne of the inflected infinitive was only
preserved with simplification of ·nn· to ·n· in a few monosyllabic verbs, as tọ̄ dọ̄ne : dọ̄n *to do*, tọ̄ sẹ̄ne : sẹ̄n *to see*.
On the loss of final ·n see §§ 147, 247.

b. THE PRETERITE.

§ 392. The normal ME. endings of the preterite are :—

Indic. {
Strong verbs sing. —, ·e, —,   pl. ·en
Weak   ,,   ,,   ·e, ·est (·es), ·e, pl. ·en

Subj. strong and weak verbs sing. ·e, pl. ·en.   OE. ·e, pl. ·en.

Pp. : strong verbs ·en, weak verbs ·ed (·d), ·t.

The personal endings of the preterite indicative were lost fairly early in the northern dialects, so that the singular and plural had the same form throughout, as **spak, māked,** &c., whereas the other dialects preserved the old difference between the singular and plural as in Chaucer.   In the northern dialects the preterite indicative came to be used at an early period for the subjunctive, as northern **band** beside Midland and southern **bounde,** pl. **bounden.**   This change had also taken place in the Midland dialects before Chaucer's time.   The past participle was rarely inflected even in early ME.   The prefix ʒe-, later i-, y- (§ 240) disappeared early in the northern dialects, and mostly also in the Midland dialects.   It remained longest in the southern dialects.   It has been preserved in the form ə- in many of the modern south Midland and south-western dialects.   For ·ed in the past participle of weak verbs the northern dialects generally had ·id, the Scottish ·it, and the west Midland ·ud (·ut), see §§ **134, 239** ; and similarly in the preterite after the loss of final ·e (§ 141).

§ 393. The final ·n of the infinitive disappeared in the OE. period in Northumbrian, whereas in the pp. of strong verbs it remained throughout the ME. period in the northern dialects.   It also disappeared fairly early in the infinitive and pp. of strong verbs in the Midland and southern dialects, and in the indicative present plural of the Midland dialects, as well as in the plural of the present subjunctive, the plural of the preterite indicative and subjunctive of all the dialects, cp. § 247.

A. STRONG VERBS

§ 394. In ME. as in OE. the strong verbs are divided into seven classes.   Before giving examples of the various classes of strong verbs, it will be useful to state here in a connected manner some of the changes which these verbs underwent in general during the ME. period :—

1. In the present of verbs belonging to the third, fourth, and fifth classes the ĕ of the first person singular and of the plural was levelled out into the second and third persons singular, as helpe, helpest, helpeþ = OE. helpe, hilp(e)st, hilp(e)þ; bẹ̄re, bẹ̄rest, bẹ̄reþ = OE. bere, bir(e)st, bir(e)þ; ẹ̄te, ẹ̄test, ẹ̄teþ = OE. ete, it(e)st, iteþ, it(t).

2. The unmutated forms of the first person singular and of the plural of the present were levelled out into the second and third persons singular, except in a few monosyllabic forms of the southern dialects, as falle, fallest, falleþ = OE. fealle, fielst, fielþ, but southern gǭ, gẹ̄st, gẹ̄þ = OE. gā, gæst, gǣþ.

3. Verbs which had double consonants in the first person singular and in the plural of the present levelled out the double consonants (except bb, gg) into the second and third persons singular, as falle, fallest, falleþ = OE. fealle, fielst, fielþ; sitte, sittest, sitteþ = OE. sitte, sitst, sit(t).

4. The old form of the second person singular of the preterite was generally preserved in early ME. in the Midland and southern dialects, as bounde, spẹ̄ke spẹ̄ke beside band (bond), spak of the first and third persons singular, but in the northern dialects the form of the first and third person singular became generalized for the singular at an early period, and similarly later in the Midland and southern dialects, which at a still later period often added -est from the present of the second person singular. Chaucer has the old beside the new form, as songe (= sunge), bẹ̄re bẹ̄re beside drank, spak.

5. In the northern dialects the preterite singular had begun to be levelled out into the plural already at the beginning of the fourteenth century, whereas in the Midland and southern dialects the old distinction between the stem-

vowels of the singular and plural forms was generally preserved throughout the ME. period, but even in Chaucer the
singular was sometimes levelled out into the plural. On
the other hand the form of the plural was sometimes levelled
out into the singular in the Midland and southern dialects,
as sę̄t(e) sę̄t(e), pl. sę̄ten sę̄ten, beside northern sat, pl.
sat(e).

6. In the second class of strong verbs the preterite plural
was generally remodelled on the past participle, as crǭpen
for older crupen (OE. crupon), pp. crǭpen (OE. cropen)
crept.

7. In OE. the preterite singular and plural of the seventh
class of strong verbs had ē or ēo, but as ēo became ę̄ in ME.
all the verbs of this class, which remained strong in ME.,
had ę̄ in the preterite, see § 65.

8. In the northern dialects the preterite indicative came
to be used at an early period for the preterite subjunctive,
which was generally also the case in Chaucer.

9. The final -n of the past participle remained throughout
the ME. period in the northern dialects, whereas in the other
dialects it disappeared fairly early, as northern cumen,
tāken, beside ycome, ytāke in the other dialects.

10. The participial ending -en became -n after liquids,
and after long vowels and diphthongs, as stǭln, bǫrn,
swǭrn; leyn, seyn, slayn (§§ 144, 147).

11. Only a few verbs preserved the operation of Verner's
Law (*EOE. Gr.* §§ 115, 116), as wę̄ren wę̄ren : was, for-
lǫr(e)n : forlę̄sen, sǫden : sę̄þen.

12. As early as the thirteenth and fourteenth centuries
many of the OE. strong verbs had begun to have weak
beside the strong forms, and some verbs had become entirely
weak before the end of the ME. period. All the French
verbs were weak in ME. except strīven (O.Fr. estriver).
ON. verbs remained strong or weak according as they were
strong or weak in ON.

FULL CONJUGATION OF A ME. STRONG VERB.

§ 395. The early ME. inflexion of bĭnden will serve as a model for the conjugation of strong verbs generally.

Present.

Indicative.

	S. and Ken.	E.M.	W.M.	N.	OE.
Sing. 1.	bīnde	bīnde	bīnde	binde	binde
2.	bintst	bīndest	bīndes(t)	bindes	bindest, bintst
3.	bint	bīndeþ, ·es	bīndeþ, ·es	bindes	bindeþ, bint
Plur.	bīndeþ	bīnden	bīnden, ·es	bindes	bindaþ

Subjunctive.

Sing. bĭnde ⎫
Plur. bĭnden ⎭ in all the dialects, OE. binde, pl. binden.

Imperative.

Sing. bĭnd in all the dialects, OE. bind.

Plur. N. bindes, but bīndeþ in the other dialects, OE. bindaþ.

Infinitive.

N. binde, but bīnden in the other dialects, OE. bindan.

Present Participle.

N. bindand, M. bīndende, S. and Ken. bīndinde, OE. bindende, cp. § 391.

Preterite.

Indicative.

	S. and Ken.	M.	N.	OE.
Sing. 1.	bond	band (bond)	band	band (bond)
2.	bounde	bounde	band	bunde
3.	bond	band (bond)	band	band (bond)
Plur.	bounden	bounden	band(en)	bunden

Subjunctive.

	S. and Ken.	M.	N.	OE.
Sing.	bounde	bounde	band	bunde
Plur.	bounden	bounden	band(en)	bunden

Participle.

ȝebounde(n)   ȝebounde(n)   bunden   (ge)bunden

The Classification of Strong Verbs.

Class I.

§ 396. OE. ī   ā (§ 51)   i   i

ME. ī   ǭ (N. ā)   i   i

bīten   bǭt (N. bāt)   biten   biten

drīven   drǭf (N. drāf)   driven   driven

And similarly abīden (bīden), agrīsen *to be horrified*, arīsen (rīsen), bistrīden, biswīken *to deceive*, clīven *to adhere*, flīten *to quarrel*, glīden, grīpen *to grip, seize*, rīden, rīnen *to touch*, rīven (ON. rīfa) *to tear*, schīnen, schrīven, slīden, slīten *to slit*, smīten, strīden, strīken, striven (O.Fr. estriver), þrīven (ON. þrīfa), wrīten, wrīþen *to twist*. On preterites like bǭte, arǭse (s = z), drǭve beside older bǭt, arǭs, drǭf, cp. §§ 140, 266, 277; and on early shortenings like droff(e, schroff(e see § 100.

§ 397. As early as the fourteenth century many of the verbs in the preceding paragraph had begun to have weak beside the strong forms either in the preterite or past participle or in both, as bīted(e, bīted; schīned(e, schīned; and similarly with grīpen, schrīven, strīken, strīven, þrīven; and with shortening of the stem-vowel, as slitte, y·slit (cp. §§ 87, 93), and similarly with flīten, slīden, slīten, smīten. Some verbs passed over entirely into the weak conjugation, as dwīnen *to disappear*, dwīned(e, dwīned; spiwen (§ 116), spiwed(e, spiwed; sīken sīchen (OE. sīcan) *to sigh*, pret. sĭȝte, pp. y·sĭȝt formed after the analogy of verbs like sǫuȝte, y·sǫuȝt (§ 426) : sēken sēchen *to seck*, from the preterite and pp. was formed the new present sīhen sīȝen sīghen in the fourteenth century ; &c.

§ 398. sīȝen, sīen sȳen=OE. sīgan (§ 122, 2) *to sink, fall* ; pret. sing. sāȝ, sǭȝ, sę̄ȝ, sey (§ 107, 5) beside late ME. weak seit seyt seyit ; pp. y·sigen (seȝen). stīȝen, stīen stȳen =OE. stīgan (§ 122, 2), steien *to ascend* ; pret. sing. stāȝ, stawe (§ 110, 4), stę̄ȝ (steiȝ) beside weak stīde, stīede, stīȝed(e, stę̄ȝed(e, pl. stiȝen, stīen stȳen (§ 122, 1), stǫwen (§ 113, 3) ; pp. stiȝen, stīen stȳen, stǫȝen beside weak stīȝed, steied. wrę̄n (OE. wrēon) *to cover* ; pret. sing. wrę̄ȝ (wreiȝ), pl. wriȝen, wrīen wrȳen ; pp. wriȝen, wrīen wrȳen. þę̄n (OE. þēon) *to thrive* ; pret. sing. þę̄ȝ (þeiȝ), pl. þǭȝen (þǫwen) ; pp. þǭȝen (þǫwen). The pret. sing. sę̄ȝ, stę̄ȝ (steiȝ), wrę̄ȝ (wreiȝ) were formed after the analogy of class II (§ 401), and þę̄n (OE. þēon, þāh, þigon, þigen) went over entirely into this class.

CLASS II.

§ 399.

	OE.	ēo		ēa	u		o
	ME.	ę̄		ę̄	ǭ (u)		ǭ
		flę̄ten *to flow*		flę̄t	flǭten (fluten)		flǭten

In early ME. the pret. plural regularly had u, but later the verbs of this class generally had ǭ from the past participle ; and similarly bręwen (§ 112, 1) *to brew*, chęwen (chǫwen, cp. § 65 note) *to chew*, clēven *to cleave*, crępen *to creep*, ȝēten *to pour*, ręwen *to rue*. bę̄den *to bid, command*, pret. sing. bę̄d beside bedd with early shortening (cp. § 100), bǭd (see § 394, 5), and bad due to mixing up of bidden (§ 410) with bę̄den, pl. buden, bǭden, bedden (see § 394, 5), pp. bǭden, late ME. bodden with shortening of the stem-vowel. schę̄ten (schūten, schǭten, cp. § 65 and note) beside schott(en with early shortening *to shoot*, pret. sing. schę̄t, pl. schǭten beside schotten ; pp. schǭten, later schotten,

schot. Many of the above verbs had weak beside the
strong forms as early as the fourteenth century, as pret. and
pp. brẹwed(e, brẹud, brued; clẹved(e (clefte, cleft with
shortening of the stem-vowel, see § 92, 2); and similarly
crẹped(e (crepte, crept); flẹted(e (flette); rẹwed(e;
schotte, schott.

§ 400. sẹþen *to seethe*, pret. sing. sẹþ, pl. sọden (suden)
beside weak sẹþed(e, pp. sọden (sọþen); chẹsen (chūsen,
chọsen *to choose*, cp. § 65 and note), pret. sing. chẹs (= OE.
céas), chās, chọs (= OE. ceás), pl. cọren (curen), chọsen,
chẹsen (cp. § 394, 5) beside weak chẹsed(e, chūsed(e, pp.
cọren, cǒrn, chọsen; and similarly frẹsen *to freeze*, forlẹsen
lẹsen *to lose* (weak pret. and pp. also leste, lest; loste, lost).
For the consonant changes due to Verner's law see *EOE. Gr.*
§ 116.

§ 401. drẹȝen, dreien (drīen drȳen, cp. § 107, 6) *to endure*,
pret. sing. drẹȝ (dreiȝ § 107, 5), pl. druȝen, drẹȝen (dreien)
with ẹ (ei) from the singular (cp. § 394, 5), pp. drọȝen,
drọwen (cp. § 113, 2); lẹȝen, leien (līȝen, līen lȳen) *to tell
lies*, pret. sing. lẹȝ (leiȝ), pl. luȝen (lowen, ou = ū, see § 122,
5), lọwen beside weak lẹȝed(e, leiȝed(e līȝed(e, lȳed(e, pp.
lọȝen, lọwen beside weak līȝed, lïed; tẹn (OE. tēon) *to draw*,
pret. tẹȝ (teiȝ), pl. tuȝen (towen, cp. § 122, 5), pp. tọȝen,
tọwen. ME. flẹn (OE. flēon) *to flee* and flẹȝen (OE. flēogan)
to fly became mixed up in the present, as flẹn (flīen flȳen),
pret. sing. flẹȝ (fleiȝ), flāȝ(e (flaw(e, pl. fluȝen (flowen),
flọȝen (flọwen) beside weak flẹde, fledde with early shortening (cp. § 100), pp. flọȝen (flọwen), flọwn (flọun) beside weak
fledd; pres. flẹȝen (*Ormulum* flẹȝhenn), fleien, flïen flȳen,
flẹn, pret. sing. flẹȝ (fleiȝ), flāȝ(e (flaw(e, flọw(e with ọw
from the plural and pp., pl. fluȝen (flowen, § 122, 5), flọȝen
(flọwen) beside late weak flȳde, pp. flọȝen (flọwen).

§ 402.

	OE.	ū	ēa	u	o
	ME.	ū (ou)	ẹ̄	ọ (u)	ọ

būȝen bouȝen (būen bouen bowen, § 122, 6) *to bow, bend.*
pret. sing. bēȝ (beiȝ), pl. buȝen (buwen, bouen bowen (§ 122,
5), beside weak bouȝed(e, bouwed(e bowed(e, pp. bōȝen,
bọwen (§ 113, 2) beside weak bowed ; schūven (schouven,
schove(n)) *to push, shove*, pret. sing. schēf, schọf (§ 394, 5)
beside weak schoved(e, schufte, pp. schọven (schuven)
beside weak schowved, schuft ; sūken (souken) *to suck*,
pret. sing. sēk, sọk (§ 394, 5) beside weak souked(e, pl.
suken, sọken, pp. sọken (sŭken) beside weak souked ;
and similarly sūpen (soupen) *to sup* ; unlūken (unlouken)
to unlock.

CLASS III.

§ 403.

OE.	i	a (o)	u	u
ME.	i	a (o), § 42	u (o=u)	u (o=u), § 9
	drinken	drank (dronk)	drunken	drunken
	spinnen	span (spon)	spunnen	spunnen

And similarly with other verbs containing a nasal + consonant other than d or b, as schrinken, sinken, stinken,
swinken *to labour, toil* ; clingen, dingen (ON. dengja) *to
beat, strike*, flingen (ON. flengja), ringen, singen, slingen
(ON. slöngva), springen, stingen, swingen, þringen *to
throng, press* ; bilimpen *to happen*, swimmen ; biginnen
(N. pret. also bigouþe, see note) ; blinnen *to cease*, rinnen
(ON. rinna) *to run*, winnen.   To this subdivision properly
belong also irnen, ernen, urnen (WS. iernan, Angl. eornan
to run, see *EOE. Gr.* § 340 note), pret. sing. arn(e, orn(e
(OE. arn, orn), pl. and pp. urnen, ornen beside weak pret.
ernde, also arnde (pp. y-arned, arnd) from the OE. weak
causative verb ǣrnan ; and rennen (ON. renna) *to run*,
pret. sing. ran (ron), pret. pl. and pp. runnen (ronnen)
beside weak pret. rende, renned(e, pp. renned.

Some of the above verbs had weak beside the strong
forms, especially in the fourteenth and fifteenth centuries, as

sinked, stinked, swinked; dinged, swinged; swimde
(pp. swimmed).

NOTE.—1. The pret. bigan (bigon) was often used as a kind of
auxiliary verb with loss of the prefix and unvoicing of the g- to k-,
whence the common forms con in the west Midland and can in
the northern dialects. And then in Scottish the new can became
mixed up with old can (§ 435) and gave rise to the analogical
pret. kouþ(e) beside bigan, bigouþ(e), see *N.E.D.* s.v.

2. The ME. for *to burn* comprises forms from four different
types of stem :—(1) bern-, the OE. strong intransitive verb WS.
biernan, Angl. beornan; (2) brinn-, the strong intransitive verb
OE. *brinnan (ON. brinna); (3) barn-, the OE. weak causative
verb bærnan; (4) brenn-, the ON. strong verb brenna. The old
strong forms of the preterite and pp. do not appear later than
Laȝamon (c. 1205), and the distinction between transitive and
intransitive was soon lost, the four types being used indiscrimina-
tively in meaning though their usage varied in different dialects,
the brinn-, brenn- types belonging chiefly to the areas more
strongly influenced by Scandinavian. In late ME. and onwards
into the sixteenth century the most common type was brenn-.
Examples are :—(1) beornen, birnen, bernen, pret. sing. born, pl.
burnen beside weak bernde; (2) brinnen, pret. brinde, brint(e,
brynned(e, pp. brind, brint; (3) barnen, pret. barnde; (4)
brennen, pret. brenn(e)de, brende, brent, pp. brend, brent.

§ 404.

ī(i, § 73) a (o) ū (u, § 73) ū (u)
bĭnden band(bond) bounden (bunden) bounden (bunden)

And similarly fĭnden, grĭnden, wĭnden; clīmben (§ 72),
pret. sing. clǫmb, clāmb (§ 72), pl. cloumben, clumben,
clāmben (§ 394, 5) beside weak clīmed(e, pp. cloumben,
clumben (clomben, o = u). For bound(e, found(e beside
band (bond), fand (fond), see § 394, 5.

§ 405.

e a o (u) o
helpen halp holpen (hulpen) holpen

The verbs of this type regularly had u in the preterite

plural in early ME., but later they generally had o from the past participle as in Chaucer. Nearly all of them had begun to have weak beside the strong forms as early as the fourteenth century, and some of them had become entirely weak before the end of the ME. period. And similarly berken, delven, kerven *to carve*, melten, smerten, sterven, swellen, swelten *to die*, werpen *to throw* (cp. § 38), ȝellen, ȝelpen *to boast*; bersten (bresten) *to burst* (cp. § 130). þreschen. Cp. § 129.

§ 406. berȝen, berwen (§ 298) *to protect, preserve*, pret. sing. barȝ, pl. bur(e)ȝen, borȝen (borwen), pp. borȝen (borwen); swelȝen (swelewen, ·owen, ·awen, swoleȝen, swolewen, ·owen) *to swallow*, pret. sing. swal(u)ȝ, swalewe beside weak swel(o)wed(e). swolewed(e), swolȝed, pp. swolȝen (swolwen, swelȝen) beside weak swelewed, ·owed, see *EOE. Gr.* § 102; wurþen, worþen (OE. weorþan, § 38) *to become*, pret. sing. warþ (wurþ, worþ), pl. wurþen, worþen (OE. wurdon), pp. worþen, wurþen (OE. worden). see *EOE. Gr.* § 116 ; ȝelden (southern ȝilden) *to recompense*. pret. sing. ȝọld (N. ȝāld, S. ȝẹ̄ld § 71), pl. ȝūlden (ȝọlden), pp. ȝọlden (cp. § 71) beside weak ȝẹ̄lded(e, pp. ȝẹ̄lded ; fiȝten (feȝten, feiȝten) *to fight*, pret. sing. fauȝt, faȝt (§ 110, 5), feiȝt (§ 107, 4), pl. fuȝten (fouȝten), pp. fŏ̄ȝten, fouȝten (§ 113, 4) ; breiden (OE. bregdan, § 107, 1) *to brandish*, pret. sing. braid breid (OE. brægd, § 106) beside weak breide braide, pl. brudden (OE. brūdon), pp. broȝden (OE. brogden), broiden beside weak braided, breided, broided ; freinen (OE. fregnan, frignan) *to ask, inquire*, pret. sing. frain frein beside weak frained(e), freined(e).

CLASS IV.

§ 407.

OE. e	æ	ǣ (ē) § 52	o
ME. ẹ̄	a	ẹ̄ (ē)	ọ̄
bẹ̄ren *to bear*	bar	bẹ̄ren (bẹ̄ren)	bọ̄ren bŏrn

And similarly **hēlen** *to conceal*, **quēlen** *to die*, **schēren** *to shear*, **stēlen** *to steal*, **tēren** *to tear*. **cumen (comen)** *to come*, pret. sing. **cōm (cam,** § 55), pl. **cōmen (cāmen)**, pp. **cumen (comen)** ; **nimen** *to take*, pret. sing. **nōm (nam,** § 55), pl. **nōmen (nāmen)**, pp. **numen (nomen)**, see § 42 note.

CLASS V.

§ 408.

OE.	e	æ	ǣ (ē) § 52	e
ME.	ē	a	ē (ē)	ē
	knēden *to knead*	**knad**	**knēden (knēden)**	**knēden**

And similarly **mēten** *to measure*, **biquēþen, quēþen** ; pret. sing. **quaþ, quad** ; **quoþ, quod** with **d** from the old pret. plural (Verner's law), and **o** with early rounding of **a** to **o** ; **quod** was the prevailing form from about 1350 to 1550 ; **wēȝen (weien,** § 107, 1) *to carry*, pret. sing. **wai (wei)** ; **was (wes,** § 43 note), pl. **wēren wēren (wāren, wōren,** § 166). Some of these verbs had also weak beside the strong forms, as pret. and pp. **kned(de, mett(e, wei(e)de** (pp. **y·wēȝed, weied,** § 107, 1).

§ 409. A number of verbs originally belonging to this class went over into class IV, as **brēken, brak, brēken (brēken, brāken), brōken** ; and similarly **drēpen** *to kill*, **spēken, trēden** (also weak **tred(d)ed(e), wēven** *to weave*, **wrēken** *to avenge* ; also pp. **knōden, quōþen.**

§ 410. **ēten** *to eat*, pret. sing. **ēt, ēt** (OE. **æt, ēt**) beside the new formation **at**, pl. **ēten, ēten**, pp. **ēten**, late ME. also **etten (ettyn)** ; and similarly **frēten** *to devour*, late ME. also weak pret. and pp. **frēted.** **ȝĕven, ȝiven** beside **given** (Orm **gifenn**), N. **gif** *to give* (§ 176), pret. sing. **ȝaf, ȝef, ȝafe, ȝave, ȝof, ȝove** beside **gaf, gaf(f)e**, pl. **ȝēven, ȝēven, ȝāven, ȝōven** (cp. § 166) beside **gēven** (Orm **gæfenn**), pp. **ȝĕven, ȝōven, ȝiven** (Orm **ȝivenn**) beside **given** (Orm also **givenn**), see

§§ 176, 292. gēten, giten (ON. geta) *to get*, pret. sing. găt(t,
get (§ 29), pl. gēten, gēten (getten, gắt(t)e(n)), pp. gēten
(getten, git(t)en, gŏt(t)en), see § 176. forȝēten, forȝiten
beside forgēten *to forget*, pret. sing. forȝat beside forgat,
pl. forȝēten, forȝēten beside forgēten, pp. forȝēten beside
forgēten. bidden (OE. biddan), also bedden (cp. §§ 92, 1,
399) in the thirteenth and fourteenth centuries *to pray, beg,
bid*, pret. sing. bad (badd, bed(d, badde) beside bēd (OE.
bēad, see § 399), pl. bēden, bēden, pp. bēden beside early
ME. bidden. sitten *to sit*, pret. sing. sat, also later satte,
pl. sēten, sēten, also later sat(t)en, pp. sēten, later ME.
also setten, sitten, satt(e. liggen, līen, līn (§§ 122, 1, 296)
to lie down, pret. sing. lai (Orm laȝȝ), cp. § 106, lei, pl. lēȝen,
lēȝen, leiȝen, leien (laien), pp. leien (lein, lain), līen, līn.
sēn (Ken. zī, zȳ) *to see*, pret. sing. saȝ, sauȝ saugh (§ 110, 5),
saw (§ 110, 4), seȝ, seiȝ seigh, sey (Chaucer say), § 107, 4,
siȝ, sī sȳ (§ 107, 6), pl. sawen (§ 110, 4), sāȝen, sauȝen,
sǭȝen, sǫwen, sēȝen (Orm sæȝhenn), seien, sīen sȳen
(§ 107, 6), pp. sēwen (OE. sewen), sawen (OE. sawen,
see *EOE. Gr.* § 350), sei(e)n sey(e)n (OE. Anglian gesegen),
sēn (OE. adj. gesīene, gesēne *visible*).

Class VI.

§ 411.

OE.	a		ō	ō	æ (a)
ME.	ā		ǭ	ǭ	ā
	fāren *to travel*		fǭr	fǭren	fāren

And similarly āken *to ache*, bāken, forsāken, grāven *to
dig* (pret. sing. grǫf), lāden *to load*, schāken, schāven,
wāden, wāken (N. wak, wakke), tāken (ON. taka), N. tak
beside N. and n. Midland tā(n, pret. also tǭ, pp. tān, see § 250.
Several of the above verbs had weak beside the strong forms
as early as the fourteenth century, as āked(e, forsāked(e,
grāved(e, schāked(e, schāved(e, tāked(e.

§ 412. hẹven (OE. hebban, § 265) *to raise, heave,* pret.
sing. hōf, hǫve (cp. §§ 140, 267) beside the analogical forms
haf, have, hẹf, hẹve, weak hẹved(e, pl. hōven, hẹven,
pp. hǫven (after the analogy of class IV, § 407), hẹven,
weak hẹved. scheppen, schippen (OE. scieppan) beside
the new formation schāpen (from the pp.) *to create,* pret. sing.
schōp, also schẹp after the analogy of class VII (§ 414) beside
weak schapte, schipte, schupte, pl. schōpen, pp. schāpen
beside weak schāped. standen (stǫnden), pret. sing. stōd,
pl. stōden, pp. standen (stǫnden).   steppen, stāpen,
stappen *to proceed,* pret. sing. stōp, stẹp after the analogy of
class VII (§ 414) beside weak stapped(e, stapte, pl. stōpen,
pp. stāpen. swẹren (OE. swerian) *to swear,* pret. sing.
swōr beside the analogical forms swar, swẹr, weak swẹred,
swāred, pl. swōren, pp. swǫren, swŏrn after the analogy
of class IV (§ 407), weak y·swẹred, y·swāred. waschen
(Ken. weschen, wesse(n), § 289) *to wash,* pret. sing. wŏsch
(wĕsch) beside weak wasched, wesched, pl. wŏschen
(wĕschen), pp. waschen (weschen), beside weak wasched
(wesched).   waxen *to grow,* pret. sing. wox (cp. § 94),
wax after the analogy of class IV (§ 407), wex (OE. wēox),
pl. woxen, wexen, pp. waxen, woxen.

§ 413. draʒen, drāʒen, drawen (§ 103, 3), early ME. also
dreiʒen, dreien *to draw,* pret. sing. drōʒ, drouʒ, drǫw (§ 114,
2), drew, Sc. drewʒ drewch (§ 115), pl. drōʒen, drǫwen,
drewen, pp. drāʒen, drawen, also dreien, drain (drayn).
And similarly gnaʒen, gnāʒen, gnawen *to gnaw.* flẹn (OE.
flēan) *to flay,* pret. sing. flōʒ (OE. flōg, flōh), flouʒ, flǫw,
also flew (§ 115), pl. flōʒen, flouʒen, flǫwen, flewen, pp.
flāʒen, flawen (OE. flagen), flain(e) (OE. flǣgen, § 106).
slẹn (OE. slēan), N. slān, slā (ON. slā, § 166), slǫn(e,
beside the analogical forms slāʒe(n), slayn, pret. sing. slōʒ,
slouʒ, slǫw, slew (§ 115), pl. slōʒen, slǫwen, slewen, pp.
slāʒen, slawen (OE. slagen), slain, slein (OE. slǣgen,
slegen, *EOE. Gr.* § 353), slān, slǫn from the present.

laȝen (Orm lahȝhenn), lāȝen, lauȝen, lauȝwen (Anglian
hlæhhen, cp. § 110, 5), leȝen, lēȝen, leiȝen, liȝen (WS.
hliehhan, cp. § 306) *to laugh*, pret. sing. lōȝ, louȝ, lọw,
N. leuȝ(e, lugh(e, see §§ 114–15, beside weak lāȝed(e, lauȝed(e,
leiȝed(e, N. lauȝt, luȝt, pl. lōȝen, lọwen, pp. laȝen, lāȝen,
lauȝen.

Class VII.

§ 414. To this class belong those verbs which originally
had reduplicated preterites. In OE. they are divided into
two subdivisions according as the preterite had ē or ēo.
But as ēo regularly became ę̄ in ME. (§ 65) all the verbs of
this class, which remained strong, have ę̄. The pret. sing.
and pl. have the same stem-vowel. The verbs are here
arranged according as in OE. the present had: ā, ǣ, ō, ea,
āw, ōw, ē, ēa.

1. OE. ā: họten, N. hāten (OE. hātan) *to bid, order, call,
name*. In OE. the passive was expressed by hātte *is* or *was
called*, pl. hātton (*EOE. Gr.* § 316). In ME. the active họten,
pret. hę̄t (OE. hēt), heȝt, hiȝt (OE. hĕht) came to mean both
to call and *to be called*. From about 1200 the pret. heȝt, hiȝt
often took final -e like the weak verbs. And both hę̄t and
hiȝt passed over to the past participle. Further heȝt(e, hiȝt(e
came to be used also for the present. From the strong
preterite hę̄t a new ME. present hę̄ten with weak preterite
hette was formed in the early fourteenth century. Thus
the common ME. forms are: họten, hāten, hę̄ten, pret.
sing. hę̄t, heȝt(e, hiȝt(e beside weak hette, pp. họten (hāten,
hatten), hę̄t, hiȝt.

schọden, schęden Orm shǣdenn (OE. scādan, scēadan)
to separate, pret. schę̄d beside weak schadde, schedde (cp.
§ 91), pp. schọden, schęden beside weak schad(d, sched(d,
late ME. also schedded.

2. OE. ǣ (ē): lę̄ten (lēten) *to let*, pret. lę̄t, lett, lat, pp.
lę̄ten (lēten), letten, latten. slępen (slēpen) *to sleep*, pret.
slę̄p beside weak slę̄ped(e (slēped(e), slepped(e, slepte,

pp. slēpen (slẹpen) beside weak slēped (slẹped), slapt, slept (cp. § 91).

3. OE. ō: fǭn (OE. fōn) beside the new formation fangen (fongen) from the past participle *to seize*. pret. fěng (OE. fēng), also the new formation fong, beside weak fanged(e (fonged(e), pp. fangen (fongen) beside weak fanged (fonged). hǭn ˎOE. hōn) beside the new formation hangen (hongen) from the past participle *to hang*, pret. hěng (OE. hēng), hing (cp. § 99), pp. hangen (hongen).

4. OE. ea: fallen (OE. feallan) *to fall*, pret. fẹl(l, fel(l, fil(l (§ 99), pp. fallen. walken (OE. wealcan) *to roll*, pret. wělk (OE. wēolc, cp. § 92, 2). pp. walken beside weak pret. and pp. walked.

fǭlden, N. fālden, S. fẹlden (OE. fealdan, § 71) *to fold*, pret. fẹld beside weak fǭlded(e, &c., pp. fǭlden, &c. beside weak fǭlded. hǭlden, N. hālden, S. hẹlden (OE. healdan, § 71) *to hold*, pret. hẹld, held (helt), hild (hilt), see § 99, pp. hǭlden, &c. wǭlden, N. wālden, S. wẹlden (OE. wealdan, § 71) *to rule*, pret. wẹld(e, wělt(e beside the new formations wǭlde, wāld(e, wẹld(e, pp. wǭlden, &c., in later ME. also weak pret. and pp. wẹlded.

5. OE. āw: blǫwen blǫuwen, N. blauwen, blau (OE. blāwan) *to blow*, pret. blęw (OE. blēow, § 112, 1), also weak blǫwed(e, pp. blǫwen, N. blawen, beside weak blǫwed. And similarly crǫwen, knǫwen, mǫwen, sǫwen, þrǫwen. swǭpen, swǭpen (§ 128) beside the new formation swẹpen *to sweep*, pret. swẹp beside the new formations swǭp(e, swǭp(e, weak swẹped(e, swepte, pp. swǭpen, swǭpen, weak swǭped, swǭped, swẹped.

6. OE. ōw, ōg: grǫwen (OE. grōwan, see § 114, 1) *to grow*, pret. grẹw beside weak grǫwed(e, pp. grǫwen. And similarly blǫwen (weak pret. also blǫude) *to blossom*, flǫwen *to flow*, rǫwen *to row*. swǭȝen, swǫwen (OE. swōgan, § 114, 2 (*b*)) *to sound*. pret. swę̄ȝ, swei (§ 107, 6), pp. swǭȝen, swǫwen.

7. OE. ē : wēpen (OE. wēpan, Goth. wōpjan) *to weep*, pret. wēp beside weak wepte (§ 92, 1), pp. wōpen (OE. wōpen) beside weak wept.

8. OE. ēa : bēten (OE. bēatan) *to beat*, pret. bēt beside shortened form bett, and weak bēted(e, bette, pp. bēten beside weak bett(e. hęwen (OE. hēawan) *to hew*, pret. hęw (hęu) beside weak hęwed(e, pp. hęwen beside weak hęwed. lēpen (OE. hlēapan) *to leap*, pret. lēp (OE. hlēop), lep(pe beside weak lēped(e, lĕpte, pp. lōpen after the analogy of class IV (§ 407, cp. also § 409).

B. WEAK VERBS

§ 415. The weak verbs, which for the most part are derivative and denominative, form by far the greater majority of all verbs. In OE. they are divided into three classes according to the endings of the infinitive, pret. indicative, and past participle. These endings are :—

Inf.	Pret.	P.P.
·an	·ede, ·de, ·te	·ed, ·d́, ·t
·ian	·ode	·od
·an	·de	·d

Each of the classes I and II contained a large number of verbs, whereas class III only contained four verbs, viz. habban *to have*, libban *to live*, secgan *to say*, and hycgan *to think*, the last of which did not survive in ME.

The OE. normal endings of the present of these three classes were : —

    I.   Sing. ·e, ·est, ·eþ, pl. ·aþ, inf. ·an
    II.   ,,   ·ie, ·ast, ·aþ, ,, ·iaþ, ,, ·ian
    III. ,,   ·e, ·ast, ·aþ, ,, ·aþ, ,, ·an

WS. generally had syncopated forms in the second and third person singular of verbs belonging to class I, as **setst, set(t)** for older **setest, seteþ**, and these syncopated forms also remained in the ME. southern dialects. The OE. verbs of class I containing an r preceded by a short vowel had an ·i· in the present first pers. singular, the present plural, the present subjunctive singular and plural, the present participle, and the infinitive, as **werie, weriaþ; werie, werien; weriende, werian** *to defend.* In ME. the Midland and northern dialects generalized the forms without ·i·, whereas the Kentish and southern dialects retained the ·i·, as M. and N. **wẹre**, S. **wĕrie**, &c., and similarly **an(d)·sweren, dẹren** *to injure*, **ẹren** *to plough*, **fẹren** *to carry*, **stiren** *to stir.*

After the ·a· had been weakened to ·e· (§ 134 (b)) the endings of class I and class III became alike; in class II the Midland and northern dialects generalized the endings without ·i·, so that in these dialects the present of all three classes fell together, whereas the endings ·ie, ·ieþ, ·ien remained in the Kentish and southern dialects. For the personal endings of the present in the various ME. dialects see § 391. The verbs of class I which had double consonants in the first person singular and the plural generally levelled out the double consonants (except **bb**, and **gg** = OE. **cg**) into the second and third person singular, as **sette, settest, setteþ** = OE. **sette, setst, set(t); telle, tellest, telleþ** = OE. **telle, tel(e)st, tel(e)þ**. In the Midland and northern dialects the verbs containing ·bb·, ·cg· in OE. were remodelled in ME. from the second and third persons singular, as **bīen bȳen** *to buy*, **aswẹven** *to stupefy*, **leien** *to lay*, beside OE. **bycgan, āswebban, lecgan**; and similarly **haven, liven, seien saien** *to say*, beside OE. **habban, libban, secgan** of the third class.

§ **416.** The OE. normal endings of the preterite and past participle of the three classes were:—

Sing. ·ede, ·edest, ·ede, pl. ·edon, pp. ·ed : fremede
I performed

I   ,,   ·de, ·dest, ·de,   ,, ·don,   ,,   ·ed : dēmde
I judged

  ,,   ·te, ·test, ·te,   ,, ·ton,   ,,   ·ed : drencte
I submerged

II   ,,   ·ode, ·odest, ·ode, ,, ·odon, ,,   ·od : lōcode
I looked

III   ,,   ·de ·dest, ·de,   ,, ·don,   ,,   ·d : hæfde
I had

The OE. verbs of class I generally had ·ede in the preterite when the stem-syllable was originally short, but ·de when the stem-syllable was originally long, and ·te after voiceless consonants. Those verbs which had ·te in OE. had it also in ME. In ME. we also often have ·te after l, m, n, and in stems ending in ·ld, ·nd, ·rd with shortening of a preceding long vowel, see § 270. Already in OE. the preterite of class III was the same as the preterite in ·de of class I. And after the ·o· had been weakened to ·e· in class II the preterite of this class became the same as the preterite in ·ede of class I. So that in early ME. the preterite sing. of all weak verbs ended either in ·ede or ·de (·te), and the plural in ·eden or ·den (·ten). The endings of the preterite indicative and the preterite subjunctive regularly fell together in ME. except that the indicative had ·est in the second person singular.

§ 417. In ME. the final ·e disappeared at an early period in those verbs which preserved the medial ·e· of ·ede, as loved (a new formation for lovęde), māked, þanked, beside hĕrde, bledde, kiste. The final ·e of the singular and the final ·en (§ 147) of the plural of all weak verbs disappeared at an early period in the northern dialects, and likewise the ·est of the second pers. singular often disappeared, so that in these dialects all forms of the singular and plural came to be alike. The final ·e also ceased to be pronounced at an early period in the Midland and southern dialects, although it continued to be written long after it had ceased to be pronounced, but the ending ·est (§ 150) of the second person singular generally remained. For the loss or retention of medial and final e in trisyllabic and polysyllabic forms see §§ 154-5.

Class I.

§ 418. Before beginning to treat the history of the preterite and past participle of the OE. first class of weak verbs in ME. it will be advisable to state here certain vowel and consonant changes which took place partly in OE. and partly in ME. :—

1. Long vowels were shortened before certain consonant combinations (§ 87), as blēden *to bleed*, bledde, ybled ; clēþen *to clothe*, cledde, cladde, ycled, yclad ; fēlen *to feel*, felte, yfelt ; hēren *to hear*, hĕrde, yhĕrd ; kēpen *to keep*, kepte, ykept ; kīþen *to make known*, kidde, ykid ; lēden *to lead*, ledde, ladde, yled, ylad ; mēten *to meet*, mette, ymet.

2. d became t after voiceless consonants in OE., and when two dentals thus came together they became tt which were simplified to t when final (§ 239), as drencte : drencan *to submerge*, cyste : cyssan *to kiss*, grētte : grētan *to greet*, and similarly in ME.

3. Double consonants were simplified in OE. before and after other consonants, as cyste : cyssan, fylde : fyllan, gewielde : gewieldan *to overpower*, gyrde : gyrdan *to gird*, sende : sendan, reste : restan (*EOE. Gr.* § 145), and similarly in ME.

4. After liquids and nasals, and in stems ending in ·ld, ·nd, ·rd we often or generally have t in the preterite and past participle, whereas OE. had d, see § 270 ; as bilte (OE. bylde), bilt *built* ; dwelte, dwelt ; felte, felt ; girte, girt ;

dremte (drempte, cp. § 251), dremt; blente, blent *blended*, sente, sent.

5. On preterites and past participles like dreinte, ydreint: drenchen; meinde, ymeind : mengen, and similarly blenchen *to flinch*, quenchen, sprengen, &c., see § 263.

§ 419. The OE. verbs with an original short stem-syllable had -ede in the preterite and -ed in the past participle, as werien *to defend*, werede, gewered; fremman *to perform*, fremede, gefremed, and similarly derian *to injure*, erian *to plough*, ferian *to carry*, styrian *to stir*, dynnan *to resound*, &c., see *EOE. Gr.* §§ 367–8. If through analogical formation the stem-syllable became long in ME. the preterite and past participle regularly had -ed, but if the stem-syllable remained short the preterite regularly had -de and the past participle -ed, as wēren, wēred, ywēred; frēmen, frēmed, yfrēmed, but stiren, stirde, ystired; dinen, dinde, ydined, but there were numerous analogical formations in both directions, see § 153. On the preterite and past participle of verbs like an(d)sweren, gaderen, see § 155.

§ 420. Verbs with an original long stem-syllable which in OE. had -de in the preterite and -ed in the past participle generally had these in ME. also, as dēlen, dēlde, ydēled, dēmen *to judge*, dēmde beside the new formation dēmed(e), ydēmed, see *EOE. Gr.* § 373. The -e- in the past participle was very often syncopated, which in OE. only took place in the inflected forms, as ydēld, yhĕrd : hēren *to hear*, and similarly deien dīen *to die*, hēlen, lēren *to teach*, stēren *to steer*, see § 151.

§ 421. When the stem-syllable ended in -d preceded by a long vowel the long vowel was shortened in the preterite and past participle (§ 91, 2), and when the -e- in the past participle had disappeared the dd was simplified to d, as blēden, bledde, ybled; lēden, ledde, ladde, yled, ylad; and similarly chīden, fēden, hīden, spēden, &c.

§ 422. When the stem ended in v, l, m, n, or nd, ld, rd

the preterite and past participle generally had **t** in ME., as lēven *to leave*, lefte, yleft beside ylēved; and similarly clēven *to cleave*. fēlen, felte, yfelt; lēnen *to lend*, lente, ylent; senden, sente, ysent; and similarly benden, blenden, wenden. bīlden, bilte, ybilt; girden, girte, ygirt, see § 270.

§ 423. þ + d became dd which was simplified to d in the past participle, as clēþen *to clothe*, cledde, cladde, ycled, yclad; kīþen *to make known*, kidde, ykid.

§ 424. Verbs which had the preterite in -te in OE. also had it in ME., as kissen, kiste, ykissed beside ykist; kēpen, kepte, ykēped beside ykept; and similarly with the following verbs which were strong in OE., but became weak in ME.: crēpen *to creep*, lēpen *to leap*, slēpen, slēpen *to sleep*, wēpen *to weep*.

§ 425. When the stem ended in t the tt was simplified to t in the past participle, as mēten, mette, ymet, and similarly grēten, swēten *to sweat*. When the stem ended in st, nt the tt was simplified to t in the preterite and past participle, as resten, reste, yrest; and similarly casten, lasten, stinten, þirsten, &c.

§ 426. OE. had a certain number of verbs belonging to class I which had umlaut in the present but not in the preterite and past participle, see *EOE. Gr.* § 379. Many of these verbs preserved this characteristic in ME., as bȳen (biggen, beggen, büggen = OE. bycgan, § 49) *to buy*, bou̯ʒte, ybou̯ʒt. tellen, tōlde (telde), ytōld (yteld); and similarly sellen. ME. new formations were: dwelde, dwelte, ydwelled, ydwelt; and similarly quellen *to kill*. rēchen *to reach*, rau̯ʒte, yrau̯ʒt; and similarly lacchen *to catch, seize*, strecchen, and the AN. loan-word cacchen. tēchen, tau̯ʒte, ytau̯ʒt. sēken (sēchen), sou̯ʒte, ysou̯ʒt; and similarly bisēken (bisēchen). bringen, brou̯ʒte, ybrou̯ʒt. þenken, þinken (þenchen), þou̯ʒte, yþou̯ʒt. me þinkeþ *it seems to me*, me þu̯ʒte, þou̯ʒte. wirken, wirchen,

worchen, wurchen (early OE. wyrcan, see § 123), pret.
wrǫuȝte (§ 113, 4), west Midland warȝte, wraȝte (OE.
worhte), pp. ywrǫuȝt (OE. geworht), cp. § 244.

§ **427.** The conjugation of the preterite of wēren *to defend*,
hēren *to hear*, tellen *to count*, and kissen *to kiss* will serve
as models of all verbs of class I :—

Indicative.

Sing.	1.	wēred(e)	hĕrde	tǫlde	kiste
	2.	wēredest	hĕrdest	tǫldest	kistest
	3.	wēred(e)	hĕrde	tǫlde	kiste
Plur.		wēred(en)	hĕrden	tǫlden	kisten

Subjunctive.

| Sing. | wēred(e) | hĕrde | tǫlde | kiste |
| Plur. | wēred(en) | hĕrden | tǫlden | kisten |

Class II.

§ **428.** It has been shown in § 415 that the ME. inflexion of
the verbs belonging to this class regularly fell together with
that of verbs of the type wēren (OE. werian) of class I, as
present singular þanke, þankest, þankeþ, plural þanken,
·es; preterite singular þanked(e), þankedest, þanked(e),
plural þanked(en); and similarly asken (axen), clensen,
clǫþen, enden, folwen, grǫpen, halwen *to hallow*, hāten,
hǫpen, lernen, līken *to please*, lǫken, offren, schewen
(schǫwen, § 111 note) *to show*, sorwen *to sorrow, grieve*,
spāren, spellen *to relate*, þǫlen *to bear, suffer*, wundren, &c.,
but loven, pret. lovęde beside loved(e), see § 153. Only
a small number of verbs had syncopated beside unsyncopated
forms in the preterite and past participle, as birēven (OE.
berēafian), birefte, bireft, beside birēved(e), birēved; clēpen

(OE. cliopian, cleopian) *to call,* clepte, yclept beside
clēpĕd(e), yclēped ; māken, māde, ymād, ymaad (§ 250)
beside māked(e), ymāked ; pleien (OE. plegian) *to play,*
pleide, ypleid beside pleied(e), ypleied.

CLASS III.

§ **429.** ME. only preserved three of the four OE. verbs
belonging to this class (§ 415), viz. haven (OE. habban),
liven (OE. libban), sei(e)n sai(e)n (OE. secgan = ME. S.
seggen, Ken. ziggen) *to say.* The presents of these verbs
were new formations from the second and third persons singular which in OE. had a single consonant, as hafast (hæfst),
hafaþ (hæfþ). In ME. the preterite and past participle
lived(e) (OE. lifde), ylived (OE. gelifd) beside the preterite
livẹde were new formations after the analogy of the second
class of verbs, see § 153. The preterite saide beside the
southern form sẹ̄de corresponded to OE. sægde beside
sǣde. The verb haven (habben) has a large number both
of contracted and uncontracted forms, for which see *N. E. D.*
s. v. The following are the more common forms of the
present and preterite indicative, the infinitive and the past
participle :—

	Present.	*Preterite.*
Sing. 1.	habbe, have, ha	hafde, havẹde, had(d)e
		(see § 43 note)
	2. havest, hast	had(d)est. had(e)st
	3. haveþ, haþ	hafde, havẹde, had(d)e
Plur.	habbeþ, -en, -es, haveþ, have(n), han	had(d)e(n)
Inf.	habbe(n), have(n)	pp. yhaved, yhadde, (y)had

AN. or O.Fr. Verbs in ME.

§ 430. All the AN. verbs were weak in ME. except **strīven** (O.Fr. estriver), which became strong. The ME. verbs were generally based on the AN. strong or accented stem-form of the present, as **accūsen, awaiten, blāmen, carien, claimen, escāpen, marien, stüdien**, &c.

§ 431. The verbs in -**ir** generally had the extended stem-form -**isch**- (§ 278), as **banischen, finischen, punischen, vanischen**, &c., but **obeyen, sēsen** *to seize*, and **rejọisen** did not have the extended stem-form. Some ME. verbs were based on the weak or end accented form of the present, as **deceiven, preien, preisen** *to praise*, **serven, deneien** beside **denȳen, coveren** beside **keveren, mọ̄ven** beside **mẹ̄ven, prọ̄ven** beside **prẹ̄ven**, see § 198.

§ 432. The preterite was formed in -**ed**, pl. **ed(en)**, and the past participle in -**ed** (see §§ 153, 155), except when the stem ended in a long vowel or diphthong, as **blāmen, blāmed; defenden, defended; assenten, assented; finischen, finisched; marien, maried; prẹ̄chen** *to preach*, **prẹ̄ched**, &c. When the stem ended in a long vowel the preterite, but not the past participle, had a syncopated beside an unsyncopated form, as **crȳen, crȳde** beside **crȳed**, pp. **crȳed**; and similarly **defȳen, espȳen**, &c. When the stem ended in a diphthong both the preterite and past participle had syncopated and unsyncopated forms side by side, as **preien** *to pray*, **preide, preid** beside **preied, preied**; and similarly **anoien, bitraien, paien**, &c.

C. MINOR GROUPS

1. Preterite-Presents.

§ 433. These verbs were originally unreduplicated strong perfects which acquired a present meaning like Gr. οἶδα = OE. **wāt** *I know*. In prim. Germanic a new weak preterite, an infinitive, a present participle, and in some verbs a strong past participle, were formed. They are inflected in the present like the preterite of strong verbs, except that the second person singular has the same stem-vowel as the first and third persons, and has preserved the old ending ·t (*EOE. Gr.* § 324). The following verbs of this type were preserved in ME. and are here arranged according to the class of strong verbs with which they are related :—

§ 434. Class I : N. **wāt** *I know*, **wās(t)**, **wāt** (cp. § 100), M. and S. **wǭt, wǭst, wǭt**, pl. **wite(n (wǣt, wǭt), wute(n**, cp. § 39 ; inf. **wite(n, wute(n** ; pres. part. **witand(e)**, **witend(e), witind(e), witing(e)** ; pret. **wiste, wuste** ; pp. **wist**. For forms like **nǭt, nāt**, pret. **niste**, see § 245.

§ 435. Class III : **an, on** *I grant*, also the new formations **unne, unnest, unne** from the plural, pl. **unnen** ; pret. **ūþe (ouþé)** ; pp. **unned**.

N. **can, canst, can**, pl. **can**, M. and S. **can (con), canst (const, cunne), can (con)**, pl. **cunnen (connen)** ; inf. **cunnen (connen)** ; subj. **cunne (conne)** ; participial adj. N. **cunnand** *cunning* ; pret. **couþe, coude** (§ 274) ; pp. **couþ**.

dar *I dare*, **darst, dar**, pl. **durren (dorren)** ; inf. **durren** ; pret. **dorste** beside the new formation **durste** with **u** from the inf. and pres. pl. ; pp. **durst**. **þarf (þar**, § 248) *I need*, **þarft (þurve), þarf (þar)**, pl. **þurven** ; pret. **þorfte** (OE. **þorfte**) beside **þurfte** formed from the inf. and pres. plural, **þorte (þurte)**.

§ 436. Class IV : M. and N. sing. and pl. **mun, mon** *shall*, *will*, pret. **munde, monde** ; ON. inf. **muna** *to remember*.

N. sing. and pl. **sal** (§ 289 note) *shall*, M. and S. **schal** (Ken. **ssel**), **schalt, schal**, pl. **schulen** beside the new formation **scholen** with **o** from the preterite, whence were formed the new singular **schul, schol** ; subj. **schule**, pret. N **suld**, M. and S. **schŏlde** beside **schǭlde** (§ 71), and **schulde** formed from the pres. plural.

§ 437. Class V : **mai may** (Orm **maȝȝ**, OE. **mæg**, § 106)

beside **mei mey** (OE. **meg,.**§ 107, 1) *I, he can,* **miʒt** (late OE.
miht) beside **maʒt, mauʒt,** Orm **mahht** (early OE. **meaht,**
§ 110, 5), **meiʒt** (§ 107), later ME. **maist(e** *thou canst,* pl.
maʒen, māʒen, mawen (§ 110, 3), also N. **mai** (may), **muʒen**
(Orm **muʒhenn**), **muwen, mowen,** mown (moun), mow
(mou, mū), see § 122, 5 ; subj. **maʒe (mawe), muʒe** (Orm
muʒhe), **muwe (mowe)**; pres. part. **maʒende** (Ken.
meʒende), **mowende, mouwinge, mowing**; inf. **muʒen**
(Orm **muʒhen**), **mowen, mown (moun), mow(mou)**; pret.
miʒte (Orm **mihhte**), **moʒt(e, muʒt(e, mouʒte.**

§ **438.** Class VI : **mōt** *may, must,* **mōst, mōt** beside later
ME. unaccented **mut(t, must, mut(t,** pl. **mōten** ; pret. **mōste**
beside the early ME. shortened and unaccented forms **moste,
muste,** pl. **mōsten** beside **mosten, musten.**

§ **439.** Class VII : N. sing and pl. **āʒ āgh** *possess, own,*
early M. **āʒ, auʒ, awe,** M. and S. **ǭʒ (ǫuʒ), ǫwe (ǫwest), ǭʒ
(ǫuʒ),** pl. **ǭʒen, ǫwen** (§ 113, 3) ; inf. N. **āʒe(n),** early M. **āʒen**
(Orm **āʒhenn**), M. and S. **ǭʒen, ǫwen ;** pret. N. **ǎʒt(e)
ǎght(e),** early M. **ǎʒte, auʒte,** M. and S. **ǫuʒte ;** pp. **āʒen,
ǫwen.**

2. Anomalous Verbs.

§ **440.**   *a.* The Substantive Verb.

Present.

	N.	M. and S.
Sing. 1.	am (es)	am (em)
2.	art (ert, es)	art (ert)
3.	es	is
Plur.	ar(e), er(e), es	are(n), arn
Sing. 1.	(bę)	bę̄
2.	bę̄s	bist (bę̄st)
3.	bę̄s	biþ (bę̄þ)
Plur.	bę̄s	bę̄n, bę̄þ
Subj.	bę̄, pl. bę̄s	bę̄, pl. bę̄n, bę̄þ

Preterite.

		M.	M.	S.
Sing.	1.	was (wes),	was (wes)	was (wes)
		§ 43 note		
	2.	was (wes)	wēre (wǭre), § 166	wēre
	3.	was (wes)	was (wes)	was (wes)
Plur.		war(e), wes	wēren (wǭren), § 166	wēren
P.P.		bēn	bēn	bēn, ybē

NOTE.—The **es** of the present second and third persons sing. in the northern dialects is of ON. origin (ON. **es** *art, is*). **es** was then extended to the first pers. sing. and to the plural ; of the same origin is the pl. form **er(e)** = ON. **ero** *they are*, and **ern** with the OE. ending ·n (OE. **earon, aron**). The OE. pl. forms **sind (sint)**, **sindon** *they are* lingered on in ME. until the thirteenth century, and then became obsolete, as **sind (sint), sinden** (Orm **sinndenn**). The **ē** in the M. and S. sing. forms **bēst** (OE. **bist**), **bēþ** (OE. **biþ**) was due to levelling out the **ē** from the other forms where it was regular.

§ **441.**   *b.*   THE VERB dǭn *to do*.

Present.

		N.	M.	S.
Sing.	1.	dǭ	dǭ	dǭ
	2.	dǭs	dǭst	dēst (dǭst)
	3.	dǭs	dǭþ	dēþ (doþ)
Pl.		dǭs	dǭn	dǭþ
Imper.		dǭ, pl. dǭs	dǭ, pl. dǭþ	dǭ, pl. dǭþ

On the forms of the second and third pers. singular, see § **394,** 2.

Pres. Part.: early ME. **dǭnde**, later N. **dǭand(e**, M. **dǭende**, S. **dǭinde, dǭing(e**, cp. § **391**.

Preterite: **dide, dede, düde** (OE. **dyde**, see § **49**) inflected like a weak preterite. P.P. **dǭn, ydǭn**, S. **ydǭ**.

§ 442.   *c.* THE VERB gān (gǭn) *to go.*

Present.

	N.	M.	S.
Sing. 1.	gā	gǭ	gǭ
2.	gās	gǭst	gēst (gǭst)
3.	gās	gǭþ	gēþ (gǭþ)
Plur.	gās	gǭn	gǭþ
Imper.	gā, pl. gās	gǭ, pl. gǭþ	gǭ, gǭþ

On the forms of the second and third pers. sing., see § 394, 2.

Preterite: ȝēde (ȝōde, § 65 note), and wente. P.P. gān, gǭn, ygǭn.

§ 443.   *d.* THE VERB willen *will.*

Present first and third pers. sing. wille, wil(e (OE. wille, third pers. wile, wille), welle, wel(e, wel(l (OE. Anglian welle) beside the new formations wole, wolle, wule, wulle from the preterites with o, u, and similarly second pers. sing. wilt (OE. wilt) beside wolt, wult, pl. willen, wilen, wiln, ·eþ, welen, wel(e, well(e beside wol(l)en, wul(l)en, ·eþ; inf. willen, wilen (Orm wilenn); pret. wŏlde (wollde, wold), wǭlde (§§ 71, 101) beside wulde formed after the analogy of schulde (§ 436), wilde formed direct from the present, northern and west Midland walde (OE. Anglian walde); pp. wŏld(e.

INDEX

The numbers after a word refer to the paragraphs in the Grammar.

220 *Index*

PRINTED IN GREAT BRITAIN
AT THE UNIVERSITY PRESS, OXFORD
BY VIVIAN RIDLER
PRINTER TO THE UNIVERSITY